Sustainability Transitions in South Africa

South Africa's transition to a greener economy features prominently in the long-term development vision of the country and is an integral part of the country's national climate change response strategy. Despite significant gains in socio-economic development since its transition to democracy, the country continues to face the triple challenges of rising unemployment, income inequality and poverty – amid a slowdown in economic growth. Sustainability transitions offer new ways of shifting the trajectory of South Africa's resource-intensive economy towards low-carbon pathways linked to the country's transformative development agenda.

Calls for inclusive approaches to greening the South African economy, which addresses the most vulnerable in society and ensures that the benefits of sustainability innovations reach all South Africans, are becoming more pronounced as sustainable development policy reforms are being implemented. The question that should be placed centre stage in South Africa's sustainability discourse is whether notions of justice and inclusivity are being sufficiently addressed in the design and implementation of policy and programme interventions.

This book explores South Africa's sustainability transition through reflections on critical policy, economic, technological, social and environmental drivers. It provides a synthesis of theoretical insights, including new models and concepts, and praxis through illustrations from South Africa's growing landscape of sustainable development policies and programmes. Finally, it assesses whether these transition pathways are beginning to reconfigure the system-level structures hindering the country's goal of 'ensuring environmental sustainability and an equitable transition to a low-carbon economy'.

Najma Mohamed is a Senior Climate and Environmental Specialist who has worked in national and international research and civil society organisations on the promotion and mainstreaming of environmental sustainability in development policies and processes.

Routledge Studies in Sustainability

www.routledge.com/Routledge-Studies-in-Sustainability/book-series/RSSTY

Sustainability Transitions in South Africa

Edited by Najma Mohamed

LONDON AND NEW YORK

First published 2019 by Routledge

2 Park Square, Milton Park, Abingdon, Oxfordshire OX14 4RN
52 Vanderbilt Avenue, New York, NY 10017

Routledge is an imprint of the Taylor & Francis Group, an informa business

First issued in paperback 2020

British Library Cataloguing-in-Publication Data
A catalogue record for this book is available from the British Library

Library of Congress Cataloging-in-Publication Data
A catalog record has been requested for this book

ISBN: 978-1-138-72799-1 (hbk)
ISBN: 978-0-367-50038-2 (pbk)

Typeset in Goudy
by Wearset Ltd, Boldon, Tyne and Wear

Contents

Figures

Tables

Boxes

Contributors

Brent Cloete is an economist with DNA Economics, and leads the firm's Climate Change and Energy Practice. He has been closely involved with the South African climate change policy process, and has an interest in the use of economic instruments to mitigate climate change. Brent has analysed the economic impact of firm decisions and government policies in several sectors, including: agriculture, water management, mining, liquid fuels, financial services, manufacturing, smelting and minerals processing, retail, power generation, forestry, sawmilling, printing and publishing, textile and clothing, and chemicals. Brent has also worked on economic development issues across Africa.

Nicola Jenkin is a doctoral candidate at the Centre for Researching Education and Labour at WITS University. She has a BA (Anthropology & Geography, Rhodes University); BSc (Hons) (Environmental & Geographical Science, University of Cape Town) and MEd (Environmental Education, Rhodes University). Her main interest lies in collaborative eco-innovation, knowledge acquisition and diffusion, and leveraging actors who enable transformative change within an innovation system. Some of her recent research is focused on sectoral sustainability, green skills, knowledge and capabilities and transformation towards a green economy, through the Greens Skills Programme.

Heila Lotz-Sisitka works in the Environmental Learning Research Centre at Rhodes University in the Faculty of Education, where she holds a South African National Research Foundation Chair in Transformative Social Learning and Green Skills Learning Pathways. The Chair's work focuses on ways in which transformative learning and green skills learning pathways can strengthen people's participation in securing more socially just and sustainable forms of life and living. It foregrounds collective agency for transformative change in society. She has a background in critical research methodologies and a long-standing commitment to furthering and extending participation in education. Her current research interests focus on the relationship between environmental learning, agency and social-ecological and social system transformation.

Najma Mohamed is an environmental scientist and writer with multi-sectoral experience in mainstreaming climate, environment and sustainable development principles in planning, policy, education and financing processes. She has worked as a Senior Climate and Environmental Specialist in developing and profiling transformative and inclusive transdisciplinary approaches to environmental sustainability in research and civil society. She holds a BSc Honours and Masters in Environmental and Geographical Science from the University of Cape Town and a PhD in Curriculum Studies focusing on Eco-Justice Education from Stellenbosch University. Najma is active in communicating on environment, climate and development issues and has published widely. She is an invited guest speaker and facilitator at local and international events, and is a member of the WE-Africa Network.

Gaylor Montmasson-Clair is a Senior Economist at Trade & Industrial Policy Strategies (TIPS), a South Africa-based economic policy think-tank, where he leads work on Sustainable Growth. He holds a Master's degree in International Affairs from the Grenoble Institute of Political Studies, France as well as a Master's degree in Energy and Environment Economics from the Grenoble Faculty of Economics, France. Gaylor has carried out extensive research and policy work on the transition to sustainable development pathways from a developing country perspective, with a focus on policy frameworks, socio-economic implications, industrial development and resource security.

Samantha Munro is an economist at DNA Economics. She obtained her Masters in Environmental Economics and her honours in Environmental Science, both with distinction. She has presented research at both local and international conferences. Her Masters thesis was published in an international journal and she also received the McGraw-Hill best Masters thesis dissertation and the 2016 AEASA first prize for best publication in a professional journal. Samantha has worked in the environmental and water sphere where she worked on environmental authorisations, audits, water footprints, water risk assessments, socio-economic assessments and resettlement action plans. She is a registered Cand. Pr. Nat Sci.

Chantal Naidoo is a Regional Advisor to the Green Climate Fund and works in African countries on the programming and mobilisation of climate finance. She has a background in the public and private finance sector in South Africa and internationally in investment banking and climate finance. Her work focuses on policies and programmes to support the financing of sustainability transitions. Chantal co-published research on 'Strategic national approaches to climate finance' building on her work with the South African National Climate Change Response Paper, design of the national Green Fund and establishing the Environmental Finance Unit of the Development Bank of Southern Africa. She is reading towards a DPhil in Technology and Innovation Management (University of Sussex) and has a MPhil in

Development Finance (University of Stellenbosch) and Bachelor of Commerce (University of Cape Town).

Shanna Nienaber is the manager of the Implementation Unit for the Water Research, Development and Innovation (RDI) Roadmap in South Africa. The Roadmap is a partnership initiative between the Department of Science and Technology (DST), Department of Water and Sanitation and the Water Research Commission (WRC). It provides a structured framework for research, high-end skills and innovation deployment to contribute to the implementation of national policy, strategy and planning in water and sanitation resources management. Shanna has a background in political science and a particular research and practitioner interest in environmental governance, systems of innovation and the science–society interface.

Johan Olivier is founding member of Inkwazi Consulting. He has extensive public sector and management experience with proven expertise and leadership in governance, project management, monitoring and evaluation, as well as both quantitative and qualitative research at the national and international level. Dr Olivier holds a PhD degree from Cornell University in the United States with specialisation in Organisational Behaviour (Cornell Business School), social movements/politics, and research methodology (statistics). He has taught at the Universities of Cape Town, Stellenbosch, Pretoria and Stanford University (US). He was appointed Extraordinary Professor at the University of Pretoria's Gordon Institute of Business Sciences in 2014.

Chantal Ramcharan-Kotze is Managing Director of Partnering for Impact (Pty) Ltd. She is a Partnership Strategist with 17 years of experience in Business Management, Public-Private Partnership (PPP) and Cross-Sector Collaboration, currently completing her doctorate with the Gordon Institute of Business Science (GIBS) – University of Pretoria. Chantal has held Executive and Senior Management roles in the Financial Services, Engineering, Biodiversity, Energy and Water sectors. She has been involved in concession, programme and platform establishment, strategy and policy development; and is currently with the South African Water Research Commission. She was awarded the African Green Futures Leadership Award in December 2017.

Presha Ramsarup's PhD focused on a systems approach to change-oriented learning pathways and sustainable development. Her PhD work uncovered systemic insights into the emergence of scarce skill occupational learning pathways. She has worked as a practising educator, professional development facilitator and environmental education advisor. She has served as a technical advisor to both provincial and national government to support the development of environmental and sustainability education within South Africa's education and training transformation process. She has worked as researcher to produce South Africa's first Environmental Sector Skills Plan and is currently the National Coordinator of the National Green Skills Project.

Her work is focused on supporting Green Skills development through an employer-led demand project to identify green jobs and researching opportunities to green traditional jobs across sectors.

Eureta Rosenberg is Professor in the Murray & Roberts Chair of Environment and Sustainability Education at Rhodes University. She obtained her PhD in Education exploring research methodologies for environmental education. Her experience in academia, civil society initiatives and consulting includes research, teaching, programme evaluation and strategic planning. She is joint national coordinator of the Green Skills programme, a founding member of the National Environmental Skills Planning Forum and Editor-in-Chief of the Southern African Journal of Environmental Education.

Nolwazi Sokhulu is a specialist in sustainable energy policy, working within the Climate Change and Energy practice at DNA Economics. She has been involved in a range of research projects relating to energy and climate change, such as the monitoring and evaluation of an energy efficiency programme and the development of a green economy strategy for a provincial government. She has previously worked as a research analyst responsible for modelling equities in the resources sector and managing investment portfolios. She holds a MSc in Global Affairs, specialising in Energy and Environmental Policy, from New York University.

Mark Swilling is Distinguished Professor of Sustainable Development in the School of Public Leadership, University of Stellenbosch, and Visiting Professor at the Universities of Sheffield and Utrecht; Academic Director of the Sustainability Institute and Co-Director of the Stellenbosch Centre for Complex Systems in Transition. He co-authored with Eve Annecke *Just Transitions: Explorations of Sustainability in an Unfair World* (Tokyo: United Nations University Press, 2012); co-edited with Adriana Allen and Andreas Lampis *Untamed Urbanism* (New York and London: Routledge); and co-edited with Josephine Musango and Jeremy Wakeford *Greening the South African Economy* (Cape Town: Juta). He is a member of UNEP's International Resource Panel and of the Board of the Development Bank of Southern Africa. He is co-lead author of *The Weight of Cities: Resource Requirements of Future Urbanization*, to be published in 2018 by the International Resource Panel.

Coleen Vogel, Distinguished Professor, Global Change Institute, University of Witwatersrand, is a Climatologist by training, focusing on Adaptation and Sustainability issues. Her research interests include systemic risk reduction, climate services, drought and the 'human dimensions' specific to global environmental change. She was one of the Chapter Lead Authors of the Africa Chapter for the Intergovernmental Panel on Climate Change, IPCC 4th Assessment Report and was also an author of the Synthesis Report for Policymakers of the 4th IPCC Assessment Report. A Nobel Peace Prize was awarded to the author team together with Al Gore for the 4th Assessment Report. Coleen was a Chapter Author on Human Security for the 5th IPCC

Assessment Report. She has been Chair and Vice Chair of international committees (for example, the International Human Dimensions Programme, now known together with other international programmes as Future Earth). She has received an international award, the Burtoni Award, for her work on climate change advocacy and the science of climate change adaptation.

Acknowledgements

The origin of this book dates back several years and is rooted in the conversations, dialogues and debates on South Africa's transition to sustainability. I would therefore first like to thank all the contributors to this volume for their commitment towards this project, and for sharing their experiences as active participants (and comrades) in crafting and implementing South Africa's transition pathways. The case contributors are also gratefully acknowledged.

I would also like to thank Earthscan for their commitment towards publishing this book, and for the insightful comments of two anonymous referees on the book proposal. A special thank you to Leila Walker for her patience and guidance in bringing the final manuscript together.

In most of the contributions to this volume, if not all, a commitment towards environmental and social justice narratives can be discerned, highlighting the vision of sustainability transition pathways in 'accelerating progress in building an equitable society'. South Africa, in spite of the great strides it has made in meeting some of its critical socio-economic challenges, still has a way to go in crafting development pathways to ensure that it stays within a 'safe and just operating space'. This book seeks to highlight some of the ingredients for working towards just and sustainable futures in South Africa.

And finally, thanks to Mohamed and Umar, for their patience, support and comfort, and for reminding and inspiring me to always live the talk.

Abbreviations and acronyms

AfDB	African Development Bank
ASGISA	Accelerated and Shared Growth Initiative for South Africa
COGTA	Department of Cooperative Governance
COSATU	Congress of South African Trade Unions
CRIBs	Climate Relevant Innovation-System Builders
CSIR	Council for Scientific and Industrial Research
DBSA	Development Bank of Southern Africa
DEA	Department of Environmental Affairs
DoE	Department of Energy
DST	Department of Science and Technology
DWS	Department of Water and Sanitation
EDD	Economic Development Department
GEAR	Growth, Employment and Redistribution
GHG	Greenhouse Gas
GW	Gigawatt
IDC	Industrial Development Corporation
ILO	International Labour Organization
IPAP	Industrial Policy Action Plan
IPP	Independent Power Producers
IRP	Integrated Resource Plan
IWRM	Integrated Water Resource Management
LTAS	Long Term Adaptation Strategies
M&E	Monitoring and Evaluation
MEC	Minerals Energy Complex
MWp	Megawatt peak
MTSF	Medium Term Strategic Framework
NAS	National Adaptation Strategy
NBI	National Business Initiative
NDP	National Development Plan
NEDLAC	National Economic Development and Labour Council
NFSD	National Framework for Sustainable Development
NGP	National Growth Path
NPC	National Planning Commission

NSI	National System of Innovation
NSSD1	National Sustainable Strategy and Development Action Plan 2011–2014
OECD	Organisation for Economic Cooperation and Development
OFO	Organising Framework for Occupations
PAGE	Partnership for Action on Green Economy
PPP	Public-Private Partnership
R&D	Research and Development
RDI	Research, Development and Innovation
RDP	Reconstruction and Development Programme
RE	Renewable Energy
REI4P	Renewable Energy Independent Power Producers Procurement Programme
REIPPPP	Renewable Energy Independent Power Producers Procurement Programme
RSA	Republic of South Africa
SACN	South African Cities Network
SALGA	South African Local Government Association
SANBI	South African National Biodiversity Institute
SDGs	Sustainable Development Goals
SHEQ	Safety, Health and Environmental Quality
SOC	State-Owned Corporations
Stats SA	Statistics South Africa
the dti	The Department of Trade and Industry
UN	United Nations
UNECA	United Nations Economic Commission for Africa
UNEP	United Nations Environment Programme
UNITAR	United Nations Institute for Training and Research
UNDP	United Nations Development Programme
WADER	Water Technologies Demonstration Programme
WEF	World Economic Forum
WRC	Water Research Commission

1 South Africa's transition to sustainability

An overview

Najma Mohamed

Introduction

The global ascendance of sustainability narratives, through the Paris Agreement on climate change and the adoption of the Sustainable Development Goals (SDGs) in 2015, has reinvigorated sustainable development discourses. This revival can be attributed primarily to the escalation of global social and environmental crises such as climate change, unemployment, inequality and environmental degradation, coupled with the financial crisis of 2008, which exposed the limitations and contradictions of existing development models (Cook *et al.*, 2012). These multiple crises also opened up new pathways for policy reforms that promote sustainable development.

Sustainable development is widely accepted globally as a policy framework in planning and development, and has featured prominently in environmental policy formulation in South Africa. Post-apartheid environmental discourse highlighted the importance of centralising social and environmental outcomes in addressing the country's development challenges and the inequities of the past. In September 2015, South Africa signed up to the 2030 Agenda for Sustainable Development. Three years before, in 2012, the country finalised its development agenda and vision for 2030, the National Development Plan (NDP), which expressed a commitment towards embarking on a just transition to a low-carbon development pathway.

South Africa's transition to a greener development pathway is reflected in the mainstreaming of environmental sustainability, and more recently climate change, in a suite of macro-economic and sector-specific policies, and a marked increase in environmental investments by the public and private sector. This is vividly illustrated in the renewable energy procurement programme, which saw the country emerge as one of the fastest growing renewable energy markets in the world. Sector- and technology-specific strategies have been instituted at the national level, supporting the development of biofuels, biogas and electric vehicle industries, for instance, while sub-national green economy strategies and plans have been developed. To date, seven of the nine provinces in South Africa have developed provincial strategies that identify the driving sectors and focus areas for green economic development at the sub-national level. Climate and environmental drivers have been central in making a case for transitioning to an employment-rich, low-carbon economy, and for developing policies, mechanisms and technologies which can build the resilience of the South African economy and society. A vision for an effective climate change response and transition to a climate resilient, efficient and equitable low-carbon economy and society thus exists.

This book explores South Africa's sustainability transition through reflections of the context and critical systems which are enabling and driving this transition – with an explicit focus on whether this transition is addressing the environment and development challenges of the country. Increasingly, questions and critiques are being raised whether current sustainability transition pathways are delivering social outcomes and whether they could catalyse the transformative structural and system reform needed to address the deep-rooted causes of rising inequalities and environmental degradation.

The environment and development challenges facing South Africa are largely structural in nature, based in part on the enduring legacy of apartheid, but also rooted in the development trajectory which the country has pursued post-apartheid. Coal-intensive electricity production is largely the reason why South Africa is amongst the top 20 CO_2 emitters in the world, with greenhouse gas emissions commensurate with those of some industrialised countries (DEA and NBI, 2017). Yet climate projections for the country paint a grim picture. In the last decades, the country has already experienced temperature increases higher than the global average, and climate change impact projections predict further warming, as well as an increase in extreme weather events like droughts, floods and heatwaves (CSIR, 2018).

The transformative vision which sought to redress the legacy of apartheid on the South African society has not resulted in the 'radical economic transformation' which the country desperately needs. Teetering on the brink of an economic downgrade, unemployment figures stand at close to 30 per cent, marginal betterments in poverty reduction are at risk of being lost and inequality remains amongst the highest in the world (see Chapter 2). South Africa's environmental performance has also not kept pace. Loss of valuable natural resources (YCELP, 2016), weak environmental governance (OECD, 2013) and resource scarcity – writ large in the recent drought and current water crisis – has highlighted not only the vulnerability of South Africa to the impact of climate change, but has unearthed the growing discontent with the governance of public resources. Ongoing service delivery protests in South Africa – centred on the provision of essential services such as water and sanitation, housing, education and energy – could be regarded as a barometer of growing civil unrest. It illustrates the need to deepen the focus of policy on the poor and vulnerable, giving life to the constitutional mandate of developing 'responsive, inclusive and accountable' governance systems befitting of a developmental state (Chigwata *et al.*, 2017: 5).

South Africa's policy commitment to a just, low-carbon, resource-efficient and pro-employment development trajectory places it amongst an increasing number of countries exploring pathways to transition to more environmentally sustainable and socially inclusive economies. In 2012, the country was ranked first in global leadership in the Global Green Economy Index due to the strength of its policy and political commitment towards greening its economy (Dual Citizen, 2012). This followed the hosting of the 17th Conference of Parties (COP 17) in 2011, the governing body that acts as the fulcrum for deliberations on global climate change commitments. By 2016, South Africa's performance had declined notably, losing the impetus created by hosting this prestigious global environmental event. The country placed 59th amongst the 80 countries covered in the Index (Dual Citizen, 2016). Further, Yale's Environmental Performance Index in 2016, which ranks countries in relation to their performance on high-priority environmental issues in two areas: protection of human health and protection of ecosystems, placed the country 81st out of the 90 countries measured (YCELP, 2016).

The marginal adjustments which have characterised much post-apartheid economic policy (Turok, 2011) has barely dented the 'powerful system of extractive industries, exploiting workers and nature to achieve economic growth' (Fioramonti, 2017: 5). A just transition towards sustainability, in which the equity and well-being of all South Africans *and* the environmental sustainability of the country's valuable natural systems is prioritised (Swilling *et al.*, 2015), promise to move beyond incremental shifts and tweaking of the current economic system. Could it deliver not merely an incremental shift but a 'substantive and transformative change towards the goal of sustainable development' (Borel-Saladin and Turok, 2013: 209)? This book explores whether 'a genuine turn to green economic activity has been made' (Sharife and Bond, 2011) through reflections on the existing environment and development context of South Africa and sustainability transitions in key systems.

From a variety of disciplinary and conceptual angles, this book brings together the reflections of researcher-practitioners in government, civil society and the private sector to explore the dynamics of South Africa's sustainability transition pathways 'empirically [and] in contextually specific ways rather than depict them in generic terms' (Swilling and Annecke, 2012: xvii). Chapters synthesise theoretical insights, including new models and frameworks, concepts and praxis, contextualised against South Africa's growing landscape of sustainability policies and programmes, to assess whether policy commitments and visions are being translated into action.

Illustrations of a broad spectrum of transition arenas – across sectors and systems, are presented as transformative niches where shifts towards more sustainability pathways can be discerned. And key challenges and recommendations for new mechanisms, concepts and frameworks to support the achievement of just sustainability pathways are outlined throughout the book, which seeks to answer the essential question: Can South Africa's current transition pathway lead towards outcomes which are both socially and environmentally just?

Just transitions: a framework for sustainable transitions in South Africa

A wide range of concepts, discourses and disciplines embody the central messages of new pathways towards sustainability, such as green economy, green growth, low-carbon development, resilience, sustainable investment, green skills and jobs, just transitions, circular economy, natural capital and climate-compatible development. These approaches offer diverging views around achieving sustainability though it is possible, as discussed in Section 1.4, to identify distinguishing features of the various discourses around greening the economy, such as a focus on economic growth, ecosystem resilience and equity and social justice.

While diverse *and* divergent concepts on sustainability abound, it remains one of the critical challenges facing the world in the 21st century – and one that continues to occupy a central role in development discourse, policy and practice. Transitions research is also increasingly being applied to understand socio-technical innovations towards sustainability, particularly the promotion, characterisation and governance of sustainability transitions (Markard *et al.*, 2012). Transitions research has been drawn upon by various contributors to this edited volume, though this work – in its totality – essentially seeks to present contextualised reflections on South Africa's sustainability transition, and is much closer aligned to the need to present 'a more nuanced and complex [transition] process' which is rooted in and determined by the 'political and economic system of path dependence' (Fakir, 2017: 29).

Pro-poor and socially inclusive pathways, which respond to the developmental challenges of poverty, inequality and unemployment, are central in crafting the notion of inclusive sustainability transitions. Drawing on existing work and empirical research on the social dimensions of sustainability transitions, this book reinforces the case for adopting a just transition framework in South Africa. A transition can be broadly defined as

> a gradual, continuous process of change where the structural character of a society (or a complex sub-system of society) transforms. Transitions are not uniform, and nor is the transition process deterministic: there are large differences in the scale of change and the period over which it occurs.
>
> (Rotmans *et al.*, 2001:16)

Transitions involve a range of possible pathways, and are often designed with long-term (30- to 50-year) end goals in mind. While the term 'just transition' has its antecedents in the organised labour movement, it has been employed in recent years by the proponents of inclusive sustainability transitions to foreground the importance of the social dimensions of sustainability transitions. Critical voices have long pointed to the neglect of the social dimensions of prevailing sustainability discourses, highlighting the need to link 'environmental sustainability with poverty reduction and social justice' (Lélé, 1991; Adams,

1995; Leach *et al.*, 2010). Heterodox economists are developing new, post-GDP economics required to delineate a 'safe and just space' for the well-being of humanity within the means of the planet (see Fioramonti, 2017; Raworth, 2017), while contemporary work is challenging the lack of social justice considerations in the mainstream orientations of prevailing green growth discourses (Centre for Inclusive Growth, 2011; UNRISD, 2012; IIED and CAFOD, 2014; Schmitz and Scoones, 2015; Fatheuer *et al.*, 2016). Environmental justice activists have identified solid ground for establishing stronger synergies between labour and community in creating a more powerful counterforce to neo-liberal sustainability discourses (Ehresman and Okereke, 2015; Evans and Phelan, 2016). From its origins in organised labour, just transitions now represents diverse views unified in their commitment towards 'going green with equity'.

The case for applying a just transitions lens to understand the dynamics of South Africa's sustainability transition pathways goes to the central aim of the book – to harness the opportunities presented by this transition for achieving transformative change. Transformative change, drawing on the definition of UNRISD 'requires changes in economic structures to promote [environmentally sustainable] employment-intensive growth patterns that ensure macro-economic stability' and which, above all, 'requires changes in social structures and relations, including addressing the growing economic and political power of elites and patterns of stratification related to class, gender, ethnicity, religion or location that can lock people (including future generations) into disadvantage and constrain their choices and agency' (2016: 5). A growing multi-stakeholder movement is agitating for transformative change, with the hope of getting the country back in line with the vision of developing a just and sustainable country in which all South Africans prosper.

Environmental policy in post-apartheid South Africa, discussed in the next section, is underscored by an equity- and rights-based discourse in which sustainable development visions include a strong emphasis on social justice. Early scholarship on sustainable development in South Africa reflected this orientation, while recent formulations of sustainability transition pathways note the systemic and structural challenges associated with transitioning from the carbon- and resource-intensive (and inefficient) economy to a low-carbon pathway. The long-term development vision, the NDP, emphasises the need for an *equitable* and *just transition* to a low-carbon economy, highlighting key principles central to this goal. Civil society voices reflect this orientation more strongly. One of the leading voices of organised labour, the Congress of South African Trade Unions (COSATU) denotes a just transition as one which 'provides the opportunity for deeper transformation that includes the redistribution of power and resources towards a more just and equitable social order' (COSATU, 2012: 52). The World Wide Fund for nature, WWF, regarded the country's transition as an 'opportunity for combining developmental and environmental goals in a new developmental approach – a just transition to a low carbon economy' (Scholtz, 2011: 1), which should highlight the structural dysfunctions of the prevailing economic model. Swilling *et al.*, reflecting on the

South African transition, posits that in South Africa 'a just transition can be understood as a structural transformation that results in the achievement of two linked goals: developmental welfarism and a sustainability transition' (2015: 2). A just transition vision can thus be discerned in South Africa's development discourse.

The driving factor which led to the adoption of just transitions as an over-arching analytical framework of this book was thus first the need to centralise equity and inclusivity, poverty reduction and employment generation in the formulation of sustainability transitions in South Africa. South Africa's trans-ition pathway not only has a distinct pro-employment focus, but multiple visions of sustainability transitions in the country converge in their commit-ment towards securing social justice as a key outcome of the country's transition pathway. Calls for inclusive approaches to greening the South African economy, which address the most vulnerable in society – urban and rural poor, women and youth – and which ensures that the benefits of green innovations reach *all* South Africans are becoming more pronounced as sustainable development-oriented policy reforms are being implemented. A just transition, which extends beyond incrementalist discourses on green economic transformation towards reformist and transformational discourses, which are unequivocally committed towards addressing the environmental *and* social dimensions of sustainability transitions, is thus needed.

Second, the need for a context-specific analytical approach which assesses *and* challenges the carbon-intensive pathway and lock-in of South Africa's coal-dependent development trajectory, revealing the structures, systems and pro-cesses which represent the powerful vested interests which support and perpetuate the 'double-speak of transformation and preservation' (Khan and Mohamed, 2016), is needed. The country has outlined an ambitious trajectory for greenhouse gas (GHG) emissions reductions, yet it remains amongst the top ten countries, globally, that continue to subsidise fossil fuels – and has further prioritised investments in coal as a long-term energy strategy. South Africa still needs to have the society-wide dialogue on how to truly craft a transition pathway which can meet the country's desired emissions reduction objectives, create employment and improve the resilience of the poor and vulnerable who are likely to be most impacted by a changing climate.

And third, sustainability policies, innovations and investments, at the global and national level, could create the discursive spaces (or niches) for more inclu-sive and environmentally sustainable economies, representing ways in which the 'old political economy can be disrupted and readjusted' (Fakir, 2017). This requires the adoption of 'middle-range explanatory frameworks that integrate global processes with local environmental action and reveal the particular out-comes experienced by people and communities living within localities and regions' (Friedmann and Rangan, 1993: 11). This book then qualifies its approach as one which employs economic, political and social considerations in exploring the partnerships, programmes and projects which are direct mani-festations of this transition pathway. The social dimensions of the green economy transition in South Africa has not been well-documented. This collection draws on the experience and insights of researcher-practitioners, who are at the cutting edge of designing and implementing transition initiatives in South Africa, to assess the social dimensions of the country's sustainability transition.

Sustainable development in South Africa: crafting pathways to environmental justice?

The rapprochement between the environment and development discourses is epitomised by the widespread adoption of the term 'sustainable development'. In Stockholm in 1972, the United Nations Conference on the Human Environment signified one of the first global efforts to reconcile environment and development objectives. This was subsequently strengthened by the 1987 Brundtland Report which defined sustainable development as 'meeting the needs of the present without compromising the ability of future generations to meet their own needs'. The concept of sustainable development has been adopted worldwide, taking centre stage in global multilateral environmental gatherings for over four decades, and culminating in the recent adoption of the SDGs which put together an integrated plan of action 'for people, planet and prosperity'. South Africa has played a leading role in the formulation of *Transforming our World: The 2030 Agenda for Sustainable Development*, the global vision underlying the SDGs. Constituting 17 goals and 169 targets, the SDGs seek to expand the ambitions of the Millennium Development Goals by seeking to adopt transformative pathways to achieve sustainable development in its three dimensions – economic, social and environmental.

Concerns exist about the diaphanous quality of the concept of sustainable development with some arguing that the concept is largely located within modernist and neo-liberal development discourses which lead to technocratic and managerial approaches to environmental governance (Lélé, 1991; Adams, 1995; Escobar, 1996), with minimal adjustments to prevailing market and governance systems. Yet the vision of sustainable development in post-apartheid South Africa, outlined in this section, emerged in a context of deep economic and socio-political reform and was premised on the constitutional mandate that 'everyone has the right to an environment that is not harmful to their health or well-being' and the right to 'ecologically sustainable development' (Republic of South Africa, 1996: 11). Sustainable development has in fact been central to environmental policymaking in South Africa.

The history of institutionalised racism has played an integral part in the creation of many environmental problems in South Africa (Durning, 1990; Ramphele and McDowell, 1991). The apartheid-era environmental governance system not only led to dispossession, forced removals and overcrowding, which contributed to the poor state of the environment, but had a profound impact on policymaking and environmental perception and attitudes. For instance, South Africa presents an image of a world conservation leader, yet the activities of the conservation movement occurred within the framework of apartheid policy

(Khan, 1997a). Historical studies document the large-scale displacement of communities in the name of conservation, limited access to land and water resources and virtually no access to protected areas for black communities (Beinart and Coates, 1995; Khan, 1997b). The environmental perception that was created was thus one which was 'wildlife-centred and preservationist'. The post-apartheid era saw the emergence of an environmental movement in South Africa, which sought to address the impact of apartheid on the environment and people through the gross maldistribution of natural resources, and reverse the 'cruel and perverse' history (and impact) of environmental policymaking (McDonald, 2002).

Following the tremendous changes that preceded the first democratic elections in 1994, numerous authors discussed the role of sustainable development in addressing environmental injustice in South Africa (Cock and Koch, 1991; Ramphele and McDowell, 1991; Munslow and Fitzgerald, 1994). The establishment of the Environmental Justice Networking Forum (EJNF) in 1992 provided an institutional form to this movement, which focused on issues of poverty, occupational and environmental health, as well as the increased participation of communities in environmental policy formulation (Cock and Fig, 2001). An environmentalism, which 'addresses the political and social dimensions of protecting the environment, and links these analyses to sustainable development through such issues as land use, urbanisation, workplace safety, employment, food policy, education and democracy' (Cole, 1994: 235) emerged. This environmental justice movement, which has been the subject of analysis (Cock and Fig, 2001; McDonald, 2002), played a central role in the 'broad, deep and inter-sectoral participation in environmental policymaking' which produced new environmental legislation in 1998.

The first decade of the South African environmental justice movement peaked in the formulation of the participatory process, the Consultative National Environmental Policy Planning Process (CONEPPP), which laid the foundations for post-apartheid environmental policymaking, ultimately taking legislative form in the National Environmental Management Act (NEMA) in 1998 – the central environmental act in the country (Cock and Fig, 2001). This process was complemented by legislative reforms, which sought to redress apartheid-era environmental injustices – in water law, land reform and protected area management for instance. Participatory policymaking took a downturn in the subsequent decade, due to a shift towards managerialist and technocratic interpretations in the implementation of environmental legislation (Oelofse et al., 2006), coupled with capacity challenges impacting enforcement, weakened civil society and a lack of inter-ministerial and inter-departmental coordination and collaboration (Cock and Fig, 2001; OECD, 2013). The environmental governance structure of the 2000s was thus one which largely failed to 'give substance' to the principle of community involvement enshrined in the NEMA, and led to policymaking which was largely 'exclusionary' (Cock and Fig, 2001). The need to revive the social and environmental foundations of the policy framework – notably the notions of equality, equity and redistribution in sustainability discourses – has been illustrated through recent work (see Perreira, 2014; Marcatelli 2015) examining how growth- and technocentric-oriented sustainability discourses (and instruments) have impacted 'both materially and discursively' on growing inequalities.

Promising shifts have been witnessed in the last five years, marking a possible revitalisation of social justice orientation, which characterised the post-apartheid environmental movement. Policymaking processes are becoming more inclusive and integrated (DEA, 2012), while intergovernmental collaboration efforts on green policymaking in South Africa is receiving global support (PAGE, 2016). Business has been responsive in taking action on climate change and resource scarcity, while civil society has begun to challenge the environmental impact of the development trajectory – highlighting the weakness of public governance structures beset by deep-rooted corruption. Legal challenges on the public discharge of constitutional and legal mandates to protect the environment, reduce GHG emissions and use state funds in an accountable and transparent manner have been mounted (and won). Circumspect interventions by the state – for instance in setting the energy mix of the country (through the procurement of nuclear energy) (SAFCEI, 2017), and in the authorisation of new coal-fired power stations (Mzamo, 2017), have been challenged in court, resulting in landmark victories which have given teeth to the country's policy framework.

The comprehensive policy and regulatory framework for environmental and natural resource management and cooperative governance, established to support the implementation of climate and environmental policies, is now under scrutiny as South Africa embarks on a 'just transition to a resource-efficient, low carbon and pro-employment growth path' (DEA, 2011a: 7). In 2009, the country committed to reducing GHG emissions through a peak, plateau and decline in its emissions. Recognising the need to shift its growth path, the government committed to reduce GHG emissions by 34 per cent by 2020 and by 42 per cent by 2025 (DEA, 2011b). This was followed by the enactment of policies, discussed throughout this book, which opened the discursive space for increased efforts towards sustainability pathways – primarily through the commitment towards transitioning to a greener economy. Figure 1.1 below sketches a timeline of the main policies, including national strategies, which characterise the sustainable development policy discourse in South Africa.

There have also been landmark policy papers and discussion documents, such as the 2006 policy papers on environmental fiscal reform (National Treasury, 2006) and carbon tax (National Treasury, 2010), which have shaped the country's transition pathway. However, continued subsidisation of the carbon-intensive coal industry, as well as the slow uptake of pricing strategies to internalise environmental externalities, such as the (postponed) carbon tax, is impeding economic reforms which could support South Africa's green economy development trajectory (OECD, 2015). A 2009 document, *Framework for South Africa's response to the international economic crisis*, produced by South Africa's

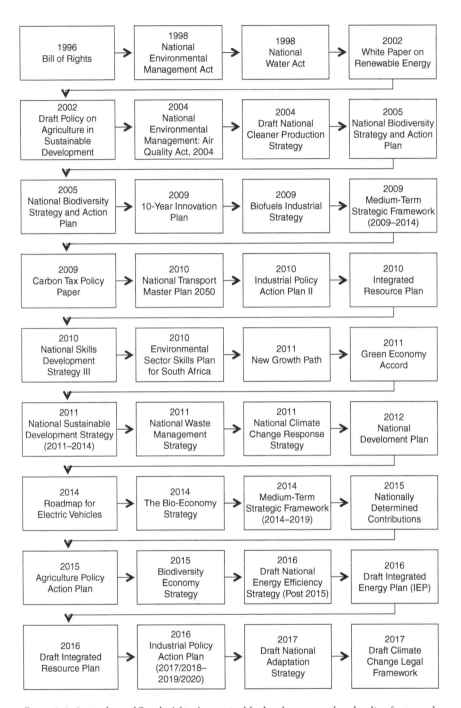

Figure 1.1 A timeline of South Africa's sustainable development-related policy framework.
Source: Author.

tripartite structure set up to facilitate social dialogue, the National Economic Development and Labour Council (NEDLAC), also set the tone for an inclusive and sustainable development pathway – as a key response to the global financial crisis. The sustainable development policy framework, the subject of analysis throughout this book, consists of cross-cutting macro-economic and sectoral policies and strategies which essentially seek to mainstream environmental sustainability.

Challenges related to policy implementation and enforcement capacity, coordination and coherence, outlined further in Chapter 5, have resulted in an 'anaemic' interpretation and implementation of the sustainable development policy landscape in South Africa. Questions abound on whether the inclusive and transformative vision of a just pathway to sustainability, which provided several inroads for 'environmental justice in the new democratic legal order' (Glazewski, 2002), has been realised. The 2008 National Environmental Management Act enshrines principles related to the achievement of environmental justice as well as equitable access to environmental resources, benefits and services – which is the bedrock on which a transition vision should be built. It has been argued that South Africa's transition to a greener economy could act as a 'lever for catalysing movement and sustaining momentum towards a more equitable and inclusive economy', but is the green economy, like sustainable development, an 'idea which is potentially purposeful, offering hope to diverse groupings, but also vulnerable to capture by powerful interests' (Khan and Mohamed, 2016: 186, 188)?

A broad spectrum of transition discourses – extending from those that adopt marginal adjustments to the political economy to those that seek more transformative structural reform – exists in South Africa. While the contributions in this book present a critique of technocentric, market-led transitions which marginalise social justice, rights and redistributive narratives, finding the transformative niches within the dominant sustainability discourses could present inroads towards catalysing more systemic shifts, as illustrated in the book chapters discussing finance (Chapter 6), skills (Chapter 8) and partnerships (Chapter 9) for instance. An outline of key sustainability transitions discourses, as captured in the growing analysis of green economy discourses, is detailed below.

South Africa's sustainability transition(s) discourses – from growth to equity

The continuum between technocentric and ecocentric approaches —reformist and transformational – evident in the environmental movement, similarly characterise sustainability transition discourses. A nascent field of analysis, largely centred on green economy discourses, presents a valuable index for understanding contemporary sustainability discourses. These discourses are being promoted by a wide range of actors and have even 'reached the core of global economic elites, which represents a change of paradigm that environmental scientists and environmentalists have been calling for decades' (Jänicke, 2012: 13).

An analysis of prevailing discourses not only assists in understanding the dominant trends (and actor networks) in sustainability pathways, but also iden-tifies the blind spots as well as the opportunities for greater convergence *and* divergence between discourses. While the 'political battles over green growth will not take place simply at the level of discourse', those with vested interests in maintaining business as usual would seek to ensure that more transformative discourses (and policies) do not make political headway (Jacobs, 2012: 18). In South Africa, tensions and contradictions between technocentric environ-mental managerialism (Oelofse *et al.*, 2006), and more radical approaches (Cock and Koch, 1991) which call for structural transformation, can also be discerned in the embryonic sustainability transition discourses. It can be seen in the con-certed efforts by powerful vested interests, allied to the state, to derail the trans-ition towards renewable energies in South Africa, or in the ways in which debates between proponents of natural capital have trumped discourses that promote the application of non-monetary indices in the valuation of nature.

Theoretical framings of green economy discourses are useful in identifying the multiplicity of pathways towards sustainability and assist in 'understanding the origins, as well as the advantages and disadvantages, of particular "green economic" strategies, and to select those most appropriate within particular cir-cumstances' (Faccer *et al.*, 2014: 645). Figure 1.2. synthesises the broad contin-uum which exists between sustainability transition discourses. Incrementalist discourses continue to operate largely within the prevailing macro-economic paradigm and are largely state- and business-led with a focus on market-based tools to drive transitions. Middle-range discourses constitute a diverse range of

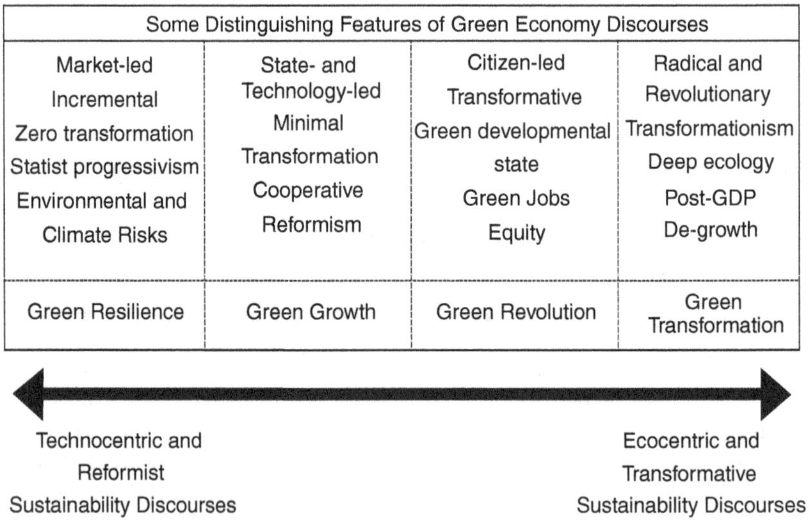

Some Distinguishing Features of Green Economy Discourses			
Market-led Incremental Zero transformation Statist progressivism Environmental and Climate Risks	State- and Technology-led Minimal Transformation Cooperative Reformism	Citizen-led Transformative Green developmental state Green Jobs Equity	Radical and Revolutionary Transformationism Deep ecology Post-GDP De-growth
Green Resilience	Green Growth	Green Revolution	Green Transformation

Technocentric and Reformist Sustainability Discourses ←——————————————→ Ecocentric and Transformative Sustainability Discourses

Figure 1.2 A continuum of sustainability and green economy discourses.

Source: Faccer *et al.* (2014), Death, (2015), Ehresman and Okereke (2015), Schmitz and Scoones (2015), Stevenson (2015).

agendas for greening economies, epitomised in the green growth discourse – defined by the OECD (2011: 9) as 'fostering economic growth and development, while ensuring that natural assets continue to provide the resources and environmental services on which our well-being relies'. Transformative discourses, which have been spearheaded by international civil society seeking to incorporate critical perspectives, such as human rights, environmental justice, well-being, gender equality and decent work, call for a structural reform of both economic and broader societal objectives. Death's (2015) analysis, which juxtaposes transitions along a continuum of green resilience and green growth, has been applied in the South African context and is useful in distinguishing the emerging transition discourses in South Africa.

While acknowledging that all four characterisations of green economy discourses, that is, green resilience, green growth, green revolution and green transformation, can be discerned in invocations of the green economy in South Africa, Death (2014) regards the dominant discourse of the green economy in the country as that of green growth. It is by capitalising on

> South Africa's 'brand' as a rising power, with a youthful and energetic population and a rich natural environment, and the country as the political and economic 'gateway to Africa', rather than its environmental and social contradictions, that South Africa [has been] … positioned as a global leader on the green economy.
>
> (Death, 2014: 2)

A state-led and, thus far, publicly financed transition pathway that prioritises technological innovations, aligns well with the existing environmental governance paradigm which is science- and technology-driven. This discourse is closely tied to that of green resilience, which emphasises environmental scarcity, climate change and resource depletion. This is evident in the ways in which the scientific community – largely comprised of natural scientists – have been central to the evidence-based policymaking processes which have supported the transition – though this is beginning to change (Swilling, 2014). The impact of the transition in shifting climate change research and the national innovation system of South Africa is discussed in Chapters 3 and 7 respectively.

While there are voices articulating green transformation and green revolution transition discourses in South Africa – agitating for green and decent jobs, just transitions, food sovereignty, climate justice and energy democracy – these have not coalesced into a coherent movement which could present a counterforce to the hegemonic green growth discourse. The language of the green economy, notably the varieties that centralise equity, was initially welcomed by environmentalists in South Africa for its radical potential. For these discourses to gain prominence, the calls for inclusive sustainability transitions, which address the most vulnerable in society, have to unite on areas of common concern. This would require that 'environmental and social justice activists' appropriate and begin to embed their concerns for the deeper structural changes required to transition to a socially and economically inclusive and greener society, within the 'construction of a development state' (Death, 2014: 3). This is already evident in the efforts to harness environmental interventions in addressing developmental challenges, such as economic empowerment, job creation and poverty alleviation, for instance.

Amongst sustainability transition discourses, a technocentric, market-led discourse of green growth is 'most embedded and widespread' in South Africa, with limited intersection with social justice, rights and redistributive discourses central to more inclusive approaches. This is beginning to change as transformative niches begin to chip away at the regime and landscape level to effect the deeper structural transformation required for systemic shifts. The chapters in this book highlight some of the key obstacles to achieving more inclusive sustainability pathways, but also present possibilities for bringing transformative discourses back into the game, and for sparking the social dialogue required to bring South Africa's sustainability transition back on track.

Conclusion

The coal-dependence of the South African economy, coupled with widening social and economic inequality, calls for a transition that should extend beyond incrementalist discourses on green economic transformation towards reformist and transformational discourses. Critical questions will have to be placed centre stage in South Africa's green economy discourse, such as: Are notions of social justice, transparency and accountability, and inclusivity being sufficiently addressed or does South Africa's green economy discourse naively assume the equitable distribution of profits and opportunities emerging from sustainable development interventions? Can the powerful vested interests impeding the country's energy transition to a post-coal future be overcome to take South Africa on a truly sustainable development pathway? And will the country be able to shift labour market dynamics to enliven a *societal* transition towards sustainability, which is about much more than green jobs?

While South Africa has undoubtedly progressed in addressing the developmental challenges of decades of injustices under apartheid, there is a real risk that rising unemployment and inequality could reverse these gains. A 2015 national study by Oxfam, describes the multi-dimensional nature of poverty and environmental change, assessing how well the country is faring in operating within a 'safe and just space' (Cole, 2015). Trends show improvements in nearly all social indicators since 1994, with social deprivation most severe in the areas of safety, income and employment. However, the country has already crossed its safe environmental boundaries for climate change, freshwater use, biodiversity loss and marine harvesting with environmental stress still growing in two dimensions – climate change and freshwater use, two critical environmental challenges in South Africa. Sustainability transitions provide an opportunity to achieve both environmental and societal well-being, addressing the impact of a changing climate on the most vulnerable, safeguarding nature, and reversing resource inefficiencies in the country. The country has taken the necessary steps towards envisioning this transition, but now needs to remain on course as it enters the difficult terrain of system shifts and structural change.

This book delves deeper into the manifestation of revitalised sustainable development paradigms in the South African landscape, assessing whether these shifts have resulted in closer links between the objectives of economic growth, equity, justice, quality of life and environmental sustainability. National development visions and commitments, as illustrated throughout this book, ostensibly remain committed to pursuing a greener development pathway, but this has to be translated into broader transformative restructuring of the economy and its key systems.

The chapters in this book explore South Africa's progress in transitioning to a socially inclusive and environmentally sustainable development pathway through an examination of both the key drivers and systems that could support the country's sustainability transition. It is structured to present the underlying context of economic growth, climate vulnerability and employment creation, all of which provide the context for South Africa's sustainability transitions, and then examines the manifestation of this transition in key socio-technical and governance systems which structure and support transitions (policies, skills, finance, research and innovation, and partnership development). Key initiatives and policies implemented in South Africa thus far, in energy, waste and water for instance, also form the subject of analysis.

Reflections on whether a just transition, which extends beyond incrementalist state-, market- and technology-led discourses on sustainability transitions, can evolve towards reformist and transformational discourses premised on social dialogue, are needed to broaden existing sustainability discourses in South Africa. Transition pathways that centralise the environmental *and* social dimensions of development, while enabling economic progress for all, thus need to be identified. This book draws on insights from policy and praxis to assess the prospects and pathways for achieving socially inclusive sustainability transitions in South Africa.

References

Adams, W.M., 1995. *Green Development: Environment and Sustainability in the Third World*. Routledge, London.

Beinart, W. and Coates, P., 1995. *Environment and History: The Taming of Nature in the USA and South Africa*. Routledge, London.

Borel-Saladin, J.M. and Turok, I.N., 2013. The Green Economy: Incremental Change or Transformation? *Environmental Policy and Governance*, 23: 209–220.

Centre for Inclusive Growth, 2011. *Going Green with Equity*. International Policy Centre for Inclusive Growth, Brasilia.

Chigwata, T.C., O'Donovan, M. and Powell, D.M., 2017. *Civic Protests and Local Government in South Africa*. Working Paper Series No. 2, The Civic Protests Barometer 2007–2016. Dullah Omar Institute, Cape Town.

Cock, J. and Fig, D., 2001. The Impact of Globalization on Environmental Politics in South Africa, 1990–2002. *African Sociological Review*, 5(2): 15–35.

Cock, J. and Koch, E., 1991. *Going Green: People, Politics and the Environment in South Africa.* Oxford University Press, Cape Town.

Cole, K., 1994. Ideologies of Sustainable Development. In Cole, K. (ed.), *Sustainable Development for a Democratic South Africa.* Earthscan, London.

Cole, M., 2015. *Is South Africa Operating in a Safe and Just Space? Using the Doughnut Model to Explore Environmental Sustainability and Social Justice.* Oxfam Research Report. Oxfam, Johannesburg.

Cook, S., Smith, K. and Utting, P., 2012. *Green Economy or Green Society? Contestation and Policies for a Fair Transition.* Occasional Paper 10. UNRISD, Geneva.

COSATU, 2012. *A Just Transition to a Low-Carbon and Climate Resilient Economy. COSATU Policy on Climate Change: A Call to Action.* COSATU, Braamfontein.

Council for Scientific and Industrial Research (CSIR), 2018. *South Africa Risk and Vulnerability Atlas 2.* CSIR, Pretoria. Available at http://sarva2.dirisa.org/ (accessed 21 February 2018).

DEA (Department of Environmental Affairs), 2011a. *National Strategy for Sustainable Development and Action Plan.* DEA, Pretoria.

DEA, 2011b. *Defining South Africa's Peak, Plateau and Decline Greenhouse Gas Emission Trajectory.* DEA, Pretoria.

DEA, 2012. *Environment Sector Research, Development and Evidence Framework. An Approach to Enhance the Sector Science–Policy Interface and Evidence-based Policy Making.* DEA, Pretoria.

DEA and National Business Initiative (NBI), 2017. *South African Vital Statistics.* Infographic. DEA and NBI, Pretoria and Johannesburg.

Death, C., 2014. The Green Economy in South Africa: Global Discourses and Local Politics. *Politikon: South African Journal of Political Studies,* 41(1): 1–22.

Death, C., 2015. Four Discourses of the Green Economy in the Global South. *Third World Quarterly,* 36(12): 2207–2224, DOI: 10.1080/01436597.2015.1068110.

Dual Citizen LLC, 2012. *Global Green Economy Index: 2012.* Dual Citizen, Washington, DC.

Dual Citizen LLC, 2016. *Global Green Economy Index: 2016.* Dual Citizen, Washington, DC.

Durning, A., 1990. *Apartheid's Environmental Toll.* Worldwatch Paper 95. Worldwatch Institute, Washington, DC.

Ehresman, T.G. and Okereke, C., 2015. Environmental Justice and Conceptions of the Green Economy. *International Environmental Agreements,* 15: 13–27.

Escobar, A., 1996. Constructing Nature: Elements for a Poststructural Political Ecology. In Peet, R. and Watts, M. (eds.), *Liberation Ecologies: Environment, Development, Social Movements.* London, Routledge.

Evans, G. and Phelan, L., 2016. Transition to a Post-Carbon Society: Linking Environmental Justice and Just Transition Discourses. *Energy Policy,* 99, DOI: 10.1010/j.enpol.2016.05.003.

Faccer, K., Nahman, A. and Audouin, M., 2014. Interpreting the Green Economy: Emerging Discourses and their Considerations for the Global South. *Development Southern Africa,* 31(5): 642–657.

Fakir, S., 2017. *Transition Realism: The Implications of Rent-Seeking to Achieve South Africa's Low-Carbon Technology Solutions.* WWF South Africa, Cape Town.

Fatheuer, T., Fuhr, L. and Unmüßig, B., 2016. *Inside the Green Economy: Promises and Pitfalls.* Greenbooks, München.

Fioramonti, L., 2017. *Wellbeing Economy: Success in a World Without Growth*. Pan Macmillan, Johannesburg.

Friedmann, J. and Rangan, H., 1993. *In Defense of Livelihood: Comparative Studies on Environmental Action*. Kumarian Press, Connecticut.

Glazewski, J., 2002. The Rule of Law: Opportunities for Environmental Justice in the New Democratic Legal Order. In McDonald, D.A. (ed.), *Environmental Justice in South Africa*. Ohio University Press, Athens.

IIED and CAFOD, 2014. *Securing Social Justice in Green Economies*. IIED, London.

Jacobs, M., 2012. *Green Growth: Economic Theory and Political Discourse Centre for Climate Change Economics and Policy*. Working Paper No. 108, Grantham Research Institute on Climate Change. London School of Economics, London.

Jänicke, M., 2012. Green Growth: From a Growing Eco-Industry to Economic Sustainability. *Energy Policy*, 48: 13–21.

Khan, F., 1997a. Time for a TRC for conservationists. *Mail and Guardian*, 7–13 November, 37.

Khan, F., 1997b. Soil Wars: The Role of the African National Soil Conservation Association in South Africa, 1953–1959. *Environmental History*, 2: 439–459.

Khan, F. and Mohamed, S., 2016. From the Political Economy of the MEC to the Political Ecology of the 'Green Economy'. In Swilling, M., Musango, J.K. and Wakeford, J. (eds.), *Greening the South African Economy: Scoping the Issues, Challenges and Opportunities*. UCT Press, Cape Town.

Leach, M., Scoones, I. and Stirling, A., 2010. *Dynamic Sustainabilities: Technology, Environment, Social Justice*. Earthscan, Oxon.

Lélé, S., 1991. Sustainable Development: A Critical Review. *World Development*, 19: 607–621.

Marcatelli, M., 2015. Suspended Redistribution: 'Green Economy' and Water Inequality in the Waterberg, South Africa. *Third World Quarterly*, 36(12): 2244–2258.

Markard, J., Raven, R. and Truffer, B., 2012. Sustainability Transitions: An Emerging Field of Research and its Prospects. *Research Policy*, 41: 955–967.

McDonald, D.A., 2002. *Environmental Justice in South Africa*. Ohio University Press, Athens.

Munslow, B. and Fitzgerald, P., 1994. South Africa: The Sustainable Development Challenge. *Third World Quarterly*, 15(2): 227–242.

Mzamo, P., 2017. Victory in SA's first climate change case. *Mining News*, 8 March 2017. www.miningne.ws/2017/03/08/victory-in-sas-first-climate-change-case/# (accessed 10 October 2017).

National Treasury, 2006. *A Framework for Considering Market-Based Instruments to Support Environmental Fiscal Reform in South Africa*. Draft Policy Paper. National Treasury, Pretoria.

National Treasury, 2010. *Reducing Greenhouse Gas Emissions: The Carbon Tax Option*. Discussion Paper for Public Comment. National Treasury, Pretoria.

OECD (Organisation for Economic Cooperation and Development), 2011. *Towards Green Growth*. OECD, Paris.

OECD, 2013. *Environmental Performance Review: South Africa*. OECD, Paris.

OECD, 2015. *Economic Survey of South Africa 2015*. OECD, Paris.

Oelofse, C., Scott, D., Oelofse, D. and Houghton, J., 2006. Shifts Within Ecological Modernization in South Africa: Deliberation, Innovation and Institutional Opportunities. *Local Environment*, 11(1): 61–78.

Partnership for Action on Green Economy (PAGE), 2016. *PAGE Annual Report 2015*. PAGE, Geneva.

Perreira, L., 2014. The Role of Substantive Equality in Finding Sustainable Development Pathways in South Africa. *McGill International Journal of Sustainable Development Law and Policy*, 10(2): 147–178.

Ramphele, M. and McDowell, C., 1991. *Restoring the Land: Environment and Change in Post-Apartheid South Africa*. Panos Publications, London.

Raworth, K., 2017. *Doughnut Economics: Seven Ways to Think like a 21st-Century Economist*. Random House Business Books, London.

Republic of South Africa, 1996. *The Constitution of the Republic of South Africa. Act 108 of 1996*. Government of South Africa, Pretoria.

Schmitz, H. and Scoones, I., 2015. *Accelerating Sustainability: Why Political Economy Matters*. IDS Evidence Report 152. STEPS Centre, University of Sussex, Brighton.

Scholtz, L., 2011. *A Discussion of Systemic Challenges for a Just Transition Towards a Low Carbon Economy*. WWF Briefing. WWF-SA, Cape Town.

Sharife, K. and Bond, P., 2011. Above and Beyond South Africa's Minerals Energy Complex. In Pillay, D., Daniel, J., Naidoo, P. and Southall, R. (eds.), *New SA Review 2: New Paths – Old Compromises*. Wits University Press, Johannesburg www.ee.co.za/wp-content/uploads/legacy/Sharife-Bond-MEC-in-New-SA-Review-2.pdf (accessed 21 February 2018).

Southern Africa Faith Communities Environment Initiative (SAFCEI), 2017. SAFCEI Press Release on High Court Ruling on Proposed Nuclear Deal. *Mail and Guardian*. Available at http://mjc.org.za/2017/04/28/safcei-press-release-on-high-court-ruling-on-proposed-nuclear-deal/ (accessed 10 October 2017).

Swilling, M., 2014. Rethinking the Science–Policy Interface in South Africa: Experiments in Knowledge Co-production. *South African Journal of Science*, 110(5/6). Available at http://dx.doi.org/10.1590/sajs.2014/2013026 (accessed 2 February 2018).

Swilling, M. and Annecke, E., 2012. *Just Transitions: Explorations of Sustainability in an Unfair World*. UCT Press, Claremont.

Swilling, M., Musango, J. and Wakeford, J., 2015. Developmental States and Sustainability Transitions: Prospects of a Just Transition in South Africa. *Journal of Environmental Policy and Planning*, DOI: 10.1080/1523908X.2015.11077.

Turok, B., 2011. *The Controversy About Economic Growth*. Jacana Media, Auckland Park.

UNRISD (United Nations Research Institute for Social Development), 2012. *Social Dimensions of the Green Economy*. UNRISD Research and Policy Brief 12. UNRISD, Geneva.

UNRISD, 2016. *Policy Innovations for Transformative Change: Summary*. UNRISD, Geneva.

Yale Centre for Environment and Policy (YCELP), 2016. *Environmental Performance Index*. Yale University, New Haven, CT.

2 Reaping the socio-economic benefits of an inclusive transition to sustainability

Brent Cloete, Samantha Munro and Nolwazi Sokhulu

Introduction

Since 1994, South Africa has made significant progress in many areas including improving access to public services, health and education, and in establishing strong institutions (The Presidency, 2014; OECD, 2017). Sound macro-economic (monetary and fiscal) policies have also created stable economic conditions. Economic growth, however, has been poor, and has slowed down significantly since the global financial crisis. A lack of micro-economic reforms has held back economic growth in South Africa, which in turn has had a negative impact on employment creation, poverty alleviation and inequality (Faulkner *et al.*, 2013; OECD, 2017).

Green growth strategies, deployed as part of a sustainability transition, have the potential to support inclusive growth and address socio-economic challenges. Yet, as this chapter shows, the same institutional and policy issues, which have constrained growth, poverty alleviation and income inequality, are also likely to hamper the sustainability transition in the absence of structural reforms. Furthermore, the transition may be delayed and even jeopardised if increasingly entrenched corruption and state capture by private interests is not addressed.

Development policy in South Africa

With democracy in 1994 came an increased focus on the socio-economic well-being of all South Africans. The 1996 Constitution of the Republic of South Africa (RSA) describes a democratic and inclusive state, guaranteeing all citizens basic human rights and "justifiable economic and social development" that is compatible with an "environment protected … for the benefit of present and future generations" (RSA, 1996, p. 11; SAHO, 2014). The Reconstruction and Development Programme (RDP) was the basis of government development policy and focused on the eradication of poverty, employment creation and reducing inequality, and established an extensive social welfare system. Implementation of the RDP was, however, impeded by organisational and fiscal challenges (RSA, 1994). Low growth was one of the main factors constraining the resources available to support the RDP.

Subsequently, in 1996, the government launched the Growth, Employment and Redistribution (GEAR) strategy to stimulate faster economic growth. GEAR incorporated the social objectives of the RDP, but also aimed to reduce the fiscal deficit, lower inflation, stabilise the exchange rate, and decrease barriers to trade and capital flows (RSA and DoF, 1996). While GEAR brought about greater macro-economic stability through a reduced fiscal deficit and lower inflation, the policy failed to achieve sufficient private investment, job creation and economic growth. In 2005, GEAR was replaced by the Accelerated and Shared Growth Initiative for South (ASGISA). ASGISA emphasised a role of a strong and coherent industrial policy to drive faster growth. In 2007, the National Industrial Policy Framework (NIPF) and Industrial Policy Action Plan (IPAP) were released (the dti, 2007a). The NIPF set out both short- and medium-term visions premised on 13 strategic programmes, while the IPAP detailed key actions and timeframes with measurable performance indicators. The IPAP promoted diversification away from traditional commodities and non-tradable services and the expansion of production within high value-added and labour-intensive sectors. Both policy documents provided a more active and interventionist approach for industrial policy and highlighted the manufacturing sector as key to South Africa's industrial development (the dti, 2007b). The IPAP is updated regularly and remains the main tool directing industrial policy in South Africa.

In 2009, the Medium Term Strategic Framework 2009–2014 was developed based on the electoral manifesto of the African National Congress (ANC) and aimed to guide short- to medium-term policy and the programme of action over the five-year electoral cycle. Since 2009 the MTSF has provided the principal guide for planning and the allocation of resources across government spheres (RSA, 2009).

In response to the global financial crisis of 2008, which led to more than a million jobs being shed in South Africa, the South African government adopted the New Growth Path (NGP) (developed by the then newly established Economic Development Department) as a strategy to address unemployment, inequality and poverty via the creation of new jobs in the private sector (CGIS, 2010). Specifically, the NGP aims to build an inclusive economy to create decent employment, sustainable livelihoods and eradicate poverty and income inequality (EDD, 2011). It placed "jobs and decent work" at the centre of economic policy. It also set out key job drivers and identified five sectors in which employment creation would be prioritised. These sectors included infrastructure; the agricultural value chain; the mining value chain; the green economy; manufacturing sectors targeted in the IPAPs; tourism; and certain high-level services. The NGP set a target of five million new jobs to be created by 2020. Four social accords were developed to set clear targets, commitments, goals and timeframes, namely Accord 1: National Skills; Accord 2: Basic Education and Partnerships with Schools; Accord 3: Local Procurement and Accord 4: Green Economy (EDD, 2011). In 2013, Accord 6: Youth Employment was also published to address the challenges of youth employment (DED, 2013).

In 2012, the National Development Plan (NDP), which provided the long-term 2030 vision for the country to eliminate poverty and reduce inequality, was developed. The plan set out six interlinked priorities:

- Uniting all South Africans around a common programme to achieve prosperity and equity.
- Promoting active citizenry to strengthen development, democracy and accountability.
- Bringing about faster economic growth, higher investment and greater labour absorption.
- Focusing on key capabilities of people and the state.
- Building a capable and developmental state.
- Encouraging strong leadership throughout society to work together to solve problems.

(NPC, 2012, p. 26)

The NDP is South Africa's primary long-term socio-economic development framework (NPC, 2012) and provides targets for investment, growth and employment creation. A holistic plan for reaching these targets exists. It further identifies key constraints on economic growth (drawing on, amongst others, the ASGISA analysis) and provides a roadmap for a more inclusive economy. To meet these objectives, the emphasis has been on improved infrastructure, basic education and skills development, and the expansion of labour-intensive sectors. The importance of improved access to economic opportunities is also highlighted via support for emerging enterprises, land reform and the inclusion of historically disadvantaged individuals via increased management and ownership opportunities. All of these strategies emphasise the need for collaboration between the public sector, the private sector and labour to achieve a more inclusive and prosperous South Africa (The Presidency, 2014). The short- and medium-term planning for the NDP is guided by the updated 2014–2019 MTSF which aims to ensure policy coherence, alignment and coordination across government plans and budgeting processes (The Presidency, 2014). Recent reiterations of the IPAP have been aligned to the vision of the NDP and the programmatic perspectives of the NGP (TIPS, 2015).

Key socio-economic challenges

The NDP is a very ambitious document that envisages a transformed, sustainable and prosperous society by 2030 (NPC, 2012). Since the inception of democracy in 1994, the South African government's main economic objectives have been job creation, the elimination of poverty and the reduction of inequality (The Presidency, 2014). Given this focus, the success of the NDP will ultimately be measured by the degree to which the lives and opportunities of the poorest South Africans are transformed (Stats SA, 2017).

The policies that have been implemented since 1994, while having increased the short-term living conditions of a large portion of the population (the impact of which will be discussed later in this chapter), have not been able to address structural poverty, unemployment and inequality. *Economic performance* during the last five years, in particular, has been disappointing. High consumer price increases for energy and food, low economic growth driven by a combination of international and domestic factors, lower investment levels, lower commodity prices, greater dependency on credit and political uncertainty meant that some gains have started to be reversed (Stats SA, 2017). As a result, the ability of the current policy and growth trajectory to achieve the NDP targets is questionable, particularly in the areas of unemployment, and poverty and inequality. In terms of economic growth, South Africa has experienced an average economic growth rate of 2.9 per cent per year since 1994. While the annual growth rate has varied significantly, as shown in Figure 2.1, the economy has only grown at more than 5 per cent per annum in three of the last 22 years (2005–2007). This highlights the ambitious nature of the GDP growth target of 5.4 per cent per annum in the NDP.

The official *unemployment rate* in South Africa, as shown in Figure 2.1, has increased from 20 per cent in 1994 to 26.7 per cent in 2016 (SARB, 2018). Over this period, unemployment only fell for more than one year in a row from 2004 to 2007 (when it fell to 22.3 per cent). Given past performance, the NDP

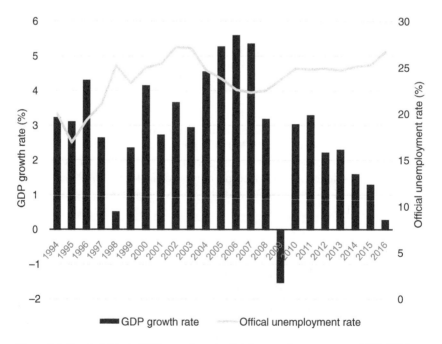

Figure 2.1 South Africa's GDP growth and official unemployment rates, 1994–2016.
Source: The World Bank Data and SARB.

target of achieving a 14 per cent unemployment rate by 2020 and 6 per cent by 2030, thus seems highly unlikely.

South Africa's volume of exports (goods and services including gold) increased by 45 per cent in real terms over the period from 1994 to 2008 at an average rate of 3.3 per cent per year. During the financial crisis of 2008, the volume of exports dropped drastically by 19 per cent. Thereafter, exports have increased at an average rate of 3.8 per cent per year from 2010 to 2015 and decreased by 0.1 per cent from 2015 to 2016 (SARB, 2017). The NDP views export growth as a key driver of economic development. It is therefore telling that South Africa is falling behind the NDP target of increasing the volume of exports by 6 per cent per year up to 2030.

South Africa, post-apartheid, initially experienced a decline in *poverty* as a result of social grants, real income growth, decelerating inflationary pressure on households, expansion of credit, and growth in informal housing (The World Bank, 2017). According to Stats SA (2017), there was also a general decline in poverty between 2006 and 2011 from 66.6 per cent to 53.2 per cent. Since 2011, the proportion of the population living in poverty has increased to 55.5 per cent in 2015. The number of persons living in extreme poverty (i.e. persons living below the Food Poverty Line of R441 inflation adjusted in 2015 per person per month) in South Africa also increased from 13.4 million in 2006 to 13.8 million in 2015 (Stats SA, 2017). The number of South Africans living in extreme poverty peaked during the aftermath of the global financial crisis, reaching 16.7 million people in 2009. Progress in reducing poverty has slowed in recent years. While weak global growth since the global financial crisis of 2008 is partially to blame, the World Bank (2017) believes that structural barriers to growth within the South African economy have played an important role in slowing poverty reduction efforts. Based on current trends, it seems unlikely that the NDP target of no individuals living below the poverty line by 2030 will be achieved.

In terms of *income inequality*, however, some limited progress has been made recently. The Gini coefficient has declined from 0.72 in 2006 to 0.68 in 2015 (Stats SA, 2017). The NDP target of reaching a Gini coefficient of 0.6 by 2030 may thus be attainable. Despite this improvement, however, South Africa is still believed to be the most unequal society in the world (*The Economist*, 2017a; *Guardian* Data Blog, 2017a; Ehrenfreund, 2017). Unsurprisingly, income inequality is seen as a significant risk to sustainable development in South Africa (NPC, 2012; Philip *et al.*, 2014).

The green economy as a driver of development

Economic growth is typically driven by the accumulation of financial, physical and human capital. This has mostly led to the exploitation and degradation of natural resources, fauna and flora, and ecosystems (or natural capital) (UNEP, 2011). Natural capital refers to the stocks of renewable and non-renewable natural resources that provide benefits in the form of ecosystem services to populations (WWF, 2016b).

The traditional, resource-intensive growth model powered by fossil fuel exploitation is often referred to as the "brown economy". From an environmental perspective, the brown economy has contributed to high levels of environmental degradation. The planetary boundaries model, first proposed by Rockström *et al.* (2009), has shown that global ecosystems, including those in South Africa, are not being maintained at a level that can sustain long-term sustainable development (Jänicke, 2011; WWF, 2016b; Cole *et al.*, 2014). Furthermore, brown economy models have perpetuated development and growth that is characteristic of wasteful consumption and production patterns; unsustainable use of ecological resources; widespread environmental and health risks; and has aided in creating unfair and inequitable societies (UNEP, 2015b). This has hampered sustainable development through the misallocation of assets (UNEP, 2011). Ignoring negative social and environmental externalities, and focusing only on the resulting artificial economic returns, has led to projects and initiatives being implemented that reduced overall societal welfare.

There is no consensus on what constitutes a green economy. Often terms such as green growth, green economy, low-carbon development are used interchangeably, although a better understanding of how these concepts are related is starting to develop (see, for example, Georgeson *et al.*, 2017). It has been recognised, however, that the core idea behind green economy approaches is to transform the traditional economy into one that recognises and accounts for not only the costs associated with financial capital but also natural and social capital (Potts *et al.*, 2014). Green economy objectives and approaches are however highly context-specific, and no definitive list of either exists (Segal and Cloete, 2012). This is demonstrated by the numerous approaches being used across the globe to support transitions to greener economies (UNDESA, 2012a; GGBP, 2014; UNEP, 2015a, 2015b; Segal and Cloete, 2012).

While the transition to a green economy will vary considerably due to a nation's local context, institutional structure, natural and human capital, as well as its current state of development, there are some commonalities in transition approaches (OECD, 2012; UNEP, 2011). Figure 2.2 shows some of these commonalities, illustrating that green economy transitions are economy-wide and are not a subset of the economy. While transitions impact all economic sectors, some sectors feature prominently in national green economy plans. A green economy also includes a set of key objectives related to sustainable development. To embed these characteristics within an economy, a number of interventions are typically required.

South Africa's development path: implications for a sustainability transition

The South African government has set a vision for the country to work towards realising an environmentally sustainable, climate change resilient, low-carbon economy and just society (UNEP, 2013; NPC, 2012). The National Development Plan (NDP) entrenches a specific vision of the green economy in the

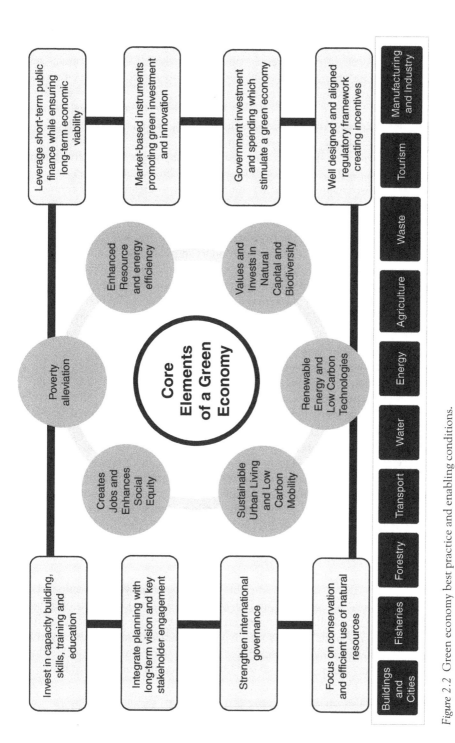

Figure 2.2 Green economy best practice and enabling conditions.

Source: Authors, based on various sources.

country's policy framework. While other policy documents, notably those developed by the Department of Environmental Affairs (DEA) (2010), frame the green economy in broader terms, the focus in the NDP is very much on addressing climate change. The NDP notes the importance of balancing this transition with the overall objectives of the country, that is, increasing employment and reducing inequality. The NDP focuses on low-carbon development (i.e. the reduction of GHG emissions), climate change resilience, skills development and job creation as key drivers of a transition.

South Africa has followed a state-led approach to developing the green economy via direct public sector initiatives and programmes, supported by market-based instruments and policy interventions to create an environment conducive to green economy projects, mobilising private sector support for green economy activities, and promoting employment and equitable growth (UNEP, 2015a). Policy interventions such as a carbon tax and the creation of finance instruments as mentioned in the NDP and National Strategy for Sustainable Development (NSSD1) speak to this market-based approach. The strong focus on job preservation and job creation cuts across policy frameworks, but is most visible in the New Growth Path and its Green Economy Accord. South Africa follows a technical and outcomes-based approach to sustainability transitions; where key indicators and specific targets are often incorporated within key policy frameworks.

While equal weight is given to state-led interventions and market mechanisms, in practice the emphasis has been on state-led interventions to date. The main market instrument, the carbon tax, is not yet in place. The Renewable Energy Independent Power Producers Procurement Programme (REI4P) (discussed later and in Chapters 3 and 5), while effectively using a market mechanism to reduce costs and stimulate competition, is very much a state-led intervention in that Eskom is the single buyer of all electricity procured. There is also currently a number of factors that constrain competition in the electricity market, including, for example, barriers to wheeling power across the national grid and the requirement for a ministerial determination before a generation licence can be issued to independent power producers generating more than 1MW of energy (see *City of Cape Town* v. *The National Energy Regulator of South Africa and the Minister of Energy*, 2017; and Montmasson-Clair, 2017).

While there is balance in terms of policy focus between greening the economy and creating new green industries (Mjimba, 2015), in terms of direct interventions, the emphasis has been on creating new green industries. The green economy in South Africa is thus typically characterised as a subset of the wider economy with different dynamics at play (see, for example, UNEP, 2013; EDD, 2011; and older iterations of the IPAP). Using the hierarchy of sustainable development terminology developed by Ten Brink *et al.* (2012), the focus in South Africa is on stimulating green growth in specific green sectors to support the move to a green economy that will deliver sustainable development. This is discussed in Chapter 1.

The policy focus in South Africa, as outlined in Chapter 5 of the NDP, has committed the country towards transitioning to a greener economy. Implementation is focused on green growth through supporting economic growth via investment in individual green industries. Treating the green economy as a subsector of the broader economy, as opposed to greening the whole economy, can lead to coordination issues and missed opportunities for advancing green economy goals in sectors not traditionally seen as "green" (Segal and Cloete, 2012). The impact of adopting an economy-wide approach to greening the South African economy is discussed less often. Mjimba (2015) mentions that the move to a green economy could present an opportunity for a "double structural transformation", where the traditional goal of economic development is reoriented, through economic diversification, towards an economic structure which balances economic, social and environmental objectives. This is no mean feat, since it requires eschewing many of the resource-intensive and highly polluting sectors and approaches, which developed countries depend on in their industrialisation pathways. Recent changes in the world economy, such as the rise of low-cost manufacturing and greener industrial development (in China in particular), mean that many of these industrialisation approaches are being questioned (Mjimba, 2015).

Given the difficulty that has accompanied economic development in African countries, and the poor performance of the South African economy over the last decade, it is surprising that the challenges of the "first" structural transformation has not received more attention within the country's sustainability discourse. Very little attention has been paid to how the same structural rigidities that have prevented the South African economy from achieving faster growth, at a time when it is being significantly outperformed by other emerging markets, could also hamper its sustainability transition.

The importance of addressing existing barriers to economic growth has been raised in the green growth literature. For example, the World Bank (2012), states that the extent to which a transition to a low-carbon economy supports growth and the creation of new green industries depends on whether existing economic policies and conditions are conducive to the creation and growth of new sectors and companies. While green growth strategies can improve welfare via economic and environmental benefits, the World Bank (2012) emphasises that "if economic growth is insufficient because of institutional or policy problems, *green growth will not boost [growth] in the absence of other structural changes*" (emphasis added). More specifically, developing new green industries at scale in South Africa is unlikely to succeed while structural barriers hamper the creation of companies (World Bank, (2011). Barriers highlighted included, for example, the regulatory burden on small companies, skills shortages and labour market rigidities. Borel-Saladin and Turok (2013) state that a lack of skilled workers in South Africa is a major barrier to the creation of green jobs, and do not believe that the optimistic estimates of green jobs in South Africa (see, for example, UNEP, 2013; EDD, 2011; Maia *et al.*, 2011) will materialise without significant reforms in education and skills development.

As discussed earlier, since 1994 South Africa has relied on a stable macro-economic environment, strong institutions and direct government interventions to drive growth. Significant micro-economic reforms, while discussed, were not implemented. Swilling *et al.* (2015) believe that this was an outcome based on the specific developmental state model that South Africa chose to implement. According to the authors, countries categorised as developmental states have typically attempted to foster economic development via long-term structural transformations that achieved human well-being linked to higher incomes and improved education and health outcomes. This was done by developing the capacity of the state to:

> coordinate the efforts of individual businesses by encouraging the emergence and growth of private economic institutions, target-specific industrial projects and sectors, resist political pressure from popular forces and, at times, also brutally suppressing them.
>
> (Swilling *et al.*, 2015, p. 3)

Developing a strong and capable state, and then deploying it to effectively change the structure of the economy to increase its productive capacity for the benefit of society at large, is referred to as "developmental welfarism" (Swilling *et al.*, 2015; Khan, 2013, p. 582). This is the model the authors believe was implemented with great success in South East Asia. In South Africa, however, government has been much more successful at providing basic services and creating a social safety net, rather than improving the productive capacity of the economy.

Extending access to basic services such as water, electricity, housing and social security has been a major achievement of the post-apartheid era (The Presidency, 2014). The proportion of households with access to piped or tap water in their dwellings, off-site or on-site, has increased from 60 per cent in 1994 to 88 per cent in 2016. Nationally, the percentage of households connected to electricity supply has increased from approximately 50 per cent in 1994 to 84.2 per cent in 2016. The percentage of households that use electricity for cooking increased from 58.0 per cent in 2002 to 76.8 per cent in 2016, while households with access to improved sanitation also increased from 62.3 per cent in 2002 to 80.9 per cent in 2016 (Stats SA, 2016).

Research by the Institute for Race Relations shows that efforts to create a social safety net in South Africa has led to a dramatic change in the make-up of the South African economy since the start of the millennium (IRR, 2017a, 2017b). In 2001, almost four million people received social grants in South Africa, while 12.5 million people were employed. By 2016, the ratio had changed sharply with more than 17 million people receiving social grants and just over 15.5m employed. In 2017, only 43.3 per cent of South Africans of working age were employed, and the number of unemployed South Africans, according to the expanded definition of unemployment which includes those who have given up looking for employment because they did not believe they would be successful, increased from 3.7 million in 1994 to 9.3 million in 2017.

Considering the period 1995 to 2005, even before the fourfold expansion of the social safety net described above, it was growth in social grants, rather than increased economic opportunities, that drove an increase in expenditure by the poor (Bhorat and Van der Westhuizen, 2012). While South Africa has developed the most progressive tax system in the world (Development Finance International and Oxfam, 2017) increased transfers and progressive taxation has not been sufficient to significantly reduce income inequality in South Africa. As mentioned earlier, South Africa remains the most unequal society in the world. The reasons for this are complex, but a lack of economic opportunity – and in particular employment opportunities – is generally viewed as the main driver of persistent high inequality in South Africa (NPC, 2011; Philip *et al.*, 2014; OECD, 2017).

The focus on the provision of social services appears to have diverted resources away from investment in physical and human capital and the modernisation of infrastructure – which is critical to future economic competitiveness and crucial to accommodating expanding populations in urbanising environments (DBSA, 2012). The NDP mentions that one of the nine primary challenges faced by South Africa is infrastructure that is "poorly located, inadequate and under-maintained" (NPC, 2012). Capital investment in South Africa peaked in the 1980s and then declined sharply until 2003, before starting to increase somewhat and then accelerating in the run-up to the 2010 Soccer World Cup, leading the National Planning Commission to conclude in its 2011 Diagnostic Overview that South Africa "effectively missed a generation of infrastructure modernisation" (NPC, 2011). The South African Institute of Civil Engineering (SAICE) mentions in its 2017 Infrastructure Report Card for South Africa that the pre-2010 large-scale infrastructure investment caused South Africa's overall infrastructure score to improve from a D+ ("at risk of failure") in 2006 to C– ("satisfactory for now") in 2011. Since then, however, a lack of maintenance has reversed these gains and the 2017 aggregate score has fallen back down to a D+ (SAICE, 2017).

Unlike the historically successful developmental states of South East Asia, where education and health outcomes were considered critical to the developmental progress, South Africa has not made the kinds of strides in these areas that would be expected after the advent of democracy. The latest World Economic Forum Global Competitiveness Report, for example, ranks South Africa 121st out of 137 countries in terms of the quality of its health and primary education systems, which is equal to the average Sub-Saharan Africa score – despite the region being significantly poorer (WEF, 2017). South Africa does do better in terms of higher education and training, but it is still ranked only 85th out of 137 countries (and this is one of the three areas where South Africa ranks worst – the other being labour market efficiency).

Rather than attempting to grow the economy and create employment, some commentators believe the focus has been on redistribution and using the fiscus to prevent large-scale unrest in what can be termed "non-developmental welfarism" (CDE, 2016; Swilling *et al.*, 2015, p. 12).

State capture: derailing South Africa's sustainability transition

South Africa relies heavily on state-owned enterprises (SOEs) to advance developmental objectives via the provision of economic and social infrastructure – and the NDP views a set of "efficient, financially sound and well-governed" SOEs by 2030 as critical to meeting its targets (NPC, 2012). Although there are around 715 SOEs in South Africa, *state-owned corporations (SOCs)*, a type of SOE, are of particular importance (PRC, 2013). They are fully corporatised, with independent boards, and are governed by both the Public Finance Management Act and the Companies Act. They are supposed to operate in accordance with the general business principles, which apply to private sector companies, generate profits and declare dividends. SOCs enjoy the greatest degree of autonomy amongst public entities and can source their own funding. There are currently 20 SOCs in South Africa (Robb, 2014). SOCs are responsible for roughly half of government's infrastructure expenditure (with three – Eskom, Transnet and South African National Roads Agency Limited (SANRAL) – accounting for 42 per cent of public sector capital formation) (SAICE, 2017; National Treasury, 2017a). Because of the size of their investments and the areas they invest in, SOCs have an important role to play in ensuring current investment patterns do not lock South Africa into an unsustainable high-carbon development path (Cloete and Venter, 2012).

Capacity in these institutions has been deteriorating for some time, driven by a high turnover of senior personnel and a lack of accountability related to poor service delivery and corruption. Despite their important role envisaged in the NDP, SOCs seem to have gone backwards since the NDP was published. More and more SOCs have been plagued by governance and performance issues, and are now widely seen as a barrier rather than a driver of growth (IMF, 2017; National Treasury, 2017b; OECD, 2017). SAICE believes that institutional weakness of SOCs is a critical factor holding back infrastructure investment in South Africa – and that the institutions responsible for overseeing and facilitating these investments are often "poorly capacitated, ambiguously mandated and badly governed" (SAICE, 2017).

SOCs have very large budgets, and often face very little competition in the markets within which they operate (National Treasury, 2017a; Robb, 2014), creating opportunities for large-scale rent seeking. As institutions have weakened, opportunities for corruption have increased. Corruption, defined as one-off, irregular actions (which has negative implications for development and was highlighted as a priority intervention in the NDP), has morphed into an even more destructive entrenched practice which the State Capacity Research Project (SCRP) (2017) calls "state capture". This entails people with established relations undertaking a systematic and well-organised set of repeated transactions, often increasing in scale, with the intent of redirecting rents from legitimate targets to private beneficiaries.

From the perspective of a transition to a greener economy in South Africa, state capture has several implications:

- It creates incentives for rent-seeking and corruption rather than innovation and entrepreneurship, limiting investment in developing the skills and capabilities required to drive transitions;
- it compounds existing structural rigidities and makes it more difficult for resources to migrate to where they are most useful during the transition to a low-carbon economy;
- it drains resources that could be used to support the transition;
- it reduces the capacity within public institutions to implement policies and initiatives that could support the transition; and
- it creates an additional barrier to implementing the transition in a way that can address inequality.

Drawing on the economic literature around rent seeking and corruption, Fakir (2017) believes that transitions should be underpinned by good economic governance. In a system characterised by unproductive rent seeking, a significant proportion of the benefits from investment in new technology will go to the politically connected. This creates a disincentive for productive economic agents to invest capital and effort in developing the skills, capacity and experience required to underpin the transition – since a large proportion of the benefits and opportunities arising from these activities will be syphoned off via corrupt means. So, while state capture is expected to significantly complicate the transition, as discussed below, Fakir (2017) highlights the risk that *unless state capture and corruption is reigned in, it is likely to delay or even prevent a sustainability transition in South Africa.*

There is a large body of academic and empirical literature that shows that the more *barriers* there are to resources moving from one application to another within an economy, the more painful and costly structural adjustments are (see, for example, Devarajan *et al.* 2011; Alton *et al.* 2014). The transition to a more sustainable economic structure already imposes additional constraints on the new industries and activities that need support (Mjimba, 2015), and existing structural rigidities have long hampered the growth of the South African economy. State capture adds an additional constraint to the deployment of resources within this already challenging environment. Whether deployed resources are efficiently utilised to support the transition to sustainability will most likely be of secondary consideration when compared to the amount of rents that can be diverted to the beneficiaries of state capture. Given that incentives are muddled, and non-market factors determine resource allocation to a large extent, this significantly reduces the impact of market-based instruments to influence decision-making. This is worrying, since these instruments form the fulcrum of the mix of policy measures currently supporting the sustainability transition in South Africa.

Widespread corruption also influences the types of projects that are preferred, and the financial and institutional mechanisms employed during implementation. The recent stalling of the widely lauded Renewable Energy Independent Power Producers Procurement Programme (REI4P), which is discussed in Chapter 5, may very well be an illustration of this. The programme was managed by an independent and highly capacitated administrative body, and the process of allocating bids to independent power producers via auctions seemed to be largely corruption free. Large, centralised infrastructure projects, like a nuclear procurement programme, however, are a much more attractive conduit for state capture largess than an efficiently run decentralised programme like REI4P (SAICE, 2017). In 2017, South Africa's nuclear procurement programme was halted when the High Court found that due process had not been followed and the process had not been transparent, did not include public participation, and had not received the required parliamentary approvals (Ensor, 2017). The judgement was in response to a legal challenge by two NGOs who raised the concern that the nuclear energy procurement process relied on an outdated Integrated Resource Plan (IRP) (which serves as the roadmap for electricity sector investment in South Africa) that was completed in 2010 (Sole and Reddy, 2017). Given this background, the recent announcement by the Minister of Energy that consultation on the revised IRP 2017 would be cut short, and that the outdated and pro-nuclear 2010 IRP would determine the future energy mix in South Africa – with the 2017 IRP only influencing the overall amount of new capacity – is widely seen as an attempt to ensure that large-scale nuclear procurement happens at any cost (Van Rensburg, 2017a; Yelland, 2017a).

Suspicions that coal supply contracts are being used to direct rents as part of state capture activities, and that South Africa's proposed nuclear procurement programme is seen as an opportunity to ratchet up these activities, has been publicly raised (Eberhard and Godinho, 2017; SCRP, 2017; Public Protector, 2016). South Africa experienced an electricity supply shock in 2007, with demand outstripping supply – which led to a series of rolling blackouts euphemistically referred to as 'load shedding'. Since then electricity prices for most users have increased six-fold and this, coupled with slow growth, has led to a situation where electricity demand in 2016 was still below its peak in 2007 (TIPS, 2017). Despite an increasing body of literature showing that renewable energy now offers the most cost-effective electricity supply option in South Africa (Wright *et al.*, 2017; Yelland, 2017b), the Minister of Energy (at the insistence of Eskom), has been unwilling to sign agreements with preferred REI4P bidders. This has raised suspicions that the REI4P may be an indirect casualty of state capture, and if so, this would illustrate the complexity of developing effective policies to drive a low-carbon transition within the context of state capture (Fakir, 2017).

State capture also has a *financial cost*. Rents are diverted from legitimate to corrupt purposes increasing the costs of targeted developmental interventions. For instance, including the nuclear allocation in the country's energy generation mix could increase the cost of new electricity generation in South Africa by up to R50 billion by 2030 (Van Rensburg, 2017a). In addition to the direct fiscal cost, there is also an indirect cost as a result of weakened capacity and oversight within SOCs. This is evident in the large contingent and real liabilities that exist because of the dire financial performance of SOCs at present (National Treasury, 2017b). Not only does this reduce the resources that can be deployed to support a sustainability transition, but it could also remove some of the short-term fiscal benefits that could come with certain policy measures such as the proposed carbon tax. The National Treasury, for example, indicated that carbon tax revenues will be used to reduce the negative distributional impacts that could accompany the tax (Republic of South Africa, 2015), whereas research by Winkler (2017) showed that carbon tax revenues could be used to effectively address energy poverty in South Africa. However, if these revenues are instead used to reduce the budget deficit (which at least in part is due to the funding requirements of SOCs) (National Treasury, 2017b), this could undermine support for the carbon tax. Resources that could have been used to support the transition, are thus being diverted to fund the direct and indirect cost of state capture.

State capture is facilitated by *weak institutions* and limited accountability. Evidence is emerging that weakened governance structures and capabilities of SOCs, government departments that influence resource allocation and oversee compliance, and even at law enforcement agencies, have been central to allowing state capture and institutionalised corruption in South Africa (Eberhard and Godinho, 2017; SCRP, 2017; Public Protector, 2016; Pauw, 2017). This not only hampers service delivery, but also reduces the capacity of public sector institutions to implement policies, projects and initiatives that can support the transition. It also means that even well-designed initiatives and programmes run the risk of being derailed by rampant corruption and rent-seeking.

Finally, it has already been mentioned that South Africa is faced with extreme inequality, and that this is largely due to limited economic opportunities. Several approaches towards sustainability transitions offer more inclusive development pathways. Green energy technologies, for example, create the possibility of a less centralised, interdependent, interactive and distributed energy system in the future. A just green transition would thus present the possibility of a fairer distribution of ownership and benefits (both in terms of economic benefit and energy services) from the energy system (WWF, 2016a). A fair and just energy transition in South Africa could thus help address many of the socio-economic challenges faced by the country, but will require a paradigm shift away from the current large-scale, rigid and centrally-planned approach to electricity supply (Essop, 2017). A lack of community ownership and meaningful participation has been highlighted as a shortcoming within the otherwise very successful REI4P programme (Wlokas, 2015; Swilling, 2017). Furthermore, Fakir (2017, p. 27) warns that in the presence of corruption and unproductive rent seeking, there is a risk that the benefits from a transition may be "cornered by the same political and economic forces that dominate the resource sector, new infrastructure or technology spend". The energy transition is currently the most visible driver of a broader sustainability transition within South Africa. If state capture leads to a continued focus on capital intensive and large-scale projects in areas like coal-fired or nuclear energy (as posited above), that are well suited to the capture of benefits, it is *highly unlikely that the sustainability transition in South Africa will be just or fair*.

Conclusion

South Africa has made significant progress in the establishment of a social safety net and the provision of improved access to public services, health and education. Despite sound macro-economic conditions, however, economic growth has been slow. As a result, unemployment, poverty and inequality remain serious developmental challenges. A lack of micro-economic reforms means that structural barriers to the development of new enterprises and sectors remain, which has stifled entrepreneurial activity. The focus on the provision of social services also appears to have diverted resources away from investment in physical and human capital and the modernisation of infrastructure that is critical to future economic competitiveness.

The South African government has embraced a transition to a greener economy as a driver of socio-economic development, and is aiming to create an environmentally sustainable, climate change resilient, low-carbon and just society. The model chosen focuses primarily on low-carbon development, climate change resilience, skills development and job creation. While a green economy holds much promise in South Africa, the same barriers and rigidities that have hampered growth may also delay the sustainability transition. It is therefore important that sustainability discourses and strategies are not divorced from broader economic reform efforts. For this to happen, a sustainability transition needs to be viewed holistically, and the focus needs to move from supporting individual "green" sectors to creating a more sustainable economy overall. While this has started happening in South Africa, it is still the exception rather than the norm.

An economic development model, which eschews the resource-intensive and polluting approaches that have historically driven industrialisation, is challenging even without the South Africa-specific factors mentioned above. In South Africa, however, the relatively strong institutions that developed since democracy have started to weaken considerably due to corruption, which has evolved into a systematic approach that has looted the public coffers. This is particularly worrying as SOCs, the public entities that spearhead infrastructure investment, and which will be responsible for most of the public investments which underpin sustainability transitions, have borne the brunt of this "state capture". Unless this trend is reversed, it is unlikely that a low-carbon, resilient and just society envisaged in the NDP will materialise.

References

Alton, T., Arndt, C., Davies, R., Hartley, F., Makrelov, K., Thurlow, J. and Umbogo, D., 2014. Introducing Carbon Taxes in South Africa. *Applied Energy*, 116, pp. 344–354.

Bhorat, H. and Van der Westhuizen, C., 2012. *Poverty, Inequality and the Nature of Economic Growth in South Africa*, Working Paper 12/151, Cape Town: Development Policy Research Unit.

Borel-Saladin, J. and Turok, I., 2013. The Impact of the Green Economy on Jobs in South Africa. *South African Journal of Science*, 109(9/10), pp. 1–4.

CDE, 2016. *Accelerating inclusive growth (CDE Growth Agenda Series Paper 3)*, Johannesburg: The Centre for Development and Enterprise, South Africa.

CGIS, 2010. *Cabinet Statement on New Growth Path*, Pretoria: Government Communications and Information Systems.

City of Cape Town v. The National Energy Regulator of South Africa and the Minister of Energy (Case 51765/2017) (2017) High Court of the Republic of South Africa, Gauteng Division, Pretoria.

Cloete, B. and Venter, F., 2012. *Carbon Lock-in: Infrastructure Investment*. [Online]. Available at www.dnaeconomics.com/assets/Usematthew/Infrastructure_Lock_In_Paper_June _2012_final2.pdf (accessed 15 January 2018).

Cole, M., Bailey, R. and New, M., 2014. Tracking Sustainable Development with a National Barometer for South Africa Using a Downscaled "Safe and Just Space" Framework. *Proceedings of the National Academy of Sciences (PNAS)*, 111(42), pp. 4399–4408.

DBSA, 2012. *The State of South Africa's Economic Infrastructure: Opportunities and Challenges*, Pretoria: Development Bank of Southern Africa.

DEA, 2010. *Green Economy Summit Report*. [Online] Available at www.sagreenfund.org. za/wordpress/wp-content/uploads/2015/04/Green-Economy-Summit.pdf (accessed February 2016).

DED, 2013. *Summary Report 1 on the Implementation of Social Accords*, Pretoria: The Presidency Republic of South Africa.

Devarajan, S., Go, D.S., Robinson, S. and Thierfelder, K., 2011. Tax Policy to Reduce Carbon Emissions in a Distorted Economy: Illustrations from a South Africa CGE model. *The B.E. Journal of Economic Analysis & Policy*, 11(1).

Development Finance International and Oxfam, 2017. *The Commitment to Reducing Inequality Index*, Oxford: Oxfam GB.

Eberhard, A. and Godinho, C., 2017. *Eskom Enquiry Reference Booklet*, Unpublished: State Capacity Research Project.

EDD, 2011. *The New Growth Path: Framework*, Pretoria: Economic Development Department.

Ehrenfreund, M., 2017. The country with the world's most progressive taxes has the world's highest income inequality. *Washington Post*, 16 July.

Ensor, L., 2017. Back to square one for Eskom as judge sets nuclear decisions aside. *Business Day*, 26 April.

Essop, T., 2017. A Just Transition to a Renewable Energy Future in South Africa. In L. Sholtz, K. Muluadzi, K. Kritzinger, M. Mabaso and S. Forder (eds.), *Renewable Energy: Facts and Futures*. Cape Town: WWF-SA, p. 40.

Fakir, S., 2017. *Transition Realism: The Implications of Rent-seeking to Achieving South Africa's Low-carbon Technology Ambitions*, Cape Town: WWF-SA.

Faulkner, D., Loewald, C. and Makrelov, K., 2013. *Achieving Higher Growth and Employment: Policy Options for South Africa*, Working Paper WP/13/03, Pretoria: South African Reserve Bank.

Georgeson, L., Maslin, M. and Poessinouw, M., 2017. The Global Green Economy: A review of Concepts, Definitions, Measurement Methodologies and their Interactions. *Geography and Environment*, 4(1), pp. 1–23.

GGBP, 2014. *Lessons from Country Experiences*, Seoul: Green Growth Best Practice Initiative.

Guardian, Data Blog, 2017a. *Inequality Index: Where are the World's Most Unequal Countries?* [Online]. Available at www.theguardian.com/inequality/datablog/2017/apr/26/inequality-index-where-are-the-worlds-most-unequal-countries (accessed 8 January 2018).

IMF, 2017. *2017 Article IV Consultation – Press Release; Staff Report; and Statement by the Executive Director for South Africa*, Washington, DC: International Monetary Fund.

IRR, 2017a. *South African Institute of Race Relations Press Release: More South Africans Receive Grants than have Jobs – A Recipe for Chaos and Violence*. [Online]. Available at http://irr.org.za/reports-and-publications/media-releases/more-south-africans-receive-grants-than-have-jobs-2013-a-recipe-for-chaos-and-violence/view (accessed 15 February 2018).

IRR, 2017b. *South African Institute of Race Relations Press Release: Only 4 in 10 People of Working Age Have a Job – IRR Report*. [Online]. Available at http://irr.org.za/reports-and-publications/media-releases/only-4-in-10-people-of-working-age-have-a-job/view (accessed 15 February 2018).

Jänicke, M., 2011. *Green Growth: From a Growing Eco-industry to a Sustainable Economy*, Berlin: Environmental Policy Research Centre.

Khan, F., 2013. Poverty, Grants, Revolution and "Real Utopias": Society Must Be Defended By Any And All. *Review of African Political Economy*, 40(138), pp. 572–588.

Maia, J., Giordano, T., Kelder, N., Bardien, G., Bodibe, M., Du Plooy, P., Jafta, X., Jarvis, D., Kruger-Cloete, E., Kuhn, G., Lepelle, R., Makaulule, L., Mosoma, K., Neoh, S., Netshitomboni, N., Ngozo, T. and Swanepoel, J., 2011. *Green Jobs: An Estimate of the Direct Employment Potential of a Greening South African Economy*, Johannesburg: Industrial Development Corporation (IDC), Development Bank of Southern Africa (DBSA); Trade and Industrial Policy Strategies (TIPS).

Mjimba, V., 2015. A Case for Industrial Policy Towards Green Economy Transition in Developing Economies. *Africa Insight*, 45(3).

Montmasson-Clair, G., 2017. *Electricity Supply in South Africa: Path Dependency or Decarbonisation?* Pretoria: Trade & Industrial Policy Strategies (TIPS Policy Brief 2/2017).

National Treasury, 2017a. *2017 Budget Review*, Pretoria: Government Printer.

National Treasury, 2017b. *Medium Term Budget Policy Statement*, Pretoria: National Treasury.

NPC, 2011. *Diagnostic Overview*, Pretoria: National Planning Commission/The Presidency.

NPC, 2012. *National Development Plan 2030: Our Future – Make it Work*, Pretoria: National Planning Commission (NPC).

OECD, 2012. *Green Growth and Developing Countries*, Paris: Organisation for Economic Cooperation and Development.

OECD, 2017. *2017 OECD Economic Surveys: South Africa (Overview)*, Paris: OECD.

Pauw, J., 2017. *The President's Keepers*. 1st edn. Cape Town: Tafelberg.

Philip, K., Tsedu, M. and Zwane, M., 2014. *The Impact of Social and Economic Inequality on Economic Development in South Africa*, New York: United National Development Programme (UNDP).

Potts, J., Lynch, M., Wilkings, A., Huppe, G., Cunningham, M. and Voora, V., 2014. *The State of Sustainability Initiatives Review: Standards and the Green Economy*, Winnipeg: International Institute for Sustainable Development.

PRC, 2013. *Presidential Review Committee (PRC) on State-owned Entities*, Pretoria: Government Printer.

Public Protector, 2016. *State of Capture*, Pretoria: Public Protector of South Africa (Report No. 6 of 2016/17).

Republic of South Africa, 2015. *Draft Explanatory Memorandum for the Carbon Tax Bill (2015)*, Pretoria: Government Printer.

Robb, G., 2014. *Competition Without Privatisation? South Africa's Experience of the Corporatisation of State-owned Enterprises*. Boksburg, 2nd South African Economic Regulators Conference (SAERC), hosted by the National Energy Regulator in collaboration with the Centre for Competition, Regulation and Economic Development (CCRED) of the University of Johannesburg.

Rockström, J., Steffen, W., Noone, K., Persson, A., Chapin III, F.S., Lambin, E.F., Lenton, T.M., Scheffer, M., Folke, C., Schellnhuber, H.J., Nykvist, B., de Wit, C.A., Hughes, T., van der Leeuw, S., Rodhe, H., Sörlin, S. and Snyder, P.K., 2009. A Safe Operating Space for Humanity. *Nature*, 461, pp. 472–475.

RSA and DoF, 1996. *Growth Employment and Redistribution*, Pretoria: The Presidency of South Africa.

RSA, 1994. *The White Paper on Reconstruction and Development*, Cape Town: Republic of South Africa.

RSA, 1996. *The Constitution of the Republic of South Africa*, Cape Town: Parliament of the Republic of South Africa.

RSA, 2009. *Medium Term Strategic Framework 2009–2014*, Pretoria: The Presidency Republic of South Africa.

SAHO, 2014. *South Africa's Key Economic Policy Changes (1994–2013)*. [Online]. Available at www.sahistory.org.za/article/south-africa%E2%80%99s-key-economic-policies-changes-1994-2013 (accessed 6 May 2014).

SAICE, 2017. *SAICE 2017 Infrastructure Report Card for South Africa*, Midrand: South African Institute for Civil Engineering.

SARB, 2017. *KBP5032 Foreign Trade: Exports of Goods and Services, Including Gold Volume Indices*, Pretoria: South African Reserve Bank.

SARB, 2018. *Official Unemployment Rate (Code: KBP7019J)*. [Online]. Available at www.resbank.co.za/Research/Statistics/Pages/OnlineDownloadFacility.aspx (accessed 5 January 2018).

SCRP, 2017. *The State Capacity Research Project Report – Betrayal of the Promise: How South Africa is Being Stolen*. [Online]. Available at www0.sun.ac.za/cst/major-project/the-state-capacity-research-project-scrp/ (accessed 1 February 2018).

Segal, N. and Cloete, B., 2012. *Combating Climate Change: How Might "Green" Growth Facilitate or Hinder SA's Developmental Objectives?* Johannesburg: Centre for Development and Enterprise (Series: Climate Change Mitigation: An Emerging Market Perspective).

Sole, S. and Reddy, M., 2017. *The Largest Procurement in SA to Date is in the Hands of the High Court in Cape Town*. [Online]. Available at http://amabhungane.co.za/article/2017-02-21-the-largest-procurement-in-sa-to-date-is-in-the-hands-of-the-western-cape-high-court (accessed 8 January 2018).

Stats SA, 2016. *General Household Survey Statistical Release P0318*, Pretoria: Statistics South Africa.

Stats SA, 2017. *Poverty Trends in South Africa: An Examination of Absolute Poverty Between 2006 and 2015*, Pretoria: Government Printer/Statistics South Africa.

Swilling, M., 2017. *Political Obstacles to a Mass Renewable Energy Programme (Key Points from Presentation to AIDC's One Million Climate Jobs)*. [Online]. Available at https://aidc.org.za/political-obstacles-mass-renewable-energy-programme-2/ and www.markswilling.co.za/talks/ (accessed 9 January 2018).

Swilling, M., Musango, J. and Wakeford, J., 2015. Developmental States and Sustainability Transitions: Prospects of a Just Transition in South Africa. *Journal of Environmental Policy & Planning*. 18(5), 650–672.

ten Brink, P., Mazza, L., Badura, T., Kettunen, M. and Withana, S., 2012. *Nature and its Role in the Transition to a Green Economy*, Nairobi: UNEP/The Economics of Ecosystems & Biodiversity.

The Economist, 2017a. Blurring the rainbow. *The Economist*, 20 May.

The Presidency, 2014. *Twenty Year Review South Africa 1994–2014*, Pretoria: The Presidency: Republic of South Africa.

the dti, 2007a. *The National Industrial Policy Framework*, Pretoria: The Presidency Republic of South Africa.

the dti, 2007b. *Industrial Policy Action Plan*, Pretoria: The Presidency Republic of South Africa.

The World Bank, 2017. *The World Bank in South Africa*. [Online]. Available at www.worldbank.org/en/country/southafrica/overview (accessed 1 February 2018).

TIPS, 2015. Reflections on the National Industrial Policy Framework and Industrial Policy Implementation in South Africa post-2007. *Policy Brief*, December, p. 7.

TIPS, 2017. *Responses to the Electricity Oversupply*, Johannesburg: TIPS Policy Brief 6/2017.

UNDESA, 2012a. *A Guidebook to the Green Economy: Issue 1: Green Economy, Green Growth, and Low-Carbon Development – History, Definitions and a Guide to Recent Publications*, New York: Division for Sustainable Development, United Nations Department of Economic and Social Affairs.

UNEP, 2011. *Towards a Green Economy: Pathways to Sustainable Development and Poverty Eradication – A Synthesis for Policy Makers*, Nairobi: United Nations Environment Programme.

UNEP, 2013. *Green Economy Scoping Study. South African Green Economy Modelling Report (SAGEM) – Focus on Natural Resource Management, Agriculture, Transport and Energy Sectors*, Nairobi: United Nations Environment Programme.

UNEP, 2015a. *Multiple Pathways to Sustainable Development: Initial Findings from the Global South*, Nairobi: United Nations Environment Programme.

UNEP, 2015b. *Uncovering Pathways Towards an Inclusive Green Economy – A Summary for Leaders*, Nairobi: United Nations Environment Programme.

Van Rensburg, D., 2017a. *Fin24.com – Nuclear Will Happen*. [Online]. Available at https://m.fin24.com/Economy/nuclear-will-happen-20171210-2 (accessed 1 February 2018).

WEF, 2017. *The Global Competitiveness Report 2017–2018*, Geneva: World Economic Forum.

Winkler, H., 2017. Reducing Energy Poverty through Carbon Tax Revenues in South Africa. *Journal of Energy in Southern Africa*, 28(3), pp. 12–26.

Wlokas, H., 2015. *A Review of the Local Community Development Requirements in South Africa's Renewable Energy Procurement Programme*, Cape Town: WWF-SA (Technical Report).

World Bank, 2011. *South Africa Economic Update – Focus on Green Growth*, Washington, DC: The World Bank.

World Bank, 2012. *Inclusive Green Growth: The Pathway to Sustainable Development*, Washington, DC: The World Bank.

Wright, J., Bishcof-Niemz, T., Van Heerden, R. and Mushwana, C., 2017. *Least Cost Electricity Mix for South Africa – Optimisation of the South African Power Sector until 2050*, Unpublished: CSIR Energy Centre Working Document (16 January 2017).

WWF, 2016a. *Signals of the Energy Transition*, Paris: WWF France.

WWF, 2016b. *Living Planet Report: Risk and Resilience in a New Era*, Switzerland: World Wildlife Fund International.

Yelland, C., 2017a. *Op-Ed: Irrational IRP Madness Grips the Energy Sector in South Africa*. [Online]. Available at www.dailymaverick.co.za/article/2017-12-12-op-ed-irrational-irp-madness-grips-the-energy-sector-in-south-africa/ (accessed 9 January 2018).

Yelland, C., 2017b. The Renewable Energy, New Coal and Gas-to-Power IPP Programmes in SA – Quo Vadis? *Fin24.com*, 11 November.

3 Climate change and vulnerability in South Africa

Sustainability transitions in a changing climate?

Coleen Vogel and Mark Swilling

Introduction

Climate change and climate variability, both complex and 'wicked' challenges (Rittel and Webber, 1973), are increasingly gaining media and policy attention by many concerned citizens across the globe, particularly post the Paris Agreement in 2015 and more recently, as severe weather events occur with apparent greater magnitude and frequency. Enhanced understanding of the biophysical and socio-economic drivers of risk to climate variability and change can provide useful junctures for deciding on future national and local development pathways and actions. Extreme weather events (such as the current drought occurring in the Western Cape and extreme storms in Gauteng Province), while difficult to attribute to climate change, have huge livelihood, development and economic implications. As such, they provide useful opportunities to re-examine current and future narratives and discourses on adaptation, vulnerability, exposures and risks to various climate hazards (Intergovernmental Panel on Climate Change (IPCC), 2014).

A number of climate change assessments note that Africa is one of the most vulnerable continents to climate change. South Africa is a semi-arid country that is strongly influenced by dominant atmospheric system controls (Tyson, 1986) which impact climate variability (Landman *et al.*, 2014). The climate system is receiving heightened attention by scientists investigating future scenarios and trajectories that may accompany climate change. Future climate change projections, for example, include significant warming trends for much of southern Africa with possible changes in rainfall patterns, magnitude and intensity (DEA, forthcoming).

Climate change and related policy and action are usually considered from two perspectives, namely adaptation and mitigation. Mitigation usually refers to human intervention to reduce the sources or enhance the sinks of greenhouse gases (Agard and Schipper, 2014). Adaptation, in human systems, seeks to moderate or avoid harm or exploit beneficial opportunities and can usually either be incremental in design (e.g. where actions are designed to maintain the system) or transformational (e.g. where the fundamental attributes of a system are restructured and transformed in response to climate change) (Agard and Schipper, 2014: 1758).

The context of South Africa, both in terms of current and future climate and hazard risk exposure and the socio-economic vulnerability to such risks, are important considerations when framing and designing developmental action. South Africa is a coal-dependent and carbon-intensive economy. Carbon dioxide is the country's most significant greenhouse gas (GHG) contributing to more than 80 per cent of GHG emissions (Swilling and Annecke, 2012). The carbon-intensive economy is directly coupled with the so-called 'mineral-energy-complex' (MEC), a critical and persistent component of the economic core of apartheid.

Notwithstanding a National Development Plan (NDP) that has tried to focus attention on various links between economic and social concerns in the country, it has been argued that '… since the late 19th century, South Africa has exploited its mineral wealth with little or no regard for the environment' (RSA, 2012: 37 and cited in Death, 2014: 2). About one-quarter of the country's coal production – the high quality coal – is exported, regularly placing it in the 'top five' coal exporters in the world. The remaining three-quarters – largely cheap, low quality coal – are used domestically. Significantly, South Africa's power stations are designed to use low quality coal, with profits from exported high quality coal cross-subsidising the cheap (and dirtier) coal.

Along with the energy-intensive economy resulting in GHG emissions, the country is also faced with a variety of social challenges that configure vulnerability. South Africa, in recent months, has undergone ratings downgrades as a result of corruption, leaving some to question the serious deficits in effective leadership and weak governance that continue to shock and ricochet through the economy, impacting the whole nation (e.g. Gqubule, 2017). Coupled with this is our role in the 'global and local carbon space'.

Multiple deprivations have also been shown to exist when using the doughnut heuristic developed by Oxfam, which uses biophysical and social boundaries – an ecological ceiling and social floor – which constrains the global adaptive space (Cole, 2015). These deprivations intersect and set the stage for a variety of climate change vulnerabilities (Cole, 2015). In 2012, safety (64 per cent) was a key concern, 52 per cent of the population was living below the national poverty line and 36 per cent of South Africans were unemployed. Mindful of these concerns, the NDP has set clear goals to reduce inequality and eliminate poverty (National Planning Commission, 2012).

Addressing these socio-economic challenges in ways that simultaneously address the consequences of a changing climate (mitigation and adaptation) is one of the major challenges confronting the country today. This is what is best described as the challenge of a just transition (Swilling and Annecke, 2012). Climate change and climate variability are key when thinking about just transitions in South Africa. However, given the limited contribution South Africa makes to total global GHG emissions, it cannot be argued that the country has only a global responsibility to introduce mitigation measures. The country's climate change response must also include vulnerability and adaptation to climate change, often areas of research, analysis and investment that are not as high profile as climate mitigation.

Climate policy in South Africa

While there is as yet no national, detailed, comprehensive assessment of the impacts and vulnerabilities of climate change (CC) across economic sectors (Midgley, 2016), some assessments of possible climate change impacts have begun to crystallise sustainability transition pathways (Loorbach and Rotmans, 2010). In the absence of a single national piece of legislation for CC (e.g. a Climate Change Act), several policy pieces and assessments (DEA, 2010, 2011) including the National Climate Change Response Policy (NCCRP) (DEA, 2011), the Long Term Mitigation Scenarios (Winkler, 2010) and Long Term Adaptation Scenarios (LTAS) (DEA, 2013), complemented by the work of the South African National Biodiversity Institute, have been undertaken. For more details on the complex development of climate change policy see Bond (2012), Hetz (2015) and Hamby *et al.* (2016). Notwithstanding these efforts, there was a call in the Intended Nationally Determined Contributions (INDC) that a goal is to '... build resilience and adaptive capacity to respond to climate change risk and vulnerability; whilst providing guidance on the integration of climate change responses into current and future development objectives' (INDC, 2015: 5). In this chapter, we argue that a comprehensive, deep and systematic assessment of the drivers of vulnerability in the country is still lacking to enable such resilience-building.

Vulnerability also features very strongly in the work being done by those developing the current National Adaptation Strategy (NAS) with calls for the development of a National Vulnerability Assessment Framework (NVAF). The aim of the National Adaptation Strategy (of which the second draft has been released for public comment) also focuses attention on the need to 'transition to a climate resilient South Africa, which will follow a development path, guided by anticipation, adaptation and recovery to a changing climate and environment to achieve our development aspirations' (DEA, 2017: 19).

To deepen the discussion about the relationship between the process of thinking about longer-term, sustainability transitions and climate change, it will be necessary to identify the specific linkages between climate change responses (mitigation and adaptation) and the key dynamics of economic production, consumption and distribution. Issues of price and government subsidies, for example, influence the declining cost of renewable energy technologies, which in turn was spurred on by the need to respond to climate change. The fact that climate drives adaptation and economics drives renewables (traditionally a 'mitigation' measure) creates a very interesting framework for discussing the relationship between climate change responses (adaptation and mitigation) and the so-called 'green economy' discourse in South Africa. A coherent and comprehensive climate change and climate variability narrative may be what is needed to achieve this. The notion of 'vulnerability', we suggest, may help to connect the complexities of climate change science to understandings related to the greening of the economy.

Notwithstanding a number of academic efforts, mainly through postgraduate research and various activist contributions and national research efforts (e.g. a

Risk and Vulnerability Atlas that begins to probe dimensions of vulnerability, including vulnerability, vulnerability drivers shaping change, and risk), the approach to date has tended to focus on vulnerability issues in isolated contexts. Adaptation projects, of which there are many, seem to be individual case studies implemented largely in response to donor funding. Many of the current outputs also tend to be static and one-off assessments, with a heavy focus on poverty reduction. Few assessments focus on human capabilities, agency and change. Further, the ways in which climate adaptation connects to the dynamics of economic development has, in many cases, been neglected.

This chapter examines the notion of 'vulnerability' in the climate change discourse and related terms such as 'mitigation' and 'adaptation'. Some key vulnerabilities and complex risks in South Africa in the energy sector, in drought risk reduction and in the urban context are explored to illustrate the complex interdependencies and challenges that require more comprehensive coordination when thinking about 'just transitions' and climate change in South Africa.

'Vulnerability' as the link between climate change and the green economy

Why focus on vulnerability when trying to examine the drivers and linkages of sustainable transitions and climate change? The notion of 'vulnerability' is a critical component in the climate change narrative, particularly from an 'adaptation' perspective. Vulnerability usually includes an external dimension (exposure) to climate variations and an 'internal dimension' comprising 'sensitivity' and 'adaptive capacity' (Fussel, 2007). Vulnerability can also be considered as either a starting point for analysis or an endpoint within wider socio-ecological systems – with a focus on an analysis of the ability to cope and respond to pressures and shocks (Agard and Schipper, 2014). For instance, 'the residual consequences that remain' after adaptation measures are implemented is referred to as levels of vulnerability (Agard and Schipper, 2014: 1769). Carefully executed vulnerability-led investigations (usually starting point assessments) can draw attention to structural inadequacies in the 'system', for example poor development planning that can exacerbate vulnerability to climate change.

Eakin *et al.* (2009) distinguish between three terms in the wider climate change discourse, namely 'adaptation', 'vulnerability' and 'resilience'. The interpretation of each gives rise to differing policy response options (e.g. with reference to greening the economy), different actors and different temporal and spatial scales of actions. A short-term view of adaptation, for example, which is usually sector-focused (e.g. water or agriculture) tries to lower risks at low economic cost and no major change in governance (Eakin *et al.*, 2009; Moser and Boykoff, 2013). Such an approach is essentially focused on maintaining elements of the system with little major structural change. The vulnerability lens being used in this chapter, is used to assist in focusing on social structures and conditions that configure vulnerabilities (Moser and Boykoff, 2013) and focuses on socio-economic restructuring and empowering the disadvantaged through careful governance and institutional changes towards a more 'just' society.

Resilience, a contested concept, focuses on the ability of larger-scale, socio-ecological systems (e.g. rangelands) to respond to climate variability, usually with a longer-term goal for building the capacity to persist, recover and renew after a disturbance (Moser and Boykoff, 2013).

The links between climate change and vulnerability are relevant for any discussion of development pathways. These include pathways towards decarbonisation and low-carbon economies, decoupling of improvements in well-being from rising levels of resource use (Swilling et al., 2016), and circular economic models. A sustainability-oriented transition – otherwise more popularly known as the 'greening' of an economy – has implications for our understanding of 'development' since it primarily means going beyond narrow, income-oriented conceptions of development. A recently formulated conception of development that achieves this in a way that is compatible with the Sustainable Development Goals (SDGs) is provided by Castells and Himanen, who argue that development can be understood as a '... social process by which humans as a collective enhance their wellbeing while creating the structural conditions for the reproduction of the process of development itself' (2014: 7).

A comprehensive critique of the implications of climate change for South Africa which could inform a 'sustainability discourse' is only beginning to emerge. Humby et al. (2016), for example, detail the various South African policies that shape legal and governance responses to climate change. Their assessment proceeds from a number of vantage points, specifically an overview of South Africa's climate policies and then using a number of knowledge frames (e.g. climate governance, sustainable development, climate mitigation and adaptation, and climate resilient development) to link development, environmental planning and climate change. The work by Humby et al. is significant because it reinforces the call by some to transcend a narrow focus on economic growth indicators. However, much of the effort to date has been focused on mitigation efforts, notably the forms of energy which may be needed to propel greener 'growth' (Jaeger et al., 2011; Global Commission on Economy and Climate, 2014). Few efforts call into question the growth paradigm which has dominated the development pathway in South Africa (Fioramonti, 2017) and which has propelled its dependence on mineral and energy production as a key driver of growth (Swilling et al., 2015).

Climate change, vulnerability and the green economy

The terms used to navigate the complex landscape of development, green economy and climate change, including vulnerability, refer to a wide range of approaches to development. By adopting a vulnerability lens, the systems and complex challenges (see next section) which would be under immense pressures to shift fundamentally in a changing climate, can more easily be demarcated.

Furthermore, this framing focuses on the systems that need to be prioritised for a just transition to occur. The nature of this change entails both adaptation and mitigation responses. Since vulnerability also changes the dynamics of the market, and hence prices, by definition the more vulnerable a system is, the more risk it carries. Perceptions of risk also influence price. This is where the link to the wider discussion of greening the economy becomes apparent.

Since 2009, with the rise of 'green Keynesianism' as one response to the global financial crisis, there has been a widening debate about the notion of a 'green economy' (see an overview from a South African perspective in Swilling *et al.*, 2015, 2016). Death (2014) proposed four conceptions of the green economy: the 'green revolution' – a radical overhauling of the system; 'green transformation' – where growth is aligned to sustainable development principles; 'green growth' – with not much change from the dominant neo-liberal paradigm, rather a mere tweaking of policies, technologies and seeking new markets for growth; and finally 'green resilience' (Death, 2014: 8). Death (2014) also reminds us to interrogate issues of power, hegemony and the control of resources of one group over another, or one paradigm (e.g. neo-liberal vs capitalist management of resources) over another (see, for example, Bond, 2012). This is discussed in Chapter 1.

Oelefse *et al.* (2006) have also examined environmental policy, processes and institutions in South Africa using an ecological modernisation approach in which techno-scientific approaches to environmental management are the focus. They note that while South African environmental policy has undergone significant changes since our democracy, we find ourselves '… in a situation of "institutional ambiguity" where there is little experience or precedent of how to proceed' (Hajer, 2004; Oelefse *et al.*, 2006: 62). They further note that because of institutional deficits, recourse to strong ecological modernisation, with the creation of strong networks that focus on development and environment, have emerged. 'Pockets of innovation', in some cases driven and serviced by consultants who are becoming the intellectual actors, reshape environmental decision-making, including the 'Africanisation of ecological modernisation' (Oelefse *et al.*, 2006: 76). The persistence of a technocratic approach to environmental governance is detailed further in Chapter 5.

Given the way the notion of vulnerability works to identify systems that are at highest risk, we adopt Death's 'green revolution' paradigm, including radical change, suggesting an approach that could respond to the call by Oelofse *et al.* (2006) for a more radical approach to environmental governance. Swilling *et al.* (2016) concur by emphasising the need for a synthesis between developmental state theory and sustainability transition theory to ensure that the meaning of 'structural transformation' is not limited to either developmental or environmental issues. When both are addressed within a coherent conceptual framework, the possibility of a 'just transition' becomes clearer. However, these emerging general narratives of 'green revolution', 'radical ecological modernisation' and 'just transition' are all very well, but where does one start?

Change happens incrementally and does not always happen systemically. Vulnerability helps to identify some of the priorities, by suggesting which systems and people are facing the greatest risk, and should inform the trajectory of investments to address these socio-economic priorities. What follows are discussions of particular arenas of intervention where developmental and environmental dynamics connect in ways that give some tangible substance to the notion of 'sustainability transitions'. The notion of vulnerability helps demarcate these systems facing new forms of risk and in which new economic dynamics are being configured.

The vulnerabilities of energy transitions in South Africa

The South African economy depends on coal as an energy source. The coal-based energy system is extremely vulnerable and is arguably in terminal decline. The International Energy Agency's *Coal Information Overview* report, for example, found that there is a limited potential for an upturn in demand for coal in the foreseeable future (IEA, 2016). By contrast, renewable forms of electricity are growing at a faster rate than fossil fuel-based energy, and this is expected to continue through to 2040 (IEA, 2016). Furthermore, variable renewables in the four largest power markets (China, United States, India and the European Union), for example, will have become the largest source of new generation capacity by 2030–2035. Furthermore, the average cost of renewable solar energy is expected to reduce by a further '40–70 per cent by 2040 and onshore wind by an additional 10–25 per cent' (IEA, 2016: 4). Subsidies per unit of new solar PV in China are expected to drop by three-quarters by 2025, and solar projects in India are expected to be competitive without subsidies by 2030 (IEA, 2016:4; Parr *et al.*, 2017).

South Africa is ideally positioned to take advantage of the global energy transition. Solar photovoltaics on commercial and residential properties, as well as additional concentrated solar power capacity, are plausible options given South Africa's vast solar radiation resources (ERC *et al.*, 2017). In particular, solar technologies were identified as making a large contribution to the decarbonisation of electricity supply in South Africa, given the technical feasibility, commitment in stated policy and currently competitive tariffs (Wright *et al.*, 2016; IPPPP, 2017).

By contrast, government investment in coal-based enterprises will become increasingly difficult to recoup as global pressures to reduce emissions occurs under the Paris Agreement. Furthermore, South Africa now faces the very real risk of perpetuating path dependence by relying on generation from coal when low-carbon technologies are a viable and cost-effective alternative. The result will be 'higher electricity prices for consumers, rendering them an even larger component of already meagre low-income household budgets' (cited in Parr *et al.*, 2017: 5).

High quality, available solar and wind resources result in higher returns on investment in renewables in South Africa (Walwyn and Brent, 2015). According to Walwyn and Brent (2015), a solar power plant in a suitable location in South Africa could generate up to 20 per cent more power for the same level of capital investment than, for example, in other locations globally. There are locations in South Africa, for example, where 2,400 kWh/m^2 is feasible, compared to 2,000 kWh/m^2 in Spain (Walwyn and Brent, 2015 cited in Parr *et al.*, 2017: 5). This helps explain why the various bid windows in the Renewable Energy Independent Power Producers Procurement Programme (REIPPPP) have been oversubscribed as foreign investors rushed to invest in South African renewables. It also explains why the economic drivers of renewable energy expansion are now more significant than climate mitigation drivers. This is reinforced by research that estimates that renewables could eventually meet 90 per cent of South Africa's energy needs (Wright *et al.*, 2017). They calculated that the costs of renewables are now roughly half the price of coal-based power over a life cycle. Given that nuclear is more expensive than coal, and that renewables can now be deployed for baseload, it follows that renewables are clearly a better alternative than nuclear (Wright *et al.*, 2017).

Renewable forms of electricity also have significant employment potential (Walwyn and Brent, 2015). While limited jobs exist during the post-construction operational phase of a renewable energy power plant, if one looks at the entire value chain from manufacturing of components, through to assembly, construction, installation and then maintenance and rehabilitation, then it is estimated that 'an average of 30 jobs per peak MW installed capacity, the overwhelming majority of which are relatively low-skilled' can be generated (Parr *et al.*, 2017: 6). Furthermore, it is noteworthy that solar energy systems tend to be decentralised relatively small systems that are mainly located in small urban towns across South Africa (Davies *et al.*, 2017).

South Africa's unreliable energy system was brought home in 2015 when a series of load-shedding events took place, colloquially known as 'blackouts'. This had a negative effect on investment and business activity slowed. According to some estimates, power interruptions since the 1990s have cut economic growth rates by as much as one percentage point (Heun *et al.*, 2010). Supply shortages that impact economic growth and certain urban settlements will also impact negatively on poor households.

Transitioning to renewable energy is the primary driver of decarbonisation in South Africa (Altiere *et al.*, 2016; Worthington, 2015). It is also the cheapest energy source. Indeed, the achievement of the Paris Agreement goals are largely premised on the speed at which major economies transition their energy systems. Given Southern Africa's high vulnerability to unmitigated climate change – which involves economic and trade risks on the one hand and geopolitical and security risks on the other – it is squarely in the country's national interests to ensure that the Paris Agreement goals of not breaching a 2°C warming scenario, is reached.

The installation of 17.8 GW of electricity generation via the REI4P from renewables including solar, wind, amongst others, over the period 2012–2030 is ambitious (Walwyn and Brent, 2015). It has proven quite successful to date.

But with some tweaks, such as revisions to the bidding and procurement process, as well as a tightening of the local content provisions (to drive local manufacturing), it could deliver even stronger social, environmental and economic benefits provided that the vested interests driving the nuclear energy agenda in the country can be overcome. The REI4P could further reduce the carbon footprint of the country, address some of the escalating costs of coal-fired electricity and also generate employment.

A focus on energy and the 'vulnerability' of energy access and provision provide one angle to climate change and sustainability challenges. Another useful way to examine underlying, structurally driven climate vulnerabilities is to focus on what is usually seen to be a climate-driven situation but is also anchored to a range of underlying vulnerabilities. Drought, for example, is increasingly drawing attention to sustainability interventions and actions that may be required.

Disaster risk reduction – implications for transitions

South Africa has long been known to be vulnerable to periods of climate stress (e.g. droughts and floods) because of its dependence on climate-sensitive economic sectors, high levels of poverty and the interrelated impacts of HIV/AIDS and other stressors. Droughts are isolated here for further discussion. For interesting examinations of floods, see Fatti and Patel (2013) and the detailed reports of the RADAR Centre of Excellence at Stellenbosch University. The poor, living in both urban and rural contexts, are often disproportionately affected relying as they do on 'sectors' that are closely linked and coupled with climate change, namely, agriculture, biodiversity, ecosystems and water supplies (Ziervogel *et al.*, 2014).

Droughts have long been *the* climate 'events' (particularly those that last for more than one season and are severe) that expose underlying vulnerabilities and structural inadequacies in development and scientific thinking on climate change. As far back as the Drought Investigation Commission of the early 1920s, efforts were being made to draw attention to both the science and policy needs of the country with reference to drought. Several investigations trying to understand and interrogate the suite of issues linking development and climate have been undertaken both in the region (Benson and Clay, 1994) and locally (e.g. Union of South Africa, 1923; Abrams *et al.*, 1992; Republic of South Africa, 2002; Vogel *et al.*, 2000; Vogel *et al.*, 2010; Vogel and Van Zyl, 2016). Since this early work, regular droughts have continued to confront the country, including the most recent drought, with far-reaching impacts. By May 2016, for example, seven out of the nine South African provinces had declared a state of provincial drought disaster and two municipalities had declared a local state of drought. The growing stress of water availability in the Western Cape also continues to focus attention on causes and consequences of climate change (Baudoin *et al.*, 2017).

In all cases, not least the National Drought Forum, established in response to the drought in the early 1990s and eventually contributing to the Reconstruction and Development Programme, attention has been focused on the close inter-connections between development and drought. Strategic directions, tabled at a meeting in 1993, which highlight the centrality of provinces (regions) in devel-opment and the need for ongoing programmes to prepare for drought (Drought Monitor, 1993), still hold relevance today.

Trying to determine estimates of the loss, damages and costs to livelihoods in both rural and urban areas that arise from droughts has also been examined. Gross-scale economic loss data are often provided (Benson and Clay, 1994), but there seems to be no national, systematic, collective data system that captures human vulnerabilities and in particular those of the poor during periods of drought (Holloway *et al.*, 2013). The state's inability to rapidly respond to drought, despite the establishment of institutional arrangements, also continues to be a major concern in the country (Vogel *et al.*, 2010; Baudoin *et al.*, 2017) placing human settlements and socio-economic con-ditions at risk.

But drought is not merely driven by complex atmospheric interactions (such as El Niño). What drought does, in a 'creeping way', is to slowly expose other drivers of vulnerability that continue to shape water availability in the country, but that all too often are not examined in a holistic manner. This includes climate *and* socio-economic-driven scarcity (DiMP, 2012) and notions of what a 'new normal', accompanying climate change, may mean. The result is that drought response measures and interventions are usually dominated by 'techno-logy speak' (e.g. desalinisation, improved early warning systems and climate service communications, etc.) in times of a drought (e.g. Cape Town 2016–2018), which although useful, may not be sustainable in the longer term since they mask the underlying vulnerabilities which could be worsened by climate change impacts.

Other options linked to longer-term transitions also need to be explored, debated and factored into policy discourses (e.g. LTAS), such as alternative methods and uses of water (e.g. drip irrigation, re-use of grey water, sustainable water management practices and changes in consumer lifestyles and business practices). Links between IWRM (Integrated Water Resource Management) and notions of decoupling, while contested, need further debate, particularly when considering options for greening the economy and sustainable transition pathways (Swilling *et al.*, 2016).

Given the history of drought in the country and also the risks of future droughts, the focus is often on how to improve the resilience of agriculture, a key sector in which the poor are involved. The responses are often focused on increasing local food security and self-sufficiency (Howden *et al.*, 2007; Dercon, 2011). Drought-resistant crops, for example, are often suggested, while climate smart agriculture is used as an entry point into thinking about how 'greening' of the economy can be used to not only reduce risks to climate change but also enhance local livelihoods. Before rapidly adopting these interventions, it is necessary to open up rigorous debate on their use and trade-offs. For instance, climate smart agriculture and agro-ecology can enhance and support the practices of smallholder farmers (Oxfam America, 2015) by ensuring that the productivity of soils is improved using non-chemical means.

Adaptation investments in response to droughts can bring opportunity costs but also expose tensions and contradictions. Low-carbon public investments, for example, can damage poor people's livelihoods but also be more labour intensive and thereby create jobs. Dercon (2011) and Raworth *et al.* (2014) argue that the role of public subsidies supporting such production could be invested in other pro-poor investments (e.g. health or education). Investing in agriculture in marginal and increasingly in drought-prone areas may also not be optimal (Dercon, 2011). Economic diversification, through economy-wide greening efforts, could result in many moving out of agriculture, migrating into cities and into new, complex and high-risk settings. Careful assessments of vulnerability in a number of contexts therefore need to be made against so-called 'greening options' particularly from longer-term sustainability perspectives (Dercon, 2011).

As can be seen by this brief example of drought – a common climate phenomenon that may become increasingly critical with climate change (IPCC, 2012, 2014) – the vulnerabilities of local communities, many of whom depend on livelihoods closely coupled with climate and weather, cannot be ignored when thinking of broader national development and future sustainability. The sad reality is that we seem to fail to learn from the wealth of experiences we have had in facing such challenges in the past. We continue to resort to short-term, technocratic and incremental efforts which supposedly enhance longer-term resilience and disaster risk reduction (e.g. Early Warning Systems), but exclude deeper investigations into the structural factors driving vulnerability, which are often exposed during times of climate risk. The recent drought in Cape Town also raises the need for more targeted research on growing urban settlements as opposed to the strong history of a rural, agricultural drought focus in South Africa. Analysis on water scarcity, the drivers, and governance responses to urban vulnerabilities to climate stress, need more concerted efforts. The costs to the economy, both direct and indirect, and most especially to many livelihoods, should be strong motivations to think much more carefully about vulnerability and resilience in planning transitions to greener economies.

Expanding what we mean by vulnerability – growing urban climate risks

The climate change vulnerability discourse has had a strong focus on sectors facing biophysical constraints. Hence, nationally led research efforts tend to focus on the vulnerability of agriculture, water, biodiversity and oceans (see LTAS reports). Notwithstanding the recent upsurge in urban adaptation and urban policy research, the climate change community has largely bypassed the need for coordinated, national policy coupled with sustainability concerns, although the National Adaptation Strategy may usher in some movement in this area. In LTAS 2, for example, the exposure of several economic sectors to

climate risks is the major focus of discussion, while there is little detailed attention to human vulnerabilities and their historic and current root causes in South
Africa (Davies, 2011), nor is there much attention to inter-sectoral concerns,
trade-offs and synergies (e.g. nexus issues such as links between food–energy–
water and what these may mean for vulnerable communities).

National effort, to date, focuses on the science of climate change, climate
projections and sectoral assessments. These often preclude a more detailed and
national, cross-sectoral and more systemic examination of the root causes of
the drivers of vulnerability to climate stresses. In one exception, a case study in
the uMkhanyakdue District in KwaZulu-Natal, Misselhorn (cited in Davies,
2011) documents the interconnecting variables and indices (namely economic
well-being, health and security, demographic structure and natural resource
dependence) to determine vulnerability to CC and CV. A national effort to
develop some social indicators of vulnerability to CC and CV has also been
attempted as part of the LTAS 2 efforts (Link*d*, 2013). This has revealed some
remarkably similar results to those identified by Misselhorn cited above. Vulnerability was examined with reference to infrastructure and services (access to
services and dwelling types); health (malnutrition and primary health care);
and socio-economic vulnerability (land ownership, household income, gender
and age profile). Composite maps of vulnerability clearly show that the provinces with large rural populations, i.e. the Eastern Cape, KwaZulu-Natal, Mpumalanga, Limpopo and North West Provinces, are the 'most socially vulnerable
to climate change' (Link*d*, 2013, 37). Specific mention was also made on the
role of income, employment and social grants in the cases examined. These
cases highlighted here all have implications for green economy pathways.
Finding ways to explore more systemic views of vulnerability that are informed
by local context, e.g. growing informality, settlement and climate-related
vulnerabilities, is exceedingly difficult but will be required in thinking about
'just' transitions to sustainability (Swilling and Annecke, 2012; Smit and
Musango, 2015).

The development of composite social, economic and environmental indicators as attempted above is, however, not always helpful – particularly if one is
using a longer-term, vulnerability lens. Kaika (2017) gives a hard-hitting review
on the use of indicators, which are developed without a more focused and systemic assessment of vulnerability to climate change and climate risks. Kaika's
(2017: 95) injunction to those thinking hard about resilience and sustainability
transitions is '… to focus instead on identifying the actors and processes that
produce the **need** to build resilience in the first place. And … [to] try to change
these factors'.

Moving on – rethinking climate change and the green economy via a vulnerability lens

This chapter contributes to the discussion about linkages between climate
change and sustainability transitions using a vulnerability lens. There is, we

argue, at a national level inadequate comprehensive and carefully coordinated attention paid to 'human' and 'social' vulnerability to climate change, that can inform and make necessary inroads into persistent issues of poverty, economic capability, natural resource use and access to services. The recent efforts to produce an NAS holds promise, though. Isolated pockets of research exist, as noted by Oelofse *et al.* (2006), providing some narratives and evidence of the complex interactions between climate change and development, but there are few comprehensive assessments.

We concur with Death, that realising the commitment to a sustainability transition will require efforts that are sustained from a wide range of actors (e.g. private sector, civil society) but will also be influenced by citizens' individual decisions (Death, 2014).

Making calls for a 'green revolution' or a 'just transition', however, becomes too abstract. Change is, by definition, incremental because it happens in time and space, not in the cognitive space of the theorist. However, given the scale of the challenge of climate change, incremental approaches are not sufficient and more transformative and transgressive approaches are required (Lotz-Sisitka *et al.*, 2015). In the current policy setting, usually determined by short-termism and party politics, the types of sustainability foci and attention may have to radically shift if we are to transition into a 'new normal' – a climate-altered world (Fioramonti, 2017).

We have also tried to argue that vulnerability helps to demarcate priority areas, like the vulnerability of our coal-based energy system and the possibility of disasters, that require more rigorous 'systems thinking'. 'Resilience', in the end, may be more about strategising on intervening in vulnerable systems to ensure structural transformation, than on tweaking the inherent properties of a system that somehow allow it to adapt – hence the need to have a developmental state with a sustainability-oriented conception of structural transformation (Swilling *et al.*, 2016). Thinking hard – including self, reflexive thinking (O'Brien, 2012: 3), and thinking as a nation – is going to be critical as the country moves forward:

> How do 'we' change the systems and structures that perpetuate environmental problems, particularly when they are maintained by powerful interests, often including our own.

Failure to 'work' on all these aspects will delay action and will heighten risks and vulnerabilities in the longer term. Every effort should be made to integrate development and greening efforts (constantly asking the questions about whose development, for what purposes and by what means, and questions of accountability of resource use in the country) into effective climate risk reduction. The country cannot afford 'mopping up efforts' after severe climate events, nor can we afford endless 'climate event' investigations. The onus thus falls on society-wide conversations about which 'developmental trajectory' can and should be chosen and what the dynamics of transition are (Swilling, 2014, 2016).

The overriding question thus remains: what will it take for a just transition towards a healthy South Africa and environment, particularly given climate change? While Swilling *et al.* (2015: 667) are correct to highlight the structural issues: '... that an integrated conception of structural transformation will be needed that is driven by a commitment to both the goals of human wellbeing and sustainability', a move and shift towards more integrated approaches across the *heart-ware – soft-ware –* and *hard-ware* spectrum for sustainability will also be required (Mohamad *et al.*, 2015, Wamsler *et al.*, 2017).

Current mechanisms, including teaching, research and policymaking, are insufficient to address global sustainability concerns (Wamsler *et al.*, 2017). What may be needed is an 'expanded consciousness', 'embodied notions of mindfulness' (Wamsler *et al.* 2017: 1) and a more effective and '... broader view of technology, not just as hardware that is transferred, ... as a set of *practices and networks* of expertise and enabling actors' (Newell and Bulkeley, 2016: 650, emphasis added). While markets have a role to play, Newell and Bulkeley (2016: 661) also caution that they are not an end to themselves '... but rather one (and not the only) tool capable of shifting socio-technical systems in lower-carbon directions'. What is urgently needed, therefore, are efforts that assist in considering, exploring and experimenting with deeper and more holistic assessments of climate change and the psychological, socio-economic and political drivers of change.

References

Abrams, L., Short, R. and Evans, J. (1992). Root Cause and Relief Restraint Report. *National Consultative Report on Drought, Secretarial and Ops Room*, Johannesburg, 8 October 1992.

Agard, J. and Schipper, L.F. (2014). Glossary to the IPCC Report, Annex II, 1757–1776.

Altiere, K., Trollip, H., Alison, T.C., Merven, B.H. and Winker, H. (2016). *Achieving Development and Mitigation Objectives Through Decarbonisation in South Africa*, Climate Policy, 16: supp. S78–S91. Available at http://dx.doi.org/10.1080/14693062.2016.115 0250 (accessed 4 May 2018).

Baudoin, M., Vogel, C., Nortje, K. and Naik, M. (2017). Living with Drought in South Africa: Lessons Learnt from the Recent El Niño Drought Period, *International Journal of Disaster Risk Reduction*, 23: pp. 128–137.

Benson, C. and Clay, E. (1994). *The Impact of Drought on Sub-Saharan African Economies: A Preliminary Examination*. ODI. Working Paper 77, London.

Bond, P. (2012). *Politics of Climate Justice, Paralysis Above, Movement Below*. University of KwaZulu-Natal Press, Scottsville.

Castells, M. and Himanen, P. (eds.) (2014). *Reconceptualising Development in the Global Information Age*, Oxford: Oxford University Press.

Cole, M. (2015). *Is South Africa Operating in a Safe and Just Space? Using the Doughnut Model to Explore Environmental Sustainability and Social Justice*, Oxfam. Available at www.oxfam.org (accessed April 2018).

Davies, C. (2011). *Climate Risk and Vulnerability: A Handbook for Southern Africa*, Pretoria, South Africa: Council for Scientific and Industrial Research, 92pp.

Davies, M., Swilling, M., Wlokas, H.L. (2017). Towards New Configurations of Urban Energy Governance in South Africa's Renewable Energy Procurement Programme. *Energy Research and Social Science*. Available at https://doi.org/10.1016/j.erss.2017. 11.010 (accessed April 2018).

DEA (Department of Environmental Affairs), (2010). *National Climate Change Response Green Paper*, Notice 1033 of 2010, Government Gazette, 25 November 2011. See the DEA website for a range of policy papers. Available at www.environment.gov.za (accessed 4 May 2018).

DEA, (2011). *National Climate Change Response Policy White Paper*, Pretoria, South Africa: Government Printer.

DEA, (2013). *Long-term Adaptation Scenarios Flagship Programme (LTAS) for South Africa, Climate trends and scenarios for South Africa*, Pretoria, South Africa.

DEA, (2017). *Department of Environmental Affairs National Adaptation Strategy*, Republic of South Africa, 2nd draft for comments.

DEA, (forthcoming). South Africa's Draft Third National Communication under the United Nations Framework Convention on Climate Change, Department of Environmental Affairs, Republic of South Africa.

Death, C. (2014). The Green Economy in South Africa: Global Discourses and Local Politics, *Politikon*, 41,1: 1–22.

Dercon, S. (2011). *Is Green Growth Good for the Poor?* World Bank Working Paper. Available at http://elibrary.worldbank; org/doi/book/10.1596/1813-9450-6231 (accessed 2 May 2018).

Disaster Mitigation for Sustainable Livelihoods Programme, DiMP (2012). *Southern Cape Drought Disaster, 'The Scramble for Water'*, Cape Town: University of Stellenbosch.

Drought Monitor, Nov/Dec., (1993). *A Forum for Rural Voices*, Report from the CFDRD's Strategic Planning Workshop, Consultative Forum on Drought and Rural Development.

Eakin, H., Tompkins, E.L., Nelson, D.R. and Anderies, J.M. (2009). Hidden Costs and Disparate Uncertainties: Trade-offs Involved in Approaches to Climate Policy, in Adger, W.N., Lorenzoni, I. and O'Brien, K.L. (eds.), *Adapting to Climate Change: Thresholds, Values, Governance*, Cambridge: Cambridge University Press, pp. 212–226.

Energy Research Centre (ERC) (2017). *The Developing Energy Landscape of South Africa: Technical Report*. Cape Town: University of Cape Town. International Food Policy Research Institute and Council for Scientific Research. Available at www.africaportal. org/publications/developing-energy-landscape-south-africa-technical-report/ (accessed 2 May 2018).

Fatti, C.E. and Patel, Z. (2013). Perceptions and Responses to Urban Flood Risk: Implications for Climate Governance in the South, *Applied Geography*, 36: 13–22.

Fioramonti, L. (2017). *Wellbeing Economy – Success in a World Without Growth*, Johannesburg: Pan Macmillan South Africa.

Fussel, H.-M. (2007). Adaptation Planning for Climate Change: Concepts, Assessment Approaches and Lessons, *Sustainability Science*, 2(2): 265–275.

Global Commission on Economy and Climate (2014). *Better Growth Better Climate: The New Climate Economy Report*. Washington, DC: World Resources Institute. Available at www.newclimateeconomy.net (accessed 4 May 2018).

Gqubule, T. (2017). *No Longer Whispering to Power: The Story of Thuli Madonsela*, Cape Town: Jonathan Ball Publishers.

Hajer, M. (2004). *Three Dimensions of Deliberate Policy Analysis: The Case of Rebuilding Ground Zero*, Paper presented at the Annual Meeting of the American Political Science Association, Chicago, 2–4 September.

Hamby, T.L., Kotze, L. Rumble, O. and Gilder, A. (eds.) (2016). *Climate Change Law and Governance in South Africa*, Cape Town: Juta and Company Pty Ltd.

Hetz, K. (2015). Contesting Adaptation Synergies: Political Realities in Reconciling Climate Change Adaptation with Urban Development in Johannesburg, South Africa, *Regional Environmental Change*, DOI 10.1007/s1013-015-0840-z.

Heun, M.K., van Niekerk, J.K., Fluri, T., Meyer, A.J., Brent, A. (2010). *Learnable Lessons on Sustainability from the Provision of Electricity in South Africa*, paper presented at the ASME 2010 4th International Conference on Energy Sustainability, Phoenix, Arizona, May 17–22, 2010.

Holloway, A., Chasi, V., de Waal, J., Drimie, S., Fortune, G., Mafuleka, G., Morojele, M., Penicela Nhambiu, B., Randrianalijaon, M., Vogel, C. and Zweig, P. (2013). *Humanitarian Trends in Southern Africa: Challenges and Opportunities*. Regional Inter-agency Standing Committee, Southern Africa. Rome: FAO.

Howden, S.M., Soussana, J.F., Tubiello, F.N., Chhetri, N., Dunlop, M. and Meinke, H. (2007). Adapting Agriculture to Climate Change. *Proceedings of the National Academy of Sciences USA*, 104: 19691–19696.

INDC, Intended Nationally Determined Contributions, South Africa. (2015). South Africa's Intended Nationally Determined Contribution (INDC), 1 August.

International Energy Agency, IEA, (2016). *Word Energy Outlook: Executive Summary*. Paris: International Energy Agency. Available at www.iea.org/Textbase/npsum/WEO 2016SUM.pdf (accessed 2 May 2018).

IPCC (Intergovernmental Panel on Climate Change), (2012). *Special Report on Managing the Risks of Extreme Events and Disasters to Advance Climate Change Adaptation: Summary for Policymakers*. Report of Working Groups I and II of the IPCC. Field, C.B., Barros, V., Stocker, T.F., Dahe, Q., Dokken, D.J., Ebi, K.L., Mastrandrea, M.D., Mach, K.J., Plattner, G.-K., Allen, S.K., Tignor, M., Midgley, P., WMO, UNEP.

IPCC, (2014). *Climate Change 2014, Impacts, Adaptation, and Vulnerability, Part B: Regional Aspects, Contribution of Working Group II to the Fifth Assessment Report of the Intergovernmental Panel on Climate Change*. Field, C.B., Barros, V.R., Dokken, D.J., Mach, K.J., Mastrandrea, M.D., Bilir, T.E., Chatterjee, M., Ebi, K.L., Estrada, Y.O., Genova, R.C., Girma, B., Kissel, E.S., Levy, A.N., MacCracken, S., Mastrandrea, P.R. and White, L.L. (eds.). Cambridge and New York: Cambridge University Press, 688pp.

IPPPP Office, *Independent Power Producers Procurement Programme: An Overview*. As at 31 March 2017, Independent Power Producers Procurement Programme Office, Johannesburg, 2017 [Online]. Available at www.ipp-projects.co.za/Publications (accessed 2 May 2018).

Jaeger, C.C., Paroussos, L., Mangalagiu, D., Kupers, R., Mandel, A., Tàbara, J.D., Botta, N., Fürst, S., Henning, E., Ionescu, C. and Lass, W. (2011). *A New Growth Path for Europe. Generating Prosperity and Jobs in the Low-Carbon Economy*. Synthesis Report PIK, University of Oxford, ICCS, Université Paris, 1.

Kaika, M. (2017). 'Don't call me resilient again!' The New Urban Agenda as Immunology … or … What Happens when Communities Refuse to be Vaccinated with 'Smart Cities' and Indicators, *Environment and Urbanization*, 29: 89–102.

Landman, W.A., Beraki, A., DeWitt, D. and Lötter, D. (2014). SST Prediction Methodologies and Verification Considerations for Dynamical Mid-summer Rainfall Forecasts for South Africa, *Water SA*, 40(4): 615–622. Available at http://dx.doi.org/10.4314/wsa.v40i4.6 (accessed 2 May 2018).

Linkd (2013). *Climate Change Risk and Vulnerability Assessment for Rural Human Settlements*, Prepared for the Department of Rural Development and Land Reform Spatial Planning and Facilitation Directorate, July 2013.

Loorbach, D. and Rotmans, J. (2010). The Practice of Transition Management: Examples and Lessons from Four Distinct Case Studies, *Futures*, 42: 237–246.

Lotz-Sisitka, H., Wals, A.E.J., Kronlid, D. and McGarry, D. (2015). Transformative, Transgressive Social Learning: Rethinking Higher Education Pedagogy in Times of Systemic Dysfunction, *Current Opinion in Environmental Sustainability*, 16: 73–80.

Midgley, G. (2016). Scientific Aspects of Climate Change and their Impacts in South Africa. In Hambly, T.L., Kotze, L., Rumble, O. and Gilder, A. (eds.), *Climate Change Law and Governance in South Africa*, Cape Town: Juta and Company Pty Ltd.

Mohamad, Z.F., Nasruddin, A., Kadir, S.N.A., Musa, M.N., Ong, B. and Sakai, N. (2015). Community-based Shared Values as a 'Heart-ware' Driver for Integrated Watershed Management: Japan-Malaysia Policy Learning Perspective, *Journal of Hydrology*, 317–327.

Moser, S. and Boykoff, M. (eds.) (2013). *Successful Adaptation to Climate Change, Linking Science and Policy in a Rapidly Changing World*, Oxford: Routledge.

National Planning Commission. (2012). *National Development Plan 2030 – Our Future Make it Work*. National Planning Commission.

Newell, P. and Bulkeley, H. (2016). Landscape for Change? International Climate Policy and Energy Transitions: Evidence from Sub-Saharan Africa, *Climate Policy*, 17: 650–663.

O'Brien, K. (2012). Global Environmental Change III: Closing the Gap Between Knowledge and Action, Progress Report, *Progress in Human Geography*, 37(4): 587–596.

Oelefse, C., Scott, D., Oelefse, G. and Houghton, J. (2006). Shifts within Ecological Liberalisation in South Africa: Deliberation, Innovation and Institutional Opportunities, *Local Environment*, 11, 1: 61–78.

Oxfam America (2015). Blog. Available at https://politicsofpoverty.oxfamamerica. org/2015/10/whats-the-danger-in-climate-smart-agriculture (accessed 2 May 2018).

Parr, B., Swilling, M. and Henry, D. (2017). *The Paris Agreement and South Africa's Just Transition*. Unpublished draft paper commissioned by the Melbourne Sustainability Institute. Melbourne: Melbourne University.

Raworth, K., Wykes, S. and Bass, S. (2014). Securing Social Justice in Green Economies: A Review and Ten Considerations for Policymakers. IIED Issue Paper. London: IIED.

Republic of South Africa, No. 57 of 2002: *Disaster Management Act, 2002*. Vol. 451 Cape Town 15 January 2003 No. 24252.

Rittel, H.W.J. and Webber, M.M. (1973). Dilemmas in a General Theory of Planning, *Policy Sciences*, 4: 155–169.

Smit, S. and Musango, J.K. (2015). Exploring the Connections Between Green Economy and Informal Economy, *SA Journal of Science*, 111(11/12). Available at http://dx.doi. org/10.17159/sajs.2015/20140535 (accessed 2 May 2018).

Swilling, M. (2014). Rethinking the Science–Policy Interface in South Africa: Experiments in Knowledge Co-production, *South African Journal of Science*, 110(5/6): 1–7.

Swilling, M. (2016). Africa's Game Changers and the Catalysts of Social and System Innovation, *Ecology and Society*, 21: 1–37. Available at http://doi.org/10.5752/ES-08226-210137 (accessed 3 May 2018).

Swilling, M. and Annecke, E. (2012). *Just Transitions, Explorations of Sustainability in an Unfair World*. Tokyo: United Nations University Press.

Swilling, M., Musango, J. and Wakeford, J. (2015). Developmental States and Sustainability Transitions: Prospects of a Just Transition in South Africa, *Journal of Environmental Policy and Planning*, DOI: 10.1080/1523908X.2015.1107716.

Swilling, M., Musango, J. and Wakeford, J., (eds.) (2016). *Greening the South African Economy*, Cape Town: Juta & Company Pty Ltd.

Swilling, M., Pieterse, E. and Hajer, M. (2018). Futuring, Experimentation and Transformative Urban Politics. Poli, R. (ed.), Handbook for Anticipation. New York: Springer. https://doi.org/10.1007/978-3-319-31737-3_24-1.

Tyson, P.D. (1986). *Climatic Change and Variability in Southern Africa*. Cape Town: Oxford University Press, 220 pp.

Union of South Africa. (1923). *Drought Investigation Commission*, Cape Times Ltd, Government Printer.

Vogel, C. and Van Zyl, K. (2016). Drought – In Search of Sustainable Solutions to a Persistent 'Wicked' Problem in South Africa. In Salzmann, N., Huggel, C., Nussbaumer, S.U. and Ziervogel, G. (eds.), *Climate Change Adaptation Strategies: An Upstream-Downstream Perspective*, Cham: Springer 197–211.

Vogel, C., Koch, I. and Van Zyl, K. (2010). 'A Persistent Truth' – Reflections on Drought Risk Management in Southern Africa, *Weather, Climate and Society*, 2: 9–22.

Vogel, C., Laing, M. and Munnik, C. (2000). Drought in South Africa, with Special Reference to the 1980–94 Period. In Wilhite, D. (ed.), *Drought. Volume 1, A Global Assessment*, Routledge Hazards and Disasters Series, 348–366, London.

Walwyn, D. and Brent, A. (2015). 'Renewable Energy Gathers Steam in South Africa', *Renewable and Sustainable Energy Reviews*, 41: 390–401.

Wamsler, C., Brossmann, J., Hendersson, H., Kristjansdottir, R., McDonald, C. and Scarampi, P. (2017). Mindfulness in Sustainability Science, Practice and Teaching *Sustainability Science*, DOI 10.1007/s11625-017-0428-2.

Winkler, H. (2010). *Taking Action on Climate Change: Long-term Mitigation Scenarios for South Africa*. Cape Town: UCT Press.

Worthington, R. (2015). *Depending on Renewable Energy: South Africa's Best Development Path*, Fossil Free Africa and 350 Africa.org.

Wright, J., Calitz, J.R., Van Heerden, P.R., Bischof-Niemz, S.T., Mushwana, C. and Senatla, M. (2017). *Formal Comments on the Integrated Resource Plan (IRP) Update Assumptions, Base Case and Observations 2016*. Available at www.csir.co.za/sites/default/files/Documents/20170331CSIR_EC_DOE.pdf (accessed 2 May 2018).

Ziervogel, G., New Mark, Archer van Garderen, E., Midgley, G., Taylor, A., Hamman, R., Stuart Hill, S., Myers, J. and Warburton, M. (2014). Climate Change Impacts and Adaptation in South Africa, *WIREs Climate Change*, 5: 605–620.

4 Sustainability transitions and employment in South Africa

A multi-dimensional approach

Gaylor Montmasson-Clair

Introduction

Jobs, jobs, jobs. Employment creation is at the centre of most policy discussions in South Africa. Persistent high levels of unemployment plague the country, with the official rate standing at 27.7 per cent in the second quarter of 2017. Including discouraged jobseekers, the unemployment rate jumped to 38.3 per cent in the same quarter. The situation amongst youth (between the ages of 15 and 24 years) is even more dramatic, with an unemployment rate of 55.9 per cent (Statistics South Africa, 2017). High levels of poverty and inequality further worsen this tragic picture, while weak economic growth and patterns of de-industrialisation have deepened the crisis. Socio-environmental challenges, primarily climate change, have compounded already destabilising dynamics in South Africa's extremely carbon-intensive and water-stressed economy.

The transition to a sustainable development pathway has been acknowledged as the long-term way forward and a response to these poly-crises. At the global level, multilateral processes, such as the Paris Agreement on Climate Change, affirm this trajectory. In South Africa, multiple policy statements have anchored (at least in theory) sustainability transitions in policy- and decision-making. The National Development Plan: Vision 2030 (NDP) envisions the transition to a low-carbon, climate resilient and just society (NPC, 2012), while the National Strategy on Sustainable Development and Action Plan 2011–2014 (NSSD1) highlights, amongst its key objectives, a "just transition towards a resource-efficient, low-carbon and pro-employment growth path" (DEA, 2011, p. 7).

At the core of the NSSD1, as well as most (if not all) policy documents, is job creation. Specifically, as depicted in Figure 4.1, the creation of so-called "green and decent jobs" is heralded as a key outcome of the transition. Despite the absence of a baseline, the New Growth Path (NGP) targets the creation of 300,000 such "green" jobs by 2030 (and 400,000 by 2040) (EDD, 2010). Complementary research efforts tend to focus on finding these "green jobs", in one form or the other. Considering 26 green technologies or programmes, the potential for potential green jobs in South Africa was estimated in 2011 to be about 462,000 by 2025 (Maia *et al.*, 2011). Similarly, the Department of Environmental Affairs' "Green Jobs Index" aims at estimating the number of green jobs

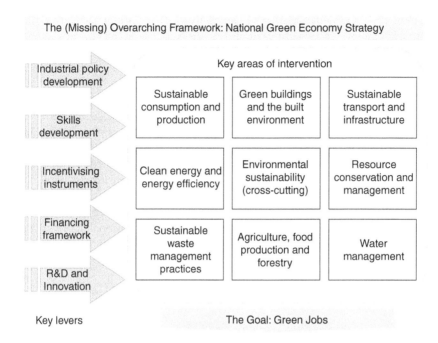

Figure 4.1 Stylised representation of the green economy based on South Africa's National Strategy for Sustainable Development and Action Plan 2011–2014.

Source: Author based on DEA (2011).

in the South African economy and generating a baseline for the country. An effort is also underway (as of June 2018) between the Partnership for Action on Green Economy (PAGE) and Statistics South Africa to develop a green jobs module which will be piloted in the 2018 Quarterly Labour Force Survey to assess the number of green jobs in the country. Skills planning work uses a different entry point, namely occupations rather than sectors or technologies, but also aims to quantify "green jobs" (see, for example, DEA, 2010).

Research and policy approaches, which generally rely on modelling, inventories, surveys and/or employment factors, remain traditional in their thinking about employment and related issues. They are highly quantitative in nature and focus on identifying, creating and counting jobs. While such approaches are instrumental in advancing the statistical and official recognition of green jobs (and skills) and identifying new employment opportunities, they fail to recognise the complexity of the transition to sustainable development from an employment perspective. Their quantitative nature provides a crude understanding of transition dynamics and does not interrogate the impacts and effects on the labour market and existing employment patterns in a developing country context.

The transition to sustainable development involves a much deeper transformation than the mere creation of "green jobs". It requires a move towards sustainable employment structures. It also means recognising the challenges and trade-offs associated with the transition, particularly in the South African context. The carbon-intensity of the economy makes the transition to a new, sustainable model of development particularly disruptive and the prospect of job losses in some sectors inevitable. Entrenched social issues, primarily high levels of unemployment and the absence of strong social safety nets, do not provide much (if any) room for a smooth transition. The role of the informal sector in the transition remains largely unexplored, despite its key role in developing country contexts. The key question is not so much how to quantify green jobs, but more about what kind of labour market dynamics the transition is likely to trigger and how to manage them.

Gaining such a strategic understanding of the transition, and how to best manage it in a South African context, calls for a multi-dimensional approach to employment and sustainability, broadening thinking on "green jobs" beyond quantitative analysis and the consideration of a wide array of economic, social and political issues. In order to grasp the implications on employment of the transition to sustainable development in South Africa, this chapter proposes such a multi-dimensional framework, building on three key and complementary components of employment: the nature of industries; the nature of occupations; and the quality of labour conditions. A typology of sustainable employment is then proposed.

The nature of industries

The nature of industries or sectors, in relation to the transition to sustainability, is the first key dimension to consider. In most cases, the nature of the industry is neglected in the discussion on "green jobs", which tends to focus solely on traditional "green" sectors, such as renewable energy and recycling, or is largely ignored in analyses, which focus on the nature of the jobs themselves. Factoring in the nature of the industry introduces new angles of analysis. Sectors can be divided into four distinct, but complementary, groups: enabling, adaptive, constrained and hindering industries.

First, *enabling* or *core industries* are economic activities which are necessary for the transition to occur. Such sectors provide the goods, services, technologies, skills and competencies that are inherently and intrinsically linked to a transition to sustainable development. These "usual suspects", without which the transition cannot take place, encompass *inter alia* the provision of renewable energy and resource-efficient technologies, waste management services, water management technologies, public transportation and natural resource management.

Importantly, such industries rely, in most cases, on the rest of the economy to operate. The platinum value chain illustrates the complexity of the transition and the role of different economic activities. The production of catalytic converters, heralded as South Africa's largest "green" export, falls squarely in the category of enabling industries, due to its contribution to air quality management. However, production relies on extractive platinum mining activities as well as energy-intensive manufacturing operations, which are largely incompatible with sustainable development principles.

Enabling industries also broadly refer to the green industries identified in South Africa's Industrial Policy Action Plan (the dti, 2017) and the "green jobs" targeted in policy documents, such as the NGP and the NSSD1. Such "green jobs" already sustain large portions of the population. For instance, the minibus taxi industry,[1] which is the main public transport system in the country, employs approximately 250,000 people. The rollout of the Gautrain high-speed train has also created 6,700 local direct jobs and an estimated total of more than 36,200 direct, indirect and induced jobs. The government-led Expanded Public Work Programme (EPWP) creates temporary and/or part-time opportunities for unemployed and poor households as a labour absorption and income transfer strategy. Approximately 13 per cent of all work opportunities created by the EPWP, that is almost one million work opportunities over the 2004–2017 period (defined as paid work for an individual for any period of time), can be considered "green jobs". Such opportunities are located in the environmental sector, through programmes which centre on ecosystem restoration, maintenance and rehabilitation, such as Working for Water, Working on Waste and Working for Forests (Mohamed, 2017).

In some cases, even from a low base, they have displayed impressive growth rates. This is the case of the employment linked to the Renewable Energy Independent Power Producers Procurement Programme (REIPPPP), which is estimated to have created about 32,500 jobs over the 2012–2017 period (DoE *et al.*, 2017). However, while their contribution to the transition is far from negligible (in fact they are at its core), such industries do not have the potential to generate employment for the whole society.

Second, *adaptive industries*, which constitute the bulk of the economy, are industries that can and need to be transitioned to more sustainable development pathways. They are adaptive in the sense that they can operate sustainably without major disruption to their business models and/or production processes, relying on enabling industries to provide the means to transition. Their contribution to the transition is based on the adaptation of their operations to incorporate sustainable practices and enabling technologies. In order to be sustainable, light manufacturing, for example, relies *inter alia* on the provision of renewable energy-based electricity, water and waste management technologies and practices, optimised energy management systems, energy efficient machineries, and "green" procurement procedures. Agriculture, forestry and fisheries, construction, and services such as tourism, personal care, finance and information and communication technologies, follow a similar logic. Importantly, while some firms are particularly pro-active in their transition and can be qualified as frontrunners or supporters, most companies are rather passive, adopting slow incremental improvements (Montmasson-Clair, 2016a).

Nevertheless, South Africa hosts a variety of pioneering companies which are championing sustainability in their business operations (even though the number of sustainable companies remains unknown).[2] The tourism industry is one such example, with the growth of the number of eco-friendly hotels and lodges in both urban (the Peech in Johannesburg, the Hotel Verde in Cape Town, the Oyster Box in Durban) and rural (Phantom Forest Eco Lodge in the Knysna Forest in the Western Cape, the Shire Eco Lodge in the Eastern Cape, the Umlani Bushcamp in the Kruger National Park) settings. Similar examples can be found in many corners of the South African economy. The textile sector displays pockets of excellence in terms of sustainability. Impahla Clothing, located in the Western Cape, is recognised as the first carbon-neutral garment manufacturer in South Africa. E'Yako Green, based in Howick in KwaZulu-Natal, manufactures, sources and supplies locally produced, waste-based, environmentally friendly corporate gifts and clothing. Another example is Gauteng-based Beyond Green Cleaning, a South African leader in environment-friendly, all-natural, effective bio-remediation cleaning and hygiene products.

These first two groups (i.e. enabling and adaptive industries) are loosely referred to as "green industries", although for different reasons. Enabling industries are considered "green" due to the purpose they fulfil, that is the end products, the goods and services they provide, irrespective of the production processes and occupations. Adaptive industries, once they have transitioned to sustainable development models, are deemed "green" as a result of their production processes and practices, that is the lifecycle of their products and services. However, the bulk of South Africa's adaptive industries remains unsustainable as at 2018.

Third, a select number of economic activities form a group of *constrained industries* (Montmasson-Clair, 2016a). Due to their production processes and/or extractive nature, such industries cannot be operated sustainably (they are not sustainable by definition) but are pro-active about the need to transform. Accordingly, transitioning such sectors to sustainable development pathways would require breakthrough technologies and a complete overhaul of their business model and operations. Despite their unsustainable patterns, such industries play a critical role in South Africa's (and the world's) socio-economic development (in terms of employment, outputs, exports, earnings, tax, etc.). Some, like the mining and linked manufacturing industries, even underpin the development of enabling technologies, by providing the necessary inputs into green technologies, such as the metals and minerals necessary for the manufacturing of wind turbines and solar-based systems (Montmasson-Clair, 2015). Others, such as cement and chemicals, provide basic commodities essential as inputs into daily life and economic activity. While such sectors are likely to be displaced (by sustainable alternatives) or materially transformed (through new technologies and processes) in the long run, they form part of the necessary "evils" which have to be actively transformed.

South Africa's chemical industry, in this respect, provides a fascinating insight. The chemical industry, dominated by petrochemical company Sasol, relies on carbon-intensive, unsustainable processes based on fossil fuels. The transition to sustainable development in the sector relies largely on the emergence of new products and production processes. Correspondingly, the development of bio-polymers, produced from natural, renewable resources, most commonly organic waste, is reshaping the sector and is set to become a major market. Countries, like Japan, and companies, such as Coca-Cola and Toyota, are leading the way. While the global market and technology development in bio-polymers remain underdeveloped, South Africa demonstrates real strength in this sector. The country possesses sufficient feedstock (such as agro-processing waste), has a history of research and development (R&D) in biocomposites (through the Mandela Bay Composites Cluster and research groups at several universities) and existing industrial capacity (such as KAP Manufacturing and Xyris Technology) (Montmasson-Clair *et al.*, 2017).

The situation of the platinum mining industries further illustrates the critical role of enabling industries and professions to the transition. While the ability of the platinum mining companies to deeply transform is conditioned on the decarbonisation of South Africa's electricity system, which is largely beyond the control of industries, performance improvement at the firm level remains important. In the short term, the potential to reduce greenhouse gas (GHG) emissions is greater and more cost effective at the industrial level than at the energy supply stage (DEA, 2014). Leveraging progress in resource management, the platinum mining industry has made strides towards better understanding, monitoring, managing and ultimately reducing resource use. Some mining companies, such as Anglo American Platinum and Lonmin, are furthermore pursuing the use of cogeneration (combined heat and power) and renewable energy sources. Others, such as Pallinghurst (with the Kell process) and Braemore Platinum (with the ConRoast process), are pursuing larger, more disruptive technological changes and introducing new shaft designs (Montmasson-Clair, 2016b).

Last but not least, *hindering industries* are made up of a limited number of sectors and companies that are in direct conflict with the transition. While these can also be significant in socio-economic terms, they largely do not form part of a sustainable economy. The most obvious example in South Africa is the coal value chain. With the limited exception of industrial usages (for example in the production of steel), coal does not feature prominently in a sustainable economy and society (Altieri *et al.*, 2015). Liquid fuels, particularly the oil industry, are in a similar, although less dramatic, situation. Even though it is possible that such sectors gain access to technologies that could improve their sustainability, transitioning to sustainable models of development calls for the phasing out of such industries. Laggards, that is firms resisting the transition despite having the techno-economic ability to transform, are also in this group of hindering industries (Montmasson-Clair, 2016a).

Managing the phasing out of hindering industries would be particularly difficult in the South African context. The domestic coal value chain is significant, with 90 per cent of the country's electricity supply relying on coal-fired power plants as well as 30 per cent of South Africa's liquid fuel being based on petrochemical company Sasol's coal- and gas-to-liquid technologies. Parts of the country, notably the Mpumalanga province, are also directly dependent on coal-related activities. Some companies have initiated a degree of diversification. Coal mining company Exxaro, through Cennergi, its joint venture with Tata Power, invested in two utility-scale wind farms (Exxaro, 2013). South Africa's electricity plan, however, remains largely coal-based, with the development of two large-scale power plants, Medupi and Kusile. The national power utility Eskom is a clear illustration of a company overtly resisting the transition to a more sustainable business model (Montmasson-Clair, 2017a). Similarly, the country appears poorly prepared for the withdrawal of the internal combustion engine and petroleum-based vehicles. While the transition could be a source of opportunities in these industries, the lack of planning and preparation for the transition away from fossil fuels poses significant risks to the economy, opening up the risks of employment shocks and social crises in the country (Deonarain and Mashiane, forthcoming; EcoMetrix Africa, 2016).

This first dimension of the interplay between employment and sustainability transitions, that is understanding the nature of the sector/industry, illustrates that no one-size-fits-all approach can be adopted when thinking about sustainability transitions. While different sectors face divergent situations and futures, all sectors have a role to play in transitioning the South African economy to sustainability. As not all industries are set to benefit, considering the nature of the industry highlights the role of adequately planning for the transition in strategic sectors that are at risk.

The nature of occupations

The second dimension relating to employment and sustainability revolves around the nature of the occupation. It refers to the spectrum of functions provided by a profession, its tasks and missions as well as the skills and competencies that are required to perform them. The nature of the occupation is either ignored by most "green jobs" and green industries analysis or considered narrowly through a focus on "core green jobs" and "green skills". Such analyses fail to recognise that most, if not all, occupations and jobs are impacted by the transition to sustainable development. While the impact is not always direct, that is requiring a change of practices, upskilling or even the disappearance of the occupation in its conventional form, all occupations are arguably at least affected at the level of human and social behaviour (recycling and reuse practices, sustainable and local purchasing and product use, resource-efficient behaviour, etc.) (Fioramonti, 2017). Based on the skills and competencies, the transition to sustainable development has diverse impacts on different employment groups: a core set of occupations can be considered as enabling the transition; the bulk of the labour market would be impacted personally rather than professionally; and a non-negligible group of jobs could be at risk.

The first group constitutes the most important occupations from the perspective of the transition, that is occupations that are core to the transition due to the nature of the job (and not the industry they are in). Such occupations are change agents in the economy and society, championing the transition to sustainability at the professional (and personal) level. Socio-environmental experts and managers, sustainable development managers, recycling champions, Safety, Health and Environment Quality (SHEQ) representatives are a few examples of what is generally referred to as "green skills" (Rosenberg *et al.*, 2016). These occupations are key enablers of the transition and can be found in all industries, even hindering industries.

As a matter of fact, such "green" skills are critical to the coal industry in a transition. Enabling occupations are instrumental at all stages of South Africa's coal value chain. The mining process relies on numerous skills and professions core to sustainable development. R&D, exploration and prospecting, resource management (energy, water, carbon, waste), logistics, land rehabilitation and remediation, environment impact mitigation and land reclamation are a few examples. In addition to the minimisation of negative externalities, the maximisation of local economic benefits requires enabling occupations in the form of community engagement, SHEQ officers, sustainable development planners, environmental economists, eco-tourism planners, green architects and small business incubators. For example, Agreenco, headquartered in Potchefstroom, in the North West Province, offers new generation rehabilitation and environmental improvement services to the mining sector. Downstream, the use of coal in industrial processes (such as electricity generation and steel making) also relies heavily on "green" skills, particularly for R&D and innovation (for new plant design and production processes, energy efficiency, and co-/tri-generation) (Rosenberg, 2015).

At the support and managerial level in the mining industry, the development of green skills is at the core of the transformation of governance, leadership, management, finance, reporting as well as training, procurement, supply chain, marketing and communication functions of the South African coal industry (Rosenberg, 2015). For example, Exxaro (2014, p. 40) has a green procurement working group and requires its staff to "buy environmentally friendly products and services, and set sustainability requirements in supplier agreements" and even to "collaborate with suppliers in addressing supply chain sustainability issues and enhance their capabilities to meet sustainability standards through supplier sustainability audits, supplier sustainability development and supplier innovations".

Regulatory functions in the industry are also critical to the sustainable operation of mining activities. Occupations responsible for research and guidelines (on water use for example), policymaking, occupational health and safety, environmental impact assessments, licence applications and approvals, monitoring, auditing and reporting, as well as enforcement and litigation, all form a component of the critical pool of green skills necessary for the sector to operate as sustainably as possible (Montmasson-Clair *et al.*, 2015; Rosenberg, 2015).

The bulk of the occupations in the economy falls into the second group. Most occupations do not have a direct impact on the transition and would be professionally marginally impacted by the transition. In this case, the transition to sustainable development has personal implications with individual- and firm-level behavioural change. To the extent that they are affected, such occupations take their cue from the change agents (which can be both employers and employees) described above. It, however, does not prevent individuals becoming sustainability champions at the personal level (both at the workplace and in their private life).

Unfortunately, most individuals lack awareness in terms of resource conservation (energy, water, waste, carbon). While personal behavioural change should be encouraged at the workplace and would make companies more sustainable, such changes are inherently individual and not linked to the successful realisation of the required tasks. As such, firms have experienced difficulties in incentivising their employees to adopt resource-efficient behaviours (e.g. sorting waste for recycling, switching off lights when not in use, using water sparingly) (OneWorld Sustainable Investments, 2010).

In some industries, such as agriculture and construction, ensuring personal behaviour changes could lead to significant advances in sustainability. Workers in these two industries, which respectively employ 810,000 and 1.36 million people in South Africa, deal with large quantities of materials, inputs, chemicals and waste, making their personal behaviour (for example, in terms of waste disposal, electricity and water use) central to the sustainability of the sectors as a whole (Didiza and Raw, 2015; Kuschke and Jordaan, 2017).

Importantly, this group includes most of the employment traditionally considered as "green" by sector-based approaches, that is the enabling industries. As discussed earlier in this chapter, such industries encompass occupations that are core to the transition due to the nature of the industry. Indeed, any employment driven by core industries is instrumental to the transition. While a share of these occupations directly provides the necessary green technologies, processes and skills for the transition (such as solar system technicians) and fall into the first group of enabling jobs, most occupations offer support functions. Indeed, even in enabling industries, the majority of the jobs are not directly related to sustainability. An accountant (unless she/he introduces new accounting systems incorporating social and environmental externalities) performs the same job in an enabling industry as in any other sector. The same is true for most managerial, administrative, support and technical occupations.

For example, the public transport sector is by definition an enabling industry, one which society relies upon to address the unsustainable (i.e. carbon-intensive and exclusive) pattern of transportation and spatial development. Employment in the sector is considered "green" due to the nature of the sector, rather than the occupations. However, jobs and skills in the industry are not sustainability specific. As such, from the perspective of the transition, people working in the public transport sector are similar to the bulk of the jobs in the rest of the economy and are primarily impacted at the personal (rather than the professional) level.

The third group corresponds to occupations that are directly at risk from the transition. These are expected to be mostly located in hindering industries as well as constrained industries, on the basis that such sectors would be phased out or dramatically transformed in the future. For example, while environmental regulations have underpinned the growth of the platinum industry since the 1970s, new sustainability-related developments are jeopardising the future of the sector, placing employment in the industry at high risk. Primary production has been declining since 2006, due to a steady and continual increase in platinum recycling. In addition, the rapid emergence of electric vehicles, which do not require catalytic converters, has the potential to jeopardise the survival of the platinum value chain. Compounding this is the rapid advancement in research programmes underway in platinum-consuming countries to identify and develop cheaper, alternative materials to replace platinum. While this has spurred on considerable investment in R&D by platinum mining companies to develop alternative uses for the metal, such as the development of fuel cells, the future of the industry remains uncertain.

Jobs at risk can also be found in other sectors, as some professions would be materially altered over time, requiring occupations to adapt (by, for instance, obtaining new skills, upgrading their technology or changing their processes) or disappear. In this category, conventional electricians and plumbers not equipped to deal with solar-based systems, mechanics without the skills to fix electric or gas-based vehicles and supply chain managers without "green procurement" skills are a few illustrations.

In addition to environmental and resource scarcity, or impacts resulting from the changing climate, which may have severe impacts on some sectors (such as agriculture and tourism), occupations can be (negatively) impacted by the transition to sustainable development through three main channels: international trade impacts, which arise from changed demand (both in quantitative and qualitative terms) for South African goods as trading partners implement policies to reduce GHG emissions; mitigation actions undertaken in South Africa to reduce GHG emissions; and efforts undertaken in South Africa to adapt to the changing environment. Vulnerable activities include mining subsectors (primarily the coal value chain), chemicals and chemical products, fertilisers and pesticides, utilities as well as the transport industry (from the shifting of freight from road to rail) (Standish *et al.*, 2017).

This second occupational dimension highlights that the transition is not restricted to the development of a limited package of "green jobs". Although mostly at the personal level, *all* jobs are set to be impacted by the transition to sustainable development. Stated differently, *all* jobs need to be altered to some extent for the transition to occur. Considering the nature of the occupation also sheds light on the key role of "green jobs" in brown industries, such as extractive activities, which form a large part of South Africa's economy.

The quality of employment

The quality of employment constitutes the third pillar of a multi-dimensional approach to employment in a sustainability context. This aspect is generally overlooked, notably by quantitative approaches, due to its qualitative nature. It is, however, critical that the qualitative conditions of labour are taken into account when thinking about the transition to sustainable development, particularly in a developing country context.

This broadly refers to the debates around the promotion of "decent work", including complex issues of socio-economic development and labour market dynamics. As defined by South Africa's Decent Work Country Programme 2010–2014, four strategic pillars form the basis of sustainable employment: the promotion of fundamental principles and rights at work; the promotion of employment and income opportunities; the expansion and improvement of social protection coverage; and the promotion of social dialogue and tripartism (Republic of South Africa, 2010).

Importantly, in South Africa, like in many other developing countries, a clear divide exists between formal and informal employment. Formal employment is governed by the Constitution as well as a set of laws, while the informal sector operates in a policy and regulatory vacuum, at the expense of workers.

The Bill of Rights (chapter 2 of the Constitution) guarantees the right to form and belong to a workers' union and for collective bargaining. The Basic Conditions of Employment Act, the Labour Relations Act, the Occupational Health and Safety Act, the Compensation for Occupational Injuries and Diseases Act and the Unemployment Insurance Fund specify the basic labour market conditions and requirements on employers. Even though further progress is required in a number of areas (such as health and family issues) (ILO, 2011a), these laws in combination determine (to the extent that they are effectively enforced) a baseline for conditions of employment in South Africa's formal sector (Aroun, 2011).

By contrast, most workers outside the formal sector are not protected by any of these regulations, have no safety nets and face high vulnerability.

> South Africa's social security coverage reflects a system designed for the needs of vulnerable white groups under apartheid, among whom unemployment was minimal, given their preferential access to jobs and education. It does not take into account the high unemployment rate, and the precarious nature of work for most workers in the informal sector and in informal employment.
>
> (DPME, 2014, p. 29)

For instance, employment in the public transportation sector displays highly disparate levels of quality. While a strong degree of formalisation exists in the transport sector as a whole, the growth of the taxi industry and the use of contractors by bus operating companies has maintained (if not increased) the key role of informal and atypical forms of employment in the sector (TETA, 2011). The taxi industry remains largely unregulated and informal in nature. In addition, oppressive employment environments within the minibus industry (both formal and informal), controlled by vehicle owners at the detriment of drivers, has resulted in relatively poor working conditions. Few taxi operators abide by the labour regulations and most taxi workers do not have a formal written contract of employment. Up to four wage systems operate in the sector (from fixed wages to percentage-based systems), further spurring tension between workers (Fobosi, 2013; TETA, 2011).

As a result of such dynamics, the majority of the South African population are not benefiting from conditions of employment which provide the opportunity for personal and professional fulfilment and growth, that is decent work. Such aspects relate to financial well-being (earnings and benefits, employment contract), working conditions (a safe and healthy workplace) as well as the professional environment (career advancement, training and upskilling, etc.). Importantly, this refers to personal choices, rather than a pre-determined indicator of "decent employment". For example, a part-time job can in some cases be a personal choice enabling personal well-being and in others an imposed situation.

Remuneration, not surprisingly, differs significantly between and within sectors. In the first quarter of 2017, average monthly earnings in South Africa (for all formal non-agricultural industries) ranged from about R12,500 (US$1,030) in the trade sector to close to R38,000 (US$3,132) in the utility sector (Statistics South Africa, 2017). South African society is also one of the most unequal in the world, with the country having the highest Palma ratio[3] in the world over the 2005–2013 period (Palma, 2016). In order to improve equality and reduce poverty, a national minimum wage agreement of ZAR 20 per hour (i.e. ZAR3,500 per month for a 40-hour week) (US$1.65 per hour or US$288 per month) is in the making as of June 2018.[4] While this does not represent a decent living wage, the agreement could, according to the South African government, uplift 6.6 million people and represents an important step forward towards inclusive development (Parliament of the Republic of South Africa, 2017).

Employment standards also differ from one sector to the next. Manufacturing, for example, offers better employment conditions than construction. The construction industry in South Africa has been characterised by precarious and short-term work arrangements, exposing workers to vulnerable and insecure employment as well as low wages, bad working conditions and poor training (Aroun, 2011).

Importantly, the emergence of green industries (i.e. enabling and adaptive industries) does not, in itself, lead to better work conditions or quality of employment (Belén Sánchez *et al.*, 2013; Montmasson-Clair, 2012). In other words, specific efforts in terms of policies and programmes are needed to ensure that the environmental and social ills are addressed simultaneously (ILO, 2011a). Particular attention must be paid to ensure that the transition is inclusive and does not deepen socio-economic marginalisation. While the transition is an opportunity to foster South Africa's socio-economic transformation and empower previously disadvantaged and currently marginalised groups of society, these co-benefits are not automatic and require planning, targeted policies and implementation to materialise.

The Employment Equity Act provides for rules against discrimination as well as for "affirmative action" (known as Broad-Based Black Economic Empowerment in South Africa [BBBEE]) in favour of previously disadvantaged populations. However, generating socio-economic progress extends beyond issues of BBBEE and remains challenging. South Africa's renewable energy journey is particularly telling in this respect. Despite the design of the REIPPPP being geared towards promoting local economic and social development, direct outcomes have been uneven. The REIPPPP has generated welcome but limited employment creation. In addition, trade unions have raised concerns about the quality and precarious nature of the jobs generated by the projects, with most employment opportunities created in the communities surrounding projects mainly for short-term construction workers and low-skilled security personnel. Indeed, skilled employment is generally sourced from the economic centres of the country, owing to the lack of available skills at the community level (Montmasson-Clair and das Nair, 2017).

The transition is likely to trigger a net movement, within the formal sector, from primary industries to secondary and tertiary activities. As long as employment remains within the formal ambit, this shift should have limited impacts (either positive or negative) on employment conditions (Maia *et al.*, 2011; UNEP, 2013). New forms of employment, either in green industries or green occupations are, however, emerging in other settings. In the informal sector, the transition to sustainable development provides multiple opportunities to foster inclusive development. Small-scale and subsistence farming, bio-processing, management and trade, recycling, upcycling and waste picking, green infrastructure, technology and construction are a few "green" activities which are occurring in South Africa's informal economy. Indeed, a large number of the jobs that would be created through ecosystem restoration (such as invasive alien clearing) or waste management are informal, providing a source of additional income, but little skills development and a short-term job rather than a career (Smit and Musango, 2015).

Waste management, one of the most important activities in a sustainable development model, plays a critical role in fostering inclusivity and alleviating poverty. However, many of the opportunities provided by waste management take the form of informal waste picking. Such jobs provide a lifeline to a large amount of unskilled people in South Africa. A sustainability transition should focus on upgrading these jobs as much as attempting to creating additional employment (ILO, 2011b). In their current form, waste-picking operations cannot be considered sustainable, as they fail to provide dignity and recognition nor an adequate social support structure. Importantly, upgrading does not mean forcing the formalisation of the activities, but providing the platform and tools for improving the conditions of waste-picking activities (Godfrey *et al.*, 2016). Waste pickers play an enabling role as "agents of change".

In addition, trade-offs do occur. The platinum mining industry offers relatively high wages but is set to shed employment in the coming decades. In addition, the harsh nature of the occupations and living conditions of mineworkers, and the delay in the economic transformation of the sector (in favour of previously disadvantaged communities) contrast with relative good performance in terms of remuneration (Makgetla and Levin, 2016). This calls for an approach considering the economic (i.e. wages) as well as socio-environmental value of employment.

Social dialogue is also an important aspect of decent work, and the greening of particular sectors may provide a new impetus for this process. Social dialogue in South Africa is historically vibrant, as illustrated by the establishment of the National Economic Development and Labour Council (Nedlac)[5] in 1994 and the signing of various quadripartite agreements. In addition, although some decline in representivity and capacity, industrial relations are largely managed through Bargaining Councils and strong trade unions, a key component for a just and fair transition to sustainable development (ILO, 2010). Attempts at creating a social compact in favour of the transition to sustainable development, such as the Green Economy Accord and the Decent Work Country Programme have, however, failed to deliver their promises (Montmasson-Clair, 2017b).

For example, the need for social dialogue in the public transport sector is urgent. The expansion of public transport in South Africa has occurred in an uncoordinated fashion, jeopardising the sustainability of the entire sector. Attempts at formalising the industry and displacing it with more structured services, such as Bus Rapid Transport (BRT), and the unmanaged development of various systems coupled with harsh working conditions, regularly triggers strikes in the industry. Indeed, growth in the largely unregulated minibus taxi industry has provided fertile ground for conflicts over route and ranking facilities. At the same time, municipalities, with support from national government, are pursuing the development of BRT systems, in direct competition with the taxi industry. This comes in addition to existing municipal and long-distance bus routes as well as mass-transport passenger rail services (Metrorail) already operating in the country. In parallel, but largely unconnected to development in the rest of the industry, a high-end high-speed train system (Gautrain) with feeder buses is operating in Gauteng. This public transport competition in the urban areas also masks the dearth of transportation services in the rural areas of the country (Deonarain and Mashiane, forthcoming).

Last but not least, the socio-economic contribution of employment matters as well. What role does a particular occupation or activity play in society? Community-based employment and care work, often disregarded due to their largely informal nature, are crucial providers of social cohesion and sustainable living, and should be recognised and rewarded. The empowerment of employees and communities, through co-decision-making processes and local ownership, is another dimension impacting the nature of employment. Most work environments only offer a platform for passive delivery of employment rather than active, involved partnerships (Fioramonti, 2017). South Africa's Community Work Programme, a community-led government employment programme under the EPWP, exemplifies the value of an area-based, local economic development approach. The programme provides an employment safety net and a source of income security to marginalised people, by providing regular rather than full-time employment. Importantly, opportunities for "useful work" are identified locally through participatory processes, creating an unprecedented sense of community spirit.

This third dimension emphasises the social upliftment required in South Africa for the transition to be truly sustainable. Improving the quality of jobs, providing equal access to opportunities, and compensating and retraining workers displaced by the greening process is critical to ensure that South Africa's transition is just in its delivery of green and decent employment opportunities. The link between economic activities and decent employment is not straightforward and must be consciously made through local stakeholder engagement and co-development.

A typology of "sustainable employment"

Based on the three components discussed in previous sections, a three-dimensional typology of South Africa's employment in a transition to sustainable development can be generated. Such a matrix, illustrated in Figure 4.2, provides an understanding of the multiple shades of green jobs, highlighting the diversity of "employment" situations from a sustainability perspective. It also depicts the dynamic concept of transitions. Such a framework shows the complexity of the dynamics at play within the sustainability transition(s) in South Africa.

It highlights the reliance of the transition on a set of enabling green jobs, incorporating both core industries and occupations. While these pockets of excellence are small in comparison to the size of the economy and the labour market, they are underpinning the nation-wide transformation. From a transition management perspective, the objective is to support the growth and development of these sectors and occupations, as they enable the transition of other sectors and professions. They may nevertheless need to evolve, particularly to improve the quality (i.e. decency) of the employment. Indeed, while some green industries operate in similar (i.e. relatively good) conditions, such as manufacturing, others (such as waste picking) do not benefit from adequate labour conditions.

Numerous "green skills" are also found in hindering and constrained industries. In this context, such occupations are critical to manage either the progressive phasing out or structural transformation of such industries. This is illustrated in Chapter 8. In the long run, these enabling skills are largely transferable from one sector to the next, ensuring their own sustainability.

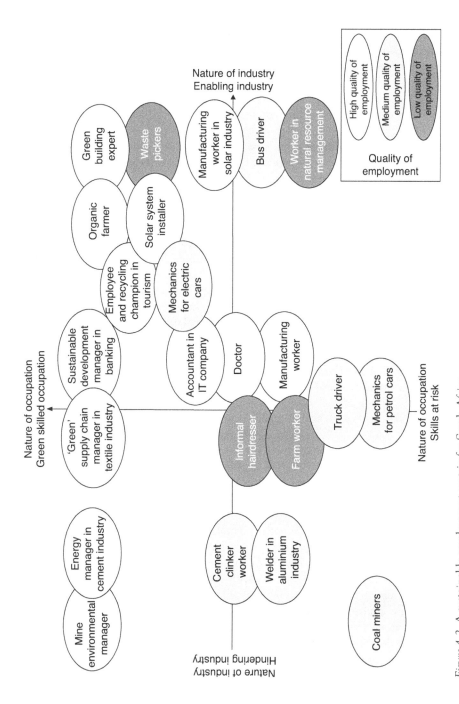

Figure 4.2 A sustainable employment matrix for South Africa.

Source: Author.

The bulk of the economy and employment however would not be negatively impacted by the transition to sustainable development. Most occupations would be marginally impacted at the professional level and would rather be altered through personal behavioural change. The same holds true for a large share of the economy, which would incrementally move towards sustainable business practices (renewable energy, resource efficiency, circular economy, social protection and awareness) but would not be fundamentally transformed. In this case, the transition is essentially conditioned on leveraging the core industries and occupations described earlier, in order to introduce new technologies and skills to conventional business practices. It also implies a marked improvement in labour market conditions, particularly in industries with low standards, such as agriculture, waste and construction. Sectors and professions which elect to be pro-active and pioneer the transition are expected to benefit from an early-mover advantage and be better off than those resisting it.

These dynamics are particularly important in an era in which technological progress, primarily the fast penetration of automation, robotics, digitalisation and artificial intelligence, is rapidly undermining traditional growth and employment strategies. New technologies are set to engender significant job losses in most sectors of the economy, such as transportation and manufacturing, and weaken workers' bargaining power, voice and ability to organise. In this respect, a sustainable development approach, by balancing economic, social and environmental considerations, offers the opportunity to harness technological progress and innovation to widen the country's social inclusivity and environmental sustainability (Norton, 2016, 2017).

In some industries and professions, however, transitioning means thinking about the phasing out of some activities and occupations. Importantly, industries that are most likely to be impacted by the transition offer relatively good working conditions (at least in monetary terms). This is particularly critical for industry-specific professions, which are hardly transferable to other sectors. In South Africa, jobs at risk, while not negligible in numbers, are concentrated in a limited number of industries (such as the coal value chain, the cement and metals industry and petrochemicals), laying the groundwork for effective policy intervention (Cloete and Robb, 2010). More broadly, much strategic planning and thinking is required to smooth the transition to provide alternative skill and employment opportunities (to both current and future workers employed in these sectors) (Rosenberg *et al.*, 2016). While such new jobs do not need be in green industries (as discussed above, such industries generate limited employment and may not constitute viable alternatives for retrenched workers), the scale of the challenge, particularly in the most affected parts of the country, raises serious challenges for transition planning.

The typology also helps understand the concept of "transition", that is where the country is starting from and where it is aiming to go. The transition is not linear in nature and indeed, not every sector and occupation needs to follow the same route. The typology enables a differentiated analysis of the policy interventions that are required to transition South Africa from an employment perspective. The diversity of situations that are defined by the ability and willingness of industries to transition, the role and characteristics of the occupations and the quality of the labour market, disqualifies any one-size-fits-all solution and calls for targeted interventions.

Conclusion

This chapter introduced new, innovative thinking about employment issues and the transition to sustainable development, applying a multi-dimensional framework for South Africa. It illustrates the complexity of the transition from an employment perspective, unpacking the multiple shades of "green" (and "brown") jobs.

A strategic typology of employment, using specific, South African examples, calls for a broader policy discussion on employment issues. The transition to sustainable development is too often depicted simplistically. For example, employment in the renewable energy industry is generally opposed to employment in the coal sector, with the expectation that the former should offset the latter going forward. Such a crude representation, contrasting new "green" activities with conventional businesses and occupations, misrepresents the full implications of the transition. A deeper, disaggregated understanding, as presented through the typology proposed in this chapter, is required to adequately grasp employment dynamics, and plan for and manage emerging trends as well as trade-offs appropriately.

An in-depth undertaking aimed at establishing a baseline of the sustainable employment spectrum should be carried out. It would provide a systemic analysis of employment in sustainability transitions and enable the development of targeted policies and programmes (for both specific sectors and occupations). Indeed, the transition to sustainable development requires a multifaceted response. At minimum, strategic plans are necessary to grow "green industries", build "green skills", transition constrained industries, phase out hindering activities, enhance the quality of the labour market (particularly in the informal sector) and raise sustainability awareness and consciousness in society as a whole. A multi-pronged response would open the door for the possibility of a smooth transition to a "low-carbon, climate resilient economy and just society" (NPC, 2012, p. 179), as envisioned by the NDP. The current emphasis on "green jobs" and "green skills" is set to only benefit a few and fail to reach its goals of addressing poverty, unemployment and inequality. A much broader conceptualisation, focused on society-wide behavioural change and the transition of all, particularly vulnerable people and communities, is required to enable an inclusive transition to sustainable development in South Africa.

Acknowledgements

I would like to gratefully acknowledge the support from the WWF Nedbank Green Trust, the Agence Française de Développement (AFD) and TIPS. Special thanks also go to Tasneem Essop, Daryl McLean, Thabo Thulare, Shakespear Mudombi and Muhammed Patel who provided comments on draft versions of this chapter.

Notes

1 In the South African context, a minibus taxi generally refers to a 16-seater van used for public transport purposes. While they operate on fixed commuter corridors, charging a fixed local rate, minibuses do not have fixed stops (apart from ranking facilities) or schedules.
2 The difficulty in defining a "sustainable company" constitutes a key obstacle in providing a clear picture. Being sustainable involves different components from one sector to the next, making it moreover virtually impossible to compare firms across industries.
3 The Palma ratio is the ratio of the richest 10 per cent of the population's share of gross national income divided by the poorest 40 per cent's share.
4 While minimum wages existed in a select number of sectors, no national standard previously existed.
5 The Nedlac is a unique statutory body that brings together representatives from government, organised labour, organised business and the community to consider all socio-economic and labour policy and legislation. Nedlac must consider all significant changes to social and economic policy before being implemented or introduced in Parliament.

References

Altieri, K., Trollip, H., Caetano, T., Hughes, A., Merven, B. and Winkler, H., 2015. *Pathways to Deep Cecarbonization in South Africa.* Paris: Sustainable Development Solutions Network and Institute for Sustainable Development and International Relations.
Aroun, W., 2011. *Climate Jobs and Manufacturing in South Africa.* Johannesburg: National Union of Metalworkers of South Africa.
Belén Sánchez, A., Martín, L., Montmasson-Clair, G., and du Plooy, P., 2013. *Green Jobs and Related Policy Frameworks: An Overview of South Africa.* Madrid: Sustainlabour.
Cloete, B., and Robb, G., 2010. *Carbon Pricing and Industrial Policy in South Africa.* Winkler, H., Marguard, A. and Jooste, M. (eds.), Presented at the Conference: Putting a Price on Carbon: Economic Instruments to Mitigate Climate Change in South Africa and Other Developing Countries, Cape Town.
DEA, 2010. *Environmental Sector Skills Plan for South Africa. A Systems Approach to Human Capacity Development and Sector Skills Planning.* (Summary document based on a more comprehensive series of working documents). Pretoria: Department of Environmental Affairs.
DEA, 2011. *National Strategy for Sustainable Development and Action Plan 2011–2014.* Pretoria: Department of Environmental Affairs.
DEA, 2014. *South Africa's Greenhouse Gas (GHG) Mitigation Potential Analysis: Technical Appendix D – Industry Sector.* Pretoria: Department of Environmental Affairs.
Deonarain, B. and Mashiane, K., forthcoming. *Transforming South Africa's Transport Sector for Sustainable Development.* Pretoria and London: Trade & Industrial Policy Strategies and Green Economy Coalition.

Didiza, S. and Raw, B., 2015. *Greening the Construction Sector – 2015 Market Intelligence Report*. Cape Town: GreenCape.

DoE, NT, DBSA, 2017. *Independent Power Producers Procurement Programme (IPPPP): An Overview as at 30 June 2017*. Pretoria and Johannesburg: Department of Energy, National Treasury and Development Bank of Southern Africa.

DPME, 2014. *Twenty-year Review – South Africa – 1994–2014*. Background paper, Social protection. Pretoria: Department of Planning, Monitoring and Evaluation.

EcoMetrix Africa, 2016. *Strategy for Policy Direction Promoting Green Road Transport Technologies in South Africa*. Pretoria: Department of Trade and Industry.

EDD, 2010. *The New Growth Path: The Framework*. Pretoria: Economic Development Department.

Exxaro, 2013. *Exxaro's Energy JV, Cennergi, Achieves Financial Closure on Two Wind Projects* [Online]. Exxaro. Available at www.exxaro.com/index.php/exxaros-energy-jv-cennergi-achieves-financial-closure-on-two-wind-projects/ (accessed 18 October 2013).

Exxaro, 2014. *Integrated Report 2013*. Pretoria: Exxaro.

Fioramonti, L., 2017. *Wellbeing Economy: Success in a World Without Growth*. Johannesburg: Pan Macmillan, SA.

Fobosi, S., 2013. *The Minibus Taxi Industry in South Africa: A Servant for the Urban Poor?* Johannesburg: Consultancy Africa Intelligence.

Godfrey, L., Vozza, A., Mohamed, N., 2016. *Transitioning South Africa to a Green Economy: Opportunities for Green Jobs in the Waste Sector*. Pretoria: Department of Environmental Affairs.

ILO (International Labour Organization), 2010. *Skills for Green Jobs in South Africa*. Geneva: International Labour Organization. Available at www.ilo.org/wcmsp5/groups/public/---ed_emp/---ifp_skills/documents/publication/wcms_142475.pdf (accessed 28 April 2018).

ILO, 2011a. *Promoting Decent Work in a Green Economy*. ILO Background Note to "Towards a Green Economy: Pathways to Sustainable Development and Poverty Eradication", UNEP, 2011. Geneva: International Labour Organization.

ILO, 2011b. *Promoting Decent Work in a Green Economy*. ILO Background Note to "Towards a Green Economy: Pathways to Sustainable Development and Poverty Eradication", UNEP, 2011. Geneva: International Labour Organization.

Kuschke, I. and Jordaan, J., 2017. *Agriculture – 2017 Market Intelligence Report*. Cape Town: GreenCape.

Maia, J., Giordano, T., Kelder, N., Bardien, G., Bodibe, M., du Plooy, P., Jafta, X., Jarvis, D., Kruger-Cloate, E., Kuhn, G., Lepelle, R., Makaulule, L., Mosoma, K., Neoh, S., Netshitomboni, N., Ngozo, T. and Swanepoel, J., 2011. *Green Jobs: An Estimate of the Direct Employment Potential of a Greening South African Economy*. Johannesburg and Pretoria: Industrial Development Corporation, Development Bank of Southern Africa and Trade and Industrial Policy Strategies.

Makgetla, N., and Levin, S., 2016. *A Perfect Storm: Migrancy and Mining in the North West Province*, Working Paper. Pretoria: Trade & Industrial Policy Strategies.

Mohamed, N., 2017. *Developing a Green Jobs Roadmap for the Expanded Public Works Programme*. Pretoria: International Labour Organization.

Montmasson-Clair, G., 2012. *Green Economy Policy Framework and Employment Opportunity: A South African Case Study*, Working Paper No. 2012–02. Trade and Industrial Policy Strategies (TIPS), Pretoria.

Montmasson-Clair, G., 2015. *Mining Value Chains and Green Growth in South Africa: A Conflictual But Intertwined Relationship*, Working Paper. Trade & Industrial Policy Strategies (TIPS), Pretoria.

Montmasson-Clair, G., 2016a. *Designing Policy Frameworks for a Climate-Compatible Industrial Development Transition in South Africa*. Pretoria: Trade & Industrial Policy Strategies and the Department of Trade and Industry.

Montmasson-Clair, G., 2016b. *Mining, Energy and Climate Change in South Africa: A Platinum Case Study*, in "Industrialisation and the Mining Economy". Presented at the TIPS Annual Forum, Trade & Industrial Policy Strategies, Johannesburg.

Montmasson-Clair, G., 2017a. *Electricity Supply in South Africa: Path Dependency or Decarbonisation?* Pretoria: Trade & Industrial Policy Strategies.

Montmasson-Clair, G., 2017b. *Governance for South Africa's Sustainability Transition: A Critical Review*. Trade & Industrial Policy Strategies and Green Economy Coalition, Pretoria and London.

Montmasson-Clair, G., das Nair, R., 2017. South Africa's Renewable Energy Experience: Inclusive Growth Lessons, in Klaaren, J., Roberts, S. and Valodia, I. (eds.), *Competition Law and Economic Regulation: Addressing Market Power in Southern Africa*. Johannesburg: Wits University Press, pp. 189–214.

Montmasson-Clair, G., Ryan, G., Gulati, M., Davies, E., 2015. *Mining and the Environment: Understanding the Impacts to Prioritise the Efforts* (Mining Phakisa Research Report). Pretoria: Trade & Industrial Policy Strategies.

Montmasson-Clair, G., Wood, C., Mudombi, S., Deonarain, B., 2017. *A Green Economy Industry and Trade Analysis: Assessing South Africa's Potential*. Pretoria: Department of Environmental Affairs, Department of Trade and Industry, Department of Science and Technology, United Nations Environment Programme and United Nations Industrial Development Organization.

Norton, A., 2016. Automation will end the dream of rapid economic growth for poorer countries. *Guardian*.

Norton, A., 2017. *Automation, the Changing World of Work, and Sustainable Development*. International Institute for Environment and Development.

NPC (National Planning Commission), 2012. *National Development Plan – Vision 2030*. Pretoria: National Planning Commission.

OneWorld Sustainable Investments, 2010. *Skills for Green Jobs in South Africa* (Unedited background study). Geneva: International Labour Organization.

Palma, J.G., 2016. *Do Nations Just Get the Inequality They Deserve? The "Palma Ratio" Reexamined*. Cambridge: Cambridge University Press.

Parliament of the Republic of South Africa, 2017. *Report of the Portfolio Committee on Labour on Budget Vote 28: Labour, and on the Strategic Plans of the Department of Labour and its Entities*. Parliament of the Republic of South Africa, Cape Town.

Republic of South Africa, 2010. *Decent Work Country Programme 2010 to 2014*. Government of the Republic of South Africa, Representative Workers', Employers' and Community Organizations and International Labour Organization, Pretoria.

Rosenberg, E., 2015. *Green Skills for the Mining Sector* (Report on Research for the Mining Qualifications Authority). Grahamstown and Johannesburg: Rhodes University Environmental Learning Research Centre and Mining Qualifications Authority.

Rosenberg, E., Rosenberg, G., Lotz-Sisitka H. and Ramsarup, P., 2016. *Green Economy Learning Assessment South Africa: Critical Competencies for Driving a Green Transition*. Pretoria and Geneva: Department of Environmental Affairs, Department of Higher

Education and Training, United Nations Institute for Training and Research and Rhodes University.

Smit, S. and Musango, J.K., 2015. Exploring the Connections Between Green Economy and Informal Economy in South Africa. *South African Journal of Science*, 111(11/12).

Standish, B., van Zyl, H. and Cohen, B., 2017. *Employment Effects of Climate Change in South Africa: National Employment Vulnerability Assessment Sector Jobs Resilience Plans* (Draft Report). Deutsche Gesellschaft für Internationale Zusammenarbeit GmbH, Department of Environmental Affairs and Economic Development Department, Pretoria.

Statistics South Africa, 2017. *Quarterly Labour Force Survey*. Quarter 2: 2017. Statistics South Africa, Pretoria.

TETA, 2011. *Sector Skills Plan 2011*. Transport Education Training Authority, Johannesburg.

the dti, 2017. *Industrial Policy Action Plan 2017/18–2019/20*. Department of Trade and Industry, Pretoria.

UNEP, 2013. *Green Economy Scoping Study: South African Green Economy Modelling Report*. United Nations Environment Programme.

5 Policies for sustainability transformations in South Africa

A critical review

Najma Mohamed and Gaylor Montmasson-Clair

Introduction

After gaining prominence in global environment and development discourses in the 1980s, sustainable development is now increasingly finding its way, in various permutations, into contemporary public policy discourse. This can be discerned in the changing international architecture, in new alliances, partnerships and agendas, as well as at the national and sub-national level where policies, strategies and programmes that support a transition to greener economies are being instituted. The 2012 United Nations Conference on Sustainable Development (Rio + 20) noted that transitions would be characterised by varied approaches, visions, models and the tools available to each country, in accordance with its national circumstances and priorities, to achieve sustainable development (United Nations, 2012). Policy and regulatory reform has been identified as one of the key tools to enable sustainability transitions (UNEP, 2011; OECD, 2012; World Bank, 2015).

South Africa, like many countries, has enacted a suite of supportive policies, regulations and incentives affirming the country's commitment to transitioning to a sustainable development pathway. The inclusion of social justice and environmental sustainability considerations in South Africa's public policies was a significant feature of post-apartheid policy reform, as discussed in Chapter 1. This has resulted in the development of a complex sustainable development policy framework. Sustainable development is widely accepted as the theoretical framework in environmental policy development and planning in South Africa, and the country's environmental legal framework is regarded as amongst the best in the world (Oelofse *et al.*, 2006).

In response to the global economic crisis, the country's vision of transitioning to a green economy has significantly enhanced the sustainable development policy discourse in the last decade. Efforts to integrate sustainability into all levels of governance have reshuffled the cards of the game and created the discursive context for deeper structural policy reform. The foundational thinking for the transition has its antecedents in the country's response to the 2009 global financial crisis (Republic of South Africa, 2009), the employment-generating potential of green economy transitions ("the promise of green and decent jobs") and the reduction of the country's greenhouse gas emissions (DEA, 2010). The country's National Development Plan: Vision 2030 (NDP), for instance, sets the goal of "South Africa's transition to an environmentally sustainable, climate change resilient, low-carbon economy and just society" (NPC, 2012: 199). However, the coal-dependence of the South African economy, coupled with widening social and economic inequality, calls for a just transition in which the challenges associated with transforming the carbon- and resource-intensive economy of South Africa must be addressed in tandem with historically based inequalities and soaring unemployment rates. This was explored in preceding chapters.

This chapter assesses the state of play in South Africa at various levels of policymaking, drawing on transformative policy reform approaches which call for integrated and holistic policymaking for sustainable development (King *et al.*, 2014; GGGI, 2016; UNRISD, 2016) as well as a policy pyramid (Figure 5.1) which presents a normative model to merge both top-down and bottom-up approaches of policymaking in a dynamic and iterative fashion. The policy pyramid proposes a cooperative governance framework, which includes social partners and is based on dialogue, engagement and co-development. Each level in the pyramid plays a complementary role in the design and implementation of evidence-based, effective and ambitious policies. A strategic, coherent vision and associated roadmaps provide the guiding blueprint for government strategies and plans, including the design and implementation of instruments and measures. Toolkits – in the form of information and education systems, monitoring, reporting and verification and monitoring and evaluation (M&E) frameworks – and implementation tools support upstream policy development.

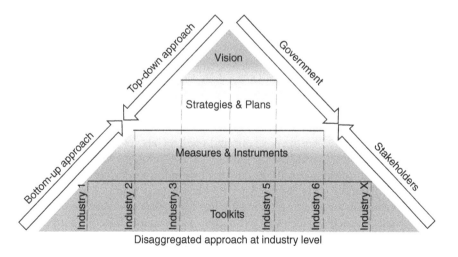

Figure 5.1 The policy pyramid.
Source: Montmasson-Clair (2017a).

The revitalisation of South Africa's sustainable development policy vision, reflecting key policy and regulatory reforms instituted in support of its sustainability transition in the last decade, is outlined in the first section of the chapter to define the prevailing policy narratives. Three cases are then assessed to interrogate, from both policy formulation *and* implementation, whether the transformative potential of sustainability policies is being realised. The final section of this chapter presents key principles needed to shift the country's transition from an enabling policy discourse, which continues to operate on the margins of economic policymaking and development planning, towards a transformative discourse which enacts the structural shifts required for a just transition.

Casting the vision: reviving sustainable development policy in South Africa

The inclusion of sustainability considerations into South Africa's public policy landscape signifies a massive and disruptive shift from traditional practices at all levels of policymaking and governance, and is an integral part of the country's response to multiple environmental, climate and development challenges. The transition to a sustainable development pathway is not just an environmental issue, but it is also primarily a socio-economic question with core implications for all aspects of economic and social life.

There is widespread agreement (UNEP, 2011; OECD, 2012; World Bank, 2015) that an enabling and coherent policy and regulatory framework, which provides confidence in the vision of a country to transition to more sustainable development pathways, requires political buy-in and support. Affirming this commitment, the South African government has not only enacted an enabling policy and regulatory framework in support of its vision, but has often played a leading role in global forums on climate and environmental action.

Building on the foundational sustainable development principle of South Africa's constitution, the short-, medium- and long-term visions of the country, as outlined in the National Strategy for Sustainable Development and Action Plan: 2011–2014 (NSSD1) (2014), the New Growth Path (NGP) (2020) and NDP (2030), all express a strong commitment to a sustainable transition pathway (Mohamed, 2014). Further, a social compact, the Green Economy Accord (EDD, 2010), agreed under South Africa's NGP, launched a partnership between government, business, labour and civil society, outlining 12 commitment areas and anticipating the creation of 300,000 new jobs in green industries in contribution to the objective of creating five million new jobs by 2020. The Accord is one of the cases discussed in detail below.

This cross-cutting macro-economic policy framework is complemented by a suite of sector-specific policies which reinforce the country's commitment to a sustainability transition, as well as a comprehensive monitoring system, the 14 Outcomes Framework, to track the operationalisation of policies. For instance, the energy, transport, waste management and construction sectors have seen the enactment of supportive "sustainability" policies and/or strategies. The policy framework includes a number of targets related to increasing the proportion of renewable energy in the country's energy mix, setting standards for energy efficiency and greener buildings, and creating green and decent jobs. In addition, sub-national initiatives, at both the municipal and provincial levels, are increasingly emerging. Figure 5.2 illustrates this policy framework.

Research is beginning to question the coherence of this policy framework, as well as the absence of the institutional structures required to coordinate green economy efforts at the national level (OECD, 2013). Kotzé (2006) frames the fragmentation of environmental governance and legislation in South Africa as "unsustainable", while Montmasson-Clair (2012, 6) reflects on how South Africa's "institutional arrangements with respect to the green economy reflect complex interconnections between a maze of institutions". Nhamo (2013) draws attention to the tensions between the policy directions, expressed in the sustainable development policy landscape, such as between the NGP as opposed to the NDP – a tension evident in the cases discussed below.

The Department of Environmental Affairs is vested with the responsibility to drive the sustainability transition for the country, but implementation is conducted by a wide array of stakeholders. The Economic Development Department supervises the Industrial Development Corporation, one of the two main state-run development finance institutions instrumental to financing the shift to a sustainable economy. The National Treasury governs the other main development finance institution, the Development Bank of Southern Africa. Direct support for industries falls under the Department of Trade and Industry, but fiscal incentives, that is, taxes and subsidies aimed at promoting behavioural and technological change, are under the mandate of the National Treasury. Then, the Department of Science and Technology is responsible for technology policy and fostering research and development in all sectors of the green economy.

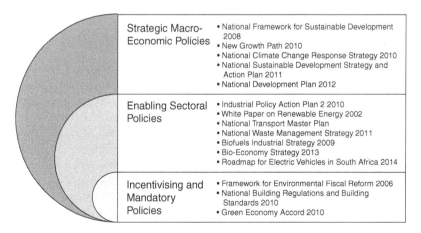

Figure 5.2 Examples of key policies supporting the sustainability transition in South Africa.

Source: Mohamed (2016).

The Departments of Rural Development and Land Reform and Agriculture, Forestry and Fisheries manage the transition in the rural (generally impoverished) parts of the country. Last, but not least, the development of the necessary skills force is spearheaded by the Departments of Labour and Higher Education and Training. The absence and/or weakness of cross-cutting and collaborative institutional structures to coordinate environmental policy implementation at the national and sub-national level is an enduring challenge in South Africa's environmental governance landscape and remains one of the main challenges in its transition pathway. While a clear vision and political commitment is essential in transition pathways, mainstreaming sustainability in public policy needs to similarly transition from the largely managerialist approach to environmental governance towards cooperative and collaborative governance.

The multiplicity of plans and strategies impacting on the transition to sustainable development, their inconsistency and misalignment, from a policy and institutional perspective, thus remain problematic. While it is essential for government (at all levels) to design dedicated strategies for climate change and other aspects of the transition to sustainable development, the mainstreaming of these "sustainability policies" into all other plans and strategies (such as the Industrial Policy Action Plan and the Integrated Energy Plan) is equally important. The policy and institutional framework does not yet display the coherence required to instil the investor confidence needed to propel this economic transition into full swing. In addition, most of the essential tools required for the transition (data, guidelines, knowledge systems, M&E systems) are not available or are incomplete, jeopardising the design and implementation of an economy-wide transition to a sustainable development pathway.

Policy reform processes have thus far been top-heavy, situated primarily at the macro-economic and sector-level, while the required levers for policy change, such as mandating policies, instruments and toolkits, have not kept pace (see Figure 5.2). Table 5.1 shows the mix of instruments that have been set up thus far – though these will have to be stepped up considerably to achieve deeper transformation.

Mainstreaming environmental sustainability and climate change in economic policymaking has also been inadequate. Despite numerous climate change strategies at national and sub-national levels, climate change considerations have not yet been integrated in other policies and, like the green economy, remain marginal in public policy implementation. For instance, while the NDP aims to provide a strategic vision and plan for the transition to a low-carbon and climate resilient economy and society, it lacks coherence and consistency across other elements of the plan, such as infrastructure investment or energy planning. The NDP defines a vision for South Africa up to 2030, but does not provide strategic and coherent planning for the country's transition to sustainable development, defining the end state of the economy and society in the long term (2050), as well as roadmaps detailing the necessary short-, medium- and long-term steps necessary to achieve the desired outcomes for sustainable development in South Africa. Roadmaps have been developed for the

Table 5.1 Examples of instruments targeted at achieving sustainable development in South Africa

Category	Sub-Categories	Examples from South Africa
Regulatory measures	Legislation Plans Standards	Standards for specific technologies or processes; mandatory energy efficiency standards from new buildings; environmental management regulations (water use licences, environmental impact assessments), fuel blending requirements
Economic measures	Taxes Offsets or Tradable Allowances Subsidies	Tax incentives for energy efficiency and for R&D; carbon tax on new vehicles, levy of plastic bags, levy on non-renewable sources of electricity, Eskom's demand-side management programmes); grant programmes for energy efficient investment (Manufacturing Competitiveness Enhancement Programme)
Direct government action	Government Procurement of Public Goods or Services Direct Infrastructure Investment	Procurement and investment in the transport sector (e.g. freight modal shift and mass public transit); Renewable Energy Independent Power Producer Procurement Programme; Industrial Symbiosis programmes
Support measures	Government Support for Voluntary Actions Support for Research and Development	Concessional finance (IDC and DBSA); Green Economy Accord; Direct funding for R&D centres
Information programmes	Public/Private programmes	Labelling programmes, National Cleaner Production Centre's support programmes; Resource efficiency campaigns (Eskom's 49M, Rand Water's Water Wise)

Source: Authors, adapted from DEA (2015).

water and waste sectors by the Department of Science and Technology, but the general lack thereof has hampered domestic efforts to shift to more sustainable development pathways. For instance, the NGP and Nationally Determined Contributions to the global climate efforts represent starting points but do not constitute a strategic, coherent and longer-term vision for the country's transition. Similarly, the Medium-Term Strategic Framework, the Industrial Policy Action Plan, the Innovation Plan and the National Strategy for Sustainable Development and Action Plan flesh out a variety of short-term interventions but fail to provide a coherent, detailed and long-term roadmap towards sustainable development for the country.

Admittedly, the task of providing an integrated vision, answering to the need to stimulate economic growth and tackling the triple developmental challenge of poverty, inequality and unemployment, while managing environmental considerations, is not straightforward. However, existing efforts remain off the mark, as policy actions continue to consider the transition to a sustainable pathway as an add-on to other developments in the country. For example, both the New Growth Plan and the Industrial Policy Action Plan frame the "green economy" as a sector. As policies are being implemented in South Africa, the absence of a more nuanced understanding carries notable risks for a transition to sustainability. The OECD's assertion that while "countries are taking steps towards green growth … much more determined efforts are needed to integrate environmental priorities into economic agendas" (OECD, 2015: 2), holds true for South Africa.

The policy narratives for a just transition exists in South Africa, yet it is becoming clear that the radical shifts required to drive the country towards a just transition remain sub-optimal. The linkages between the transition to sustainability and socio-economic considerations, such as poverty, employment, inequality, competitiveness, rural development and natural resource management, and the inclusion of the informal economy, largely remain weak. Calls for inclusive approaches to greening the South African economy (Musyoki, 2012; Infodev, 2013; Smit and Musango, 2015; Swilling *et al.*, 2015), which address the most vulnerable in society and which ensure that the benefits of green innovations reach all South Africans, are becoming more pronounced. Evidence of inclusive and pro-poor approaches to greening the South African economy exist (see UNECA, 2015 and Hlahla *et al.*, 2016), though these are by no means at the core of green economy project and programme implementation. Further, in stark contrast to the initial social dialogue epitomised in the Green Economy Accord, policy implementation has occurred with a virtual exclusion of social partners, notably civil society. The voices of civil society have been marginal to the policy- and decision-making processes of South Africa's transition, leading to a transition pathway which is largely state- and market-led and in which government, industry and financial institutions craft and implement a technocratic and marketised transition pathway where notions of equity, justice and inclusion are marginal (see Scoones *et al.*, 2015).

Transitions to sustainable development involve a complex balancing act on multiple fronts, managing short-term trade-offs between economic, social and environmental outcomes. While the transition is expected to bring multiple long-term benefits, in the form of stronger, more resilient growth, increased competitiveness, higher and better employment, reduced inequality and increased welfare (UNEP, 2013), it remains beset with difficulties and trade-offs to be addressed in the short term, particularly to minimise the socio-economic costs of transitions (Cloete and Robb, 2010; Montmasson-Clair, 2015). Moreover, the social benefits and outcomes of sustainable development are not always automatic and have to be induced and directed through effective policies to fully materialise. This reality and the implications in terms of governance have not been fleshed out in the South African context beyond generic, high-level policy considerations, as illustrated by the following case studies.

Policies for sustainability – deepening national policy visions towards action

The cases discussed below present examples of key policy processes which have been central to the country's transition pathway. They illustrate the challenges of implementing a transformative transition in a country that largely remains entrenched on a highly unsustainable pathway due to its reliance on fossil fuels (primarily coal), energy-intensive value chains, and carbon-intensive transport systems.

From a socio-economic perspective, in addition to displaying severe levels of unemployment, the South African society remains one of the most unequal in the world, while investor confidence in the country has plummeted in recent years. While making the case for an economic transition in this context presents a challenge, the post-apartheid sustainable development policy discourse has effectively linked environmental sustainability with poverty reduction and social justice. National policy visions, such as the NDP, thus incorporate amongst their guiding principles a clear commitment to an inclusive transition that is just, ethical, transformative and participatory (NPC, 2012). On many accounts though, the recent policy reform processes fall short in mainstreaming environmental principles in the country's development vision, leading to policy processes which have been more "evolutionary than revolutionary".

From the NFSD to the NDP: shifting sustainability to the margins?

The development of the National Framework for Sustainable Development (NFSD) (DEA, 2008) in 2008 was followed by the approval of the NSSD1 (DEA, 2011) by the South African government. The framework and strategy were formulated in response to an international environmental commitment, agreed at the World Summit of Sustainable Development (hosted by South Africa in 2002), to formulate national strategies for sustainable development.

The strategy presents a well-structured argument and approach for adopting a systemic approach to mainstreaming sustainability which should be integrated across the country's governance system. It puts forward five strategic priorities which speak to many of the challenges outlined above, including the need for enhancing governance and institutional structures for integrated planning and implementation. The NSSD1 also set out nine sectoral focus areas for transitioning to a green economy, which have remained central to the analysis of the country's sustainability transition – often framed as a green economy transition (see Figure 4.1). It presents not only an understanding of sustainable development, but an attendant action plan and indicators to guide the monitoring of policy implementation. However, a lack of political support, as well as the fact that the environment ministry has no enforcement power over other ministries, has led to limited uptake of both the framework and the NSSD1 which "never received the priority it deserved as a planning tool" (Rennkamp, 2012: 7). The action plan has largely not been implemented while the proposed update to the NSSD1, which extends till 2014, has not been forthcoming. The strategy thus effectively ends in 2014.

The development of the NDP created hopes of sustainability mainstreaming. The NDP indeed envisions that, "by 2030, South Africa's development transition to an environmentally sustainable, climate change-resilient, low-carbon economy and just society will be well underway" (NPC, 2012: 199). The NDP also generated high-level political support, while the establishment of the independent National Planning Commission in the Presidency provides, in theory, the institutional clout to promote intergovernmental collaboration and implementation. Further, the NDP has largely been integrated into government administration and planning, most notably through the Medium Term Strategic Framework, the strategic action plan reflecting the commitments made in the election manifesto of the governing party. However, while there is some coherence between the NSSD1 and the NDP, the NDP does not appear to build on existing environmental policy and fails to recognise ecological systems as the foundation of a resilient future economy (WWF, 2012).

There are also several contradictions between the NDP and the development pathways outlined in other policy documents (Rennkamp, 2012; CDE, 2013). For instance, the IPAP and the 10-year Innovation Plan envisage a skills and innovation-based transition to a knowledge economy, while the energy planning in the NDP suggests a traditional infrastructure-driven approach to economic development through the exploitation of natural resources, especially coal. Further, there are contradictions between the sectors identified for an employment-rich sustainability transition – not only within the broader policy landscape but also by the growing body of work detailing the potential for enhancing transition pathways in agriculture, the built environment and the wildlife industry, for instance (Musvoto *et al.*, 2015; Taylor *et al.* 2015; PAGE, 2017).

The NDP, however, strongly asserts the social dimension of the transition, noting the need for an equitable transition in which the poor and vulnerable are protected from the "costs" of a transition, such as increased costs of energy, food and transport, job losses in carbon-intensive industries, and promoting an employment-rich transition pathway. It has laid important foundations for South Africa's sustainability transition – notwithstanding the lack of inclusion of the sustainable development framework and sectoral plans and strategies.

The NDP is also well aligned with the Sustainable Development Goals (SDGs), which UN member states will use to frame their agendas and policies up until 2030 (NBI, 2016; Wits School of Governance, 2016). A mapping exercise comparing the SDG targets and objectives of the NDP revealed "a highly overlapping, reinforcing framework that can be used to structure collective action and drive development outcomes" (NBI, 2016: 2). Over 90 per cent of the NDP's 72 stated objectives can be mapped to the 169 SDG targets. The NDP has de facto become the primary reference point for deliberations on the domestication of the SDGs, superseding the NSSD1 and effectively elevating the SDGs to the highest level of policymaking.

However, the NDP has not adequately framed a transformative vision – which would depict a post-carbon (post-coal) society that is environmentally sustainable and socially just. There are growing concerns about the slow pace of implementation of the NDP and the ambitious targets that had been set, as discussed in Chapter 2. Furthermore, the timeframe of 2030 cannot be considered "long term" when planning for a transition, and a 2050 timeframe would have lent itself to more meaningful and effective transition planning. Clear roadmaps detailing the short-, medium- and long-term steps necessary to achieve the desired outcomes for sustainable development in South Africa are also needed. The lack thereof has hampered domestic efforts to shift to more sustainable development pathways.

Energy policy in South Africa: from path dependency to deep decarbonisation? (Montmasson-Clair, 2017b)

Given that South Africa is amongst the most carbon-intensive economies in the world, "shifting the trends of energy investment is at the heart of a just transition to a sustainable, equitable society" (Worthington, 2015: 23). Renewable energy (RE) technologies have experienced an exponential growth globally from 800 GW of generation capacity in 2004 to more than 2,000 GW in 2016 (REN21, 2017). Forecasts predict that RE technologies, predominantly solar- and wind-based systems, will further expand in the coming decades, overcoming coal-based electricity by around 2030 (IEA, 2015). South Africa is no exception and RE has entered the country's electricity landscape as a significant trend. However, despite recent progress, the full potential of RE technologies, which is reported to have the potential to meet 100 per cent of the country's energy needs by 2050 (Worthington, 2015), has yet to be harnessed.

The commissioning of RE-based electricity generation capacity was a clear policy choice set by the 2003 White Paper on Renewable Energy and introduced in the 2010 Integrated Resource Plan for Electricity (DoE, 2011). This is particularly important as electricity supply accounts for about 60 per cent of the country's direct greenhouse gas (GHG) emissions (DEA, 2013). RE has experienced an exponential growth in South Africa due to a strong political directive that launched the Renewable Energy Independent Power Producers Procurement Programme (REIPPPP) in 2011. The REIPPPP, a competitive bidding process for procuring RE projects, has been the main conduit for entry into the utility-scale RE sector. The programme has grown significantly. By June 2017, the programme had procured 6,422 MWp of RE generation capacity from 112 preferred bidders, of which 3,152 MWp had been connected and was feeding electricity into the national grid (DoE et al., 2017).

The programme has already triggered more than R200 billion of investment in the country, and is reported to have created approximatively 32,500 jobs (DoE et al., 2017). It also constituted a welcome opportunity to increase the developmental benefits associated with infrastructure projects, by including enhanced socio-economic objectives in the project evaluation process. These account for 30 per cent of the project evaluation, along with price (70 per cent). These enhanced requirements have, however, not been without challenges for project developers, financiers and the government alike, and particularly for community development (DoE *et al.*, 2017; Mthembi, 2015). Despite some success, the REIPPPP, and the growth of the RE sector in South Africa, are facing critical challenges. There was a virtual standstill in the REIPPPP for over a year due to delays by the state-owned energy utility to sign the power purchase agreement of 37 duly procured plants, with some signs that these will be concluded in 2018. As of February 2018, the future of the REIPPPP remains uncertain and there are indications that the programme will not continue in its current form, and will shift its focus from RE to coal and gas, despite the growing public sentiment that the coal industry has had its time – "just as telegraphs had their moment, just as stone tools had their era" (Khambule, 2017). The intractable support for coal-based energy is reflected in the central role afforded to coal in energy policy in South Africa.

While the IRP factors in the transition to a lower-carbon and more environmentally friendly energy mix, the persistent domination of coal-based electricity remains at its core. Coal-based electricity is expected to grow in megawatt of generation capacity, notably with the construction of the two large-scale Medupi and Kusile power plants. The 2013 review of the IRP, which proposed more aggressive scenarios aimed at setting the electricity sector on a genuine low-carbon development path compatible with the country's emission targets, was never adopted. Although coal-related subsidies have been significantly reduced in the country over the past few years, notably through the increase in electricity prices, substantial support is still directed at the development of fossil fuels. The exact amount of fossil fuel subsidies provided in South Africa is difficult to ascertain and numbers largely diverge. Their scale nevertheless remains impressive and the country is the fifth largest provider of coal subsidies in percentage of GDP terms.

Decisions on technological choices in the energy space have substantial implications for the country's sustainability transition. The development of carbon capture and storage, the expansion of nuclear energy, the rollout of a gas industrialisation programme, fracking and the development of a hydrogen economy are examples of initiatives that do not garner unanimous support. For instance, the government's announcement that it would procure additional nuclear energy was met with vehement opposition by civil society organisations calling for a just transition to sustainable energy. A coalition of civil society organisations challenged the government's decision to procure nuclear energy and was successful in having the decision declared unconstitutional (SAFCEI, 2017), while the Department of Environmental Affairs' authorisation of a coal power station was overturned (in light of the country's greenhouse gas emission targets), hastening much-awaited climate change legislation in South Africa (Mzamo, 2017).

Despite the fact that the transition away from fossil fuel-based (particularly coal-based) energy systems (for electricity generation but also transportation) should underpin the transition to sustainable development in South Africa, (powerful) support for coal-fired electricity production has remained unshaken. These vested interests found unlikely allies in the members of the Coal Transportation Forum, who undertook industrial action in March 2017 protesting against the signing of REIPPPP projects, on the basis that RE would result in job losses in the coal industry (Dludla, 2017). However, the coal industry has in the last decade actively shifted towards automation, which has lessened the need for coal transport. Thus, while shifts to RE could impact on job losses in the coal sector, the impact of an RE transition is much less significant than ongoing changes within the coal sector itself. Further, the industry, which has reported a coal surplus for the last five years, also has to be cognisant of the implications of global shifts away from coal (through fossil fuel divestment) on the future of the industry.

The complex challenges facing a just energy transition in South Africa highlight the need for social dialogue around the transformation of the fossil fuel energy system. The necessity and possibility of further decarbonising of the country's electricity supply by increasing the share of RE technologies, which have proved increasingly cost-competitive, reaching levels similar to, if not lower than, coal-fired power plants, exists (Altieri *et al.* 2015; DoE *et al.*, 2017). However, significant vested interests alongside massive state support to maintain the domination of the coal industry over electricity supply in South Africa, persist. Active efforts are required to incorporate a low-carbon transition in electricity policy planning, phase out fossil fuel subsidies, and address the competing visions and vested interests which threaten the development, to their optimal potential, of RE technologies in South Africa. Social dialogue, which underpinned the country's transition, has not kept pace as policy implementation processes are rolled out in the country.

The Green Economy Accord: a missed opportunity to build an effective national partnership (Montmasson-Clair, 2017a)

The NGP, developed by the Economic Development Department in 2009 (EDD, 2009), lays out avenues to create five million new jobs in South Africa by 2020. It is part of a broader policy to shift the country towards a more labour-intensive trajectory, in turn contributing to a more cohesive and equitable economy and society. The NGP targets the so-called "green economy" (natural resource management, waste management and recycling, renewable energy and energy efficiency) as one of the key "sectors" for job creation in South Africa and aims at creating 300,000 additional direct jobs by 2020 (and more than 400,000 by 2030), including 80,000 in manufacturing in the green economy (EDD, 2009).

As part of a set of multi-stakeholder initiatives in support of the NGP and an attempt to cement a national partnership, the South African government and social partners (organised labour, business and community constituents) signed a Green Economy Accord in November 2011. The Accord was characterised as "one of the most comprehensive social partnerships on the green economy anywhere in the world" by South African President Jacob Zuma and "groundbreaking" by leading trade unionist Zwelinzima Vavi (Seeliger and Turok, 2016). The ILO's *Guidelines for a Just Transition* (2015, 5) notes that "strong social consensus on the goal and pathways to sustainability is fundamental … and social dialogue has to be an integral part of the institutional framework for policymaking and implementation at all levels". The Green Economy Accord features prominently as an illustration of best practice in a global review of social dialogue and sustainable development (ILO, 2012), and is lauded as a formal quadripartite agreement which has set quantifiable targets, identified an implementation timeframe and established mechanisms for evaluation and monitoring.

The Accord identifies points of agreement as well as specific tasks to be carried out by each constituency for a series of 12 commitments covering *inter alia* renewable energy, energy efficiency, solar water heaters, green investment, recycling, public transportation and rail freight, biofuels, clean-coal initiatives, the promotion of localisation and green jobs, and access to electricity for all.

Importantly, commitments are diverse in scope and specificity, with some containing targets and deadlines while others are broad statements of intent. Ten of them are also not new but were merely reiterated (and sometimes enhanced) in a more public-facing exercise ahead of the COP17 in Durban, South Africa. Unfortunately, in the spirit of consensus, while the NGP recognises the need to consider trade-offs between the present costs and future benefits of a green economy, the Accord considers the green economy as an add-on to the rest of the economy, focusing only on co-benefits and avoiding controversial topics. This makes the ambition of the Accord relatively modest and a missed opportunity for meaningful social dialogue on an economic transition to a sustainable development pathway. Commitments are also heavily focused on energy- and technology-related issues, neglecting other dimensions, such as water, waste, biodiversity and ecosystems which contribute significantly to the country's climate adaptation efforts.

As part of M&E, all parties to the Accord were due to meet on a regular basis (at least twice a year), under the auspices of the Economic Development Department, to review progress and to assess what changes and additions are required. Yet, there is limited evidence of ongoing assessment of the Accord's implementation. The lack of capacity, expertise and clout of the Economic Development Department, the absence of implementation plans and the failure of some departments (responsible for implementation) to take ownership of the commitments have, however, undermined the Accord (Seeliger and Turok, 2016). Progress towards the targets and other commitments is inadequately monitored and no enforcement mechanism exists at this point in time, resulting in the Accord being more of a voluntary measure than a regulatory requirement (Seeliger and Turok, 2016). As a result, progress has been extremely uneven and essentially linked to other dynamics, specific to each sector. Some areas have gained momentum due to sectoral transitions and have progressed well, while the Accord has not helped unlock sectors where additional policy stimulus was needed.

Since the formulation of the Accord, there have nonetheless been significant developments from social partners in support of the country's sustainability transitions. Business has launched and participated in a number of key programmes, such as the donor-funded Private Sector Energy Efficiency Programme; established the South African leg of the voluntary Carbon Disclosure Project; and has instituted annual climate change reporting – the 2017 version of which presented the climate change efforts of 803 investors representing US$100 trillion in assets (NBI, 2017). Private finance has been significant in activating the country's 'green' investment landscape, notably in RE and energy efficiency, and remains a significant, often untapped source of finance. In a similar vein, civil society has also stepped up actions, partnering in a number of landmark programmes (several of which feature in this book, notably in Chapter 9) and networks which seek to coordinate actions for sustainable development. Labour unions have presented a policy vision for a just transition to sustainable development (COSATU, 2012) and are beginning to intensify their efforts as the impacts of transitioning to a sustainability pathway on the world of work become more evident. Community constituents across the country are also partnering in grass-roots actions on climate change and the greening of local economies (Mohamed, 2015; Hlahla *et al.* 2016).

The policy pyramid approach adopted in this chapter considers social dialogue as an essential feature of a collaborative, inclusive and dynamic process required for sustainability transition policies. It is "a driver *and* governance instrument for sustainable development" (Hermans *et al.*, 2017), which could significantly enhance the social outcomes of sustainability transitions. In the end, the Green Economy Accord now appears as more of a public relations exercise than the creation of a social compact on the sustainability transition in South Africa.

Towards a transformative sustainable development policy transition in South Africa

A sustainable development policy framework integrates divergent policy strands and should, in principle, combine social, environmental and economic objectives and result in holistic outcomes (Raworth *et al.*, 2014). The analysis of both the policy vision, as well as three of the central policy processes in South Africa's sustainability transition attest to the fact that, in South Africa, sustainable development policy goals "hide" across diverse sectoral plans (Rennkamp, 2012), and are not yet sufficiently mainstreamed and integrated in economic policymaking. Further, while this policy vision creates a discursive context in support of an inclusive, employment-rich and pro-poor transition (Ganda and Ngwakwe, 2014; Swilling *et al.*, 2015), there is mounting concern that the country's transition has not been socially inclusive (Khambule, 2017), and could reinforce and reproduce inequalities (Marcatelli, 2015).

The growing body of work exploring the integration of social justice in sustainable development policymaking (Leach *et al.* 2010; IIED and CAFOD, 2014; King *et al.*, 2014; Raworth *et al.* 2014; GGGI, 2016; UNRISD, 2016) highlights a number of principles which can enable more transformative sustainability pathways. Of these, social dialogue, policy coherence and consistency, inclusive and reflexive transition planning, collaborative governance and prioritisation of the poor and vulnerable in policymaking would be of particular value in shifting from South Africa's technocentric, managerialist sustainability pathway towards a just transition which addresses poverty reduction, pervasive and growing unemployment and inequality, and enlivens participatory democracy. Much of these principles are already contained in the country's policy vision but are virtually absent in the institutional machinery. While South Africa is by no means lagging in its integration of social objectives in economic policymaking, the country needs to up its game to reap the social benefits of sustainable development-related policies by implementing social safeguards and setting transformative policy goals and actions which would lead to social and environmental justice. Further, the SDG vision, which is underscored by integrated and holistic policymaking, presents an additional impetus for the type of transformational policy action that is needed in the country.

In order to institute a societal transition envisioned in the policy framework of the country, there is a need to create an enabling environment for active citizenry and participatory processes of *social dialogue* around the goals of the country's sustainability transition. The National Planning Commission, responsible for drafting the NDP, initiated a social partner-driven process for developing pathways for a just transition that maximises socio-economic outcomes of a low-carbon, climate resilient development pathway. The aim is to build an understanding of the transition from a citizenry perspective, and to define and contextualise the sustainability transition from the bottom up. The NSSD1 vision of working towards a sustainable society, building environmental knowledge and awareness, changing attitudes and behaviour towards more environmentally sustainable consumption and production practices, and promoting participation in environmental protection, lies at the heart of social dialogue, which needs to be harnessed as an instrument and driver of governance for sustainable development.

Policy coherence and consistency is needed to develop a transition vision for a sustainable South African economy and society that gives substance to the constitutional mandate and the sustainable development framework, in addition to the country's international commitments. Currently, South Africa has multiple plans and strategies impacting on the transition to sustainable development. In addition to the implementation challenges discussed earlier, the inconsistency and misalignment of these plans and strategies, from a policy and institutional perspective, remains problematic, hindering the effectiveness of the policy framework. This includes the broader misalignment between the existing sustainability goals with other policies, as illustrated in the case of energy policy. This lack of clarity, coherence and certainty applies equally to the mix of policy incentives and measures. For instance, as of February 2018, there is still no agreement in South Africa on the preferred instruments on carbon pricing. Long-term policy coherence, clarity and certainty across 32 green economy-related policies, strategies and measures (PAGE, 2017) are key to implementing a sustainability transition and notably in garnering the confidence of the private sector, which remains central to implementing and financing sustainability transitions.

The NDP is clear in that the country has to embark on a "managed transition", building on existing processes and capacities to enable society to change in a structured and phased manner. *Transition planning*, which is adaptive, reflexive and complex, requires a shift away from traditional linear policy processes. According to the typology of transition phases developed by Rotmans *et al.* (2001), South Africa is still largely at the predevelopment stage and is yet to reach take-off (system shifts), breakthrough (structural change) and stabilisation. Transition management requires long-term planning and multi-level, cross-sectoral thinking, as well as the boldness to undertake system innovation while simultaneously undertaking system improvements (Rotmans *et al.*, 2001). It requires the policy dexterity to assess a range of possible development paths (and technology choices), and the ability to assess the trade-offs between long-term ambition and short-term concerns. A number of possible sustainability pathways should be developed for discussion and debate, clearly highlighting the transition goals, including short-term (<5 years), medium-term (5–15 years) and long-term (15–50 years) interventions, and the steps and mechanisms to achieve them. Given the rapidly changing socio-economic and global environments, such pathways should be regularly updated to remain relevant and in line with transition goals. Acknowledging the contested nature of the debates, this forward-looking exercise should lay the foundation for specific plans and strategies aimed at maximising the benefits and mitigating the trade-offs, particularly for the most vulnerable segments of society and the economy.

Collaborative governance for transitions needs to be inclusive and participatory, not only facilitating policy coordination and alignment both vertically and horizontally, but ensuring that front-line workers who spearhead policy implementation become champions of transformative policies at the sub-national level (Leach *et al.*, 2010). In South Africa, political leadership in environmental governance has largely been directed at international negotiations, with minimal translation into fundamental domestic transformation. Enhancement of the Intergovernmental Committee on Climate Change, as recommended by Giordano *et al.* (2011), or the re-establishment of the Green Growth Task Team, under the leadership of the Presidency, could promote high-level intergovernmental collaboration on mainstreaming climate change and sustainable development in policymaking. Institutionally, despite the existence of official channels aimed at facilitating coordination and alignment, the governance of the transition to a sustainable model of development remains a key challenge. For collaborative governance systems to evolve further, both inter- and intra-governmental coordination at the strategic as well as planning, design and implementation levels should be meaningfully enhanced by democratising the policy process through the inclusion of social partners, in line with the aim of encouraging co-development of policies and strengthening coherence of the policy framework.

Pro-poor policymaking, which promotes the empowerment of the poor and vulnerable, extends the coverage of social protection, promotes social innovation, recognises the role of the informal economy, and strengthens the livelihoods, assets and capabilities of the poor, is essential for sustainable and equitable restructuring of economies. The impacts of the transition on South Africa's most vulnerable populations are yet to be fully understood and addressed in a coherent fashion. This is central to sustainability transitions (Khor, 2011; Dercon, 2012; GGGI, 2016). A small body of work has emerged to begin to address the impact of greening economies on the poor and vulnerable in the informal economy (Smit and Musango, 2015), enterprise development (Hlahla *et al.*, 2016), social innovation (Mohamed, 2015), and the employment dimension of sustainability transitions (see Chapter 4). Seekings (2014) asserts that the establishment of representative democracy in South Africa (which essentially constituted institution- and coalition-building to protect the interests of sections of the urban working, middle, and upper classes) provided weak impetus to pro-poor policymaking and did not result in any substantial empowerment of the poorest citizens. This, in truth, represents the reality of many countries that are subjected to different shades of political and economic repression, which continues to marginalise the poor. If the current trend of sustainability policies is to represent a transformative eco-social and pro-poor turn in policymaking, then social justice, equity and redistribution have to be integrated in a more meaningful way.

Conclusion

Going forward, tremendous opportunities exist for improving the policy framework in support of South Africa's just transition to a sustainable development pathway. Governance should be enhanced at all levels of policymaking in both a top-down and bottom-up framework. Clarity and consensus need to be reached on the transition goals for the country and the approaches to achieve it. Policy alignment and implementation must be promoted from a socio-economic and an environmental perspective, with priority given to addressing South Africa's triple challenge of poverty, unemployment and inequality. The mix of policy and regulatory measures should be grounded in the socio-economic realities of the country, and the adequate tools, particularly information and data, must be developed.

Ultimately, the transition to sustainability is a long-term endeavour which will take several decades, the planning of which has to begin now. From a public policy perspective, designing and implementing a policy framework for a sustainability transition is not a one-off exercise, but a dynamic, iterative and participatory process. This is the underlying condition *sine qua non* to ensuring the long-term sustainability of policy actions and, by extension, the transition to sustainable development in South Africa.

References

Altieri, K., Trollip, H., Caetano, T., Hughes, A., Merven, B. and Winkler, H., 2015. *Pathways to Deep Decarbonization in South Africa*. SDSN – IDDRI, New York.

Centre for Development Enterprise (CDE), 2013. *Policy Gridlock: Comparing the Proposals Made in Three Economic Policy Documents*. CDE, Johannesburg.

Cloete, B. and Robb, G., 2010. *Carbon Pricing and Industrial Policy in South Africa*. Presentation at the Conference, Putting a Price on Carbon: Economic Instruments to Mitigate Climate Change in South Africa and Other Developing Countries, University of Cape Town. Available at http://carbonprice.ercblogs.co.za/wp-content/uploads/2010/04/04_Cloete,Robb.pdf (accessed 10 October 2017).

COSATU, 2012. *A Just Transition to a Low-Carbon and Climate Resilient Economy. COSATU Policy on Climate Change: A Call to Action*. COSATU, Braamfontein.

DEA (Department of Environmental Affairs), 2010. *National Climate Change Response White Paper*. DEA, Pretoria.

DEA, 2011. *National Strategy for Sustainable Development and Action Plan*. DEA, Pretoria.

DEA, 2013. *GHG Inventory for South Africa: 2000–2010*. DEA, Pretoria.

DEA, 2015. DEROS Explanatory Note No. 2: Development of Mix of Measures for Sectors and Subsectors of the Economy. DEA, Pretoria.

DEAT (Department of Environmental Affairs and Tourism), 2008. *People – Planet – Prosperity: A National Framework for Sustainable Development in South Africa*. DEAT, Pretoria.

Dercon, S., 2012. *Is Green Growth Good for the Poor?* World Bank Policy Research, Working Paper 6231. The World Bank, Washington, DC.

Dludla, N., 2017. South African coal truck drivers protest against renewables. *Reuters*, 1 March 2017. Available at www.reuters.com/article/us-safrica-power/south-african-coal-truck-drivers-protest-against-renewables-idUSKBN1683OC (accessed 30 April 2018).

DoE, 2011. *Integrated Resource Plan for Electricity 2010–2030*. DoE, Pretoria.

DoE, NT, DBSA, 2017. *Independent Power Producers Procurement Programme (IPPPP): An Overview as at 30 June 2017*. Department of Energy, National Treasury and Development Bank of Southern Africa, Pretoria and Johannesburg.

EDD (Economic Development Department), 2009. *New Growth Path*. EDD, Pretoria.

EDD, 2010. *Green Economy Accord*. EDD, Pretoria.

Ganda, F. and Ngwakwe, C.C., 2014. The Role of Social Policy in Transition Towards a Green Economy: The Case of South Africa. *Environmental Economics*, 5(3): 32–41.

Giordano, T., Hall, L., Gilder, A. and Parramon, M., 2011. *Governance of Climate Change in South Africa*. DEA, Pretoria.

Global Green Growth Institute (GGGI), 2016. *Pro-poor, Inclusive Green Growth: Experience and New Agenda*. GGGI, Seoul.

Hermans, M., Huyse, H. and Van Ongevalle, J., 2017. *Social Dialogue as a Driver and Governance Instrument for Sustainable Development*. ILO-ITUC Issue Paper. ITUC, Geneva.

Hlahla, S., Goebel, A. and Hill, T.R., 2016. Green Economy: A Strategy to Alleviate Urban Poverty and Safeguard the Environment? KwaZulu-Natal, South Africa. *Urban Forum*, 27: 113–127.

IIED and CAFOD, 2014. *Securing Social Justice in Green Economies*. IIED, London.

ILO (International Labour Organization), 2012. *Social Dialogue for Sustainable Development. A Review of National and Regional Experiences*. ILO, Geneva.

ILO, 2015. *Guidelines for a Just Transition. Towards Environmentally Sustainable Economies and Societies for all*. ILO, Geneva.

infoDev, 2013. *Inclusive Green Growth: Findings from Community Outreach through the Climate Innovation Center in South Africa*. InfoDev: Washington, DC.

International Energy Agency (IEA), 2015. *World Energy Outlook 2015*. IEA, Paris.

Khambule, H., 2017. A transition to renewable energy will not be just until there are a greater percentage of winners. *Huffington Post*, 2 May 2017.

Khor, M., 2011. *Risks and Uses of the Green Economy Concept in the context of Sustainable Development, Poverty and Equity*. South Centre Research Paper 40. South Centre, Geneva.

King, P., Olhoff, A. and Urama, K., 2014. Policy Design and Implementation. In Green Growth Best Practice (GGBP), *Green Growth in Practice: Lessons from Country Experiences*. GGBP, Seoul.

Kotzé, L.J., 2006. Improving Unsustainable Environmental Governance in South Africa: The Case for Holistic Governance. *Potchefstroom Electronic Law Journal*, 9(1): 75–118.

Leach, M., Scoones, I. and Stirling, A., 2010. *Dynamic Sustainabilities. Technology, Environment, Social Justice*. Earthscan, Oxon.

Marcatelli, M., 2015. Suspended Redistribution: 'Green Economy' and Water Inequality in the Waterberg, South Africa. *Third World Quarterly*, 36(12): 2244–2258.

Mohamed, N., 2014. The Green Fund: Establishment, Process and Prospects. *Green Fund Policy Brief*, 1. Available at www.sagreenfund.org.za/wordpress/wp-content/uploads/2016/11/GF-Policy-Brief-1.pdf (accessed 30 April 2018).

Mohamed, N., 2015. *From the Margins to the Mainstream? Social Innovation in Support of South Africa's Low Carbon Transition*. Paper presented at International Conference on Innovation for Sustainability under Climate Change and Green Growth, 26–28 May 2015.

Mohamed, N., 2016. *The Implications of Macro-Economic Drivers for Anticipating Green Skills in Support of South Africa's Green Economy Transition*. Unpublished Paper presented at Green Skills Programme Report Back and Round Tables held at University of the Witwatersrand, Johannesburg, 21 April 2016.

Montmasson-Clair, G., 2012. *Green Economy Policy Framework and Employment Opportunity: A South African Case Study*. TIPS Working Paper No. 2012–02. Trade and Industrial Policy Strategies (TIPS), Pretoria.

Montmasson-Clair, G., 2015. *The Two Shall Become One: Overcoming the Stalemate Between Industrial and Climate Change Policies*. TIPS, Pretoria.

Montmasson-Clair, G., 2017a. *Governance for South Africa's Sustainability Transition: A Critical Review*. Trade & Industrial Policy Strategies and Green Economy Coalition, Pretoria and London.

Montmasson-Clair, G., 2017b. *Electricity Supply in South Africa: Path Dependency or Decarbonisation?* TIPS Policy Brief 02/2017. Trade & Industrial Policy Strategies, Pretoria.

Mthembi, F., 2015. Lost in Procurement: An Assessment of the Development Impact of the Renewable Energy Procurement Programme. In Mistra, 2015, *Earth, Wind and*

Fire: Unlocking the Political, Economic and Security Implications of Discourse on the Green Economy. MISTRA, Johannesburg.

Musvoto, C., Nortje K., De Wet, B., Mahumani, B.K. and Nahman, A., 2015. Imperatives for an Agricultural Green Economy in South Africa. *South African Journal of Science*, 111(1/2). Available at http://dx.doi.org/10.17159/sajs.2015/20140026 (accessed 17 January 2018).

Musyoki, A., 2012. *The Emerging Policy for Green Economy and Social Development in Limpopo, South Africa*. UNRISD Occasional Paper 8. UNRISD, Geneva.

National Planning Commission (NPC), 2012. *National Development Plan 2030: Our Future – Make It Work*. NPC, Pretoria.

NBI (National Business Initiative), 2016. *Business Action in Support of the NDP*. NBI, Parktown.

NBI, 2017. *CDP South Africa Climate Change 2017: Executive Summary*. NBI, Parktown.

Nhamo, G., 2013. Green Economy Readiness in South Africa: A Focus on the National Sphere of Government. *International Journal of African Renaissance Studies – Multi-, Inter- and Transdisciplinarity*, 8(1): 115–142.

Oelofse, C., Scott, D., Oelofse, D. and Houghton, J., 2006. Shifts Within Ecological Modernization in South Africa: Deliberation, Innovation and Institutional Opportunities. *Local Environment*, 11(1): 61–78.

OECD (Organisation for Economic Cooperation and Development), 2012. *Green Growth in Developing Countries – A Summary for Policymakers*. OECD, Paris.

OECD, 2013. *Environmental Performance Review: South Africa*. OECD, Paris.

OECD, 2015. *Towards Green Growth? Tracking Progress*. OECD, Paris.

PAGE (Partnership for Action on Green Economy), 2017. *Green Economy Inventory for South Africa: An Overview*. PAGE, Geneva.

Raworth, K., Wykes, S. and Bass, S., 2014. *Securing Social Justice in Green Economies: A Review and Ten Considerations for Policymakers*. IIED Issue Paper. IIED, London.

Renewable Energy Policy Network for the 21st Century (REN21), 2017. *Renewables 2016 Global Status Report*. REN, Paris.

Rennkamp, B., 2012. *Sustainable Development Planning in South Africa: A Case of Over-Strategizing?* Energy Research Centre, University of Cape Town, Rondebosch.

Republic of South Africa, 2009. Framework for South Africa's Response to the International Economic Crisis. NEDLAC, Johannesburg.

Rotmans, J., Kemp, R. and Van Asselt, M., 2001. More Evolution Than Revolution: Transition Management in Public Policy. *Foresight*, 3(1): 15–31.

SAFCEI, 2017. Judgement Made on the SA Government's Secret Trillion Rand Nuclear Court Case. *Polity*. Available at www.polity.org.za/article/safcei-judgement-made-on-the-sa-governments-secret-trillion-rand-nuclear-court-case-2017-04-26 (accessed 10 October 2017).

Scoones, I., Leach, M. and Newell, P., 2015. *The Politics of Green Transformations*. Routledge, Oxon.

Seekings, J., 2014. *South Africa: Democracy, Poverty and Inclusive Growth Since 1994*. CDE, Johannesburg.

Seeliger, L. and Turok, I., 2016. The Green Economy Accord: Launchpad for a Green Transition? In Swilling, M., Musango, J. and Wakeford, J. (eds.), *Greening the South African Economy: Scoping the Issues, Challenges and Opportunities*. UCT Press, Cape Town.

Smit, S. and Musango, J.K., 2015. Exploring the Connections Between Green Economy and Informal Economy in South Africa. *South African Journal of Science*, 111(11/12).

Swilling, M., Musango, J. and Wakeford, J., 2015. Developmental States and Sustainability Transitions: Prospects of a Just Transition in South Africa. *Journal of Environmental Policy & Planning*, DOI: 10.1080/1523908X.2015.1107716.

Taylor, W.A., Lindsey, P.A. and Davies-Mostert, H., 2015. *An Assessment of the Economic, Social and Conservation Value of the Wildlife Ranching Industry and its Potential to Support the Green Economy in South Africa*. The Endangered Wildlife Trust, Johannesburg.

UNEP (United Nations Environment Programme), 2011. *Towards a Green Economy: Pathways to Sustainable Development and Poverty Eradication. A Synthesis for Policy Makers*. UNEP, Nairobi.

UNEP, 2013. *Green Economy Modelling Report of South Africa – Focus on Natural Resource Management, Agriculture, Transport and Energy Sectors*. UNEP, Nairobi.

United Nations, 2012. *Report of the United Nations Conference on Sustainable Development*. Rio de Janeiro, Brazil 20–22 June 2012. United Nations, New York.

United Nations Economic Commission for Africa (UNECA), 2015. *Inclusive Green Growth in South Africa: Selected Case Studies*. UNECA, Addis Ababa.

United Nations Research Institute for Social Development (UNRISD), 2016. *Policy Innovations for Transformative Change: Summary*. UNRISD, Geneva.

Wits School of Governance, 2016. *Aligning the Sustainable Development Goals (SDGs) to the NDP: Towards Domestication of the SDGs in South Africa*. OR Tambo Debate Series 6. Wits School of Governance, Johannesburg.

World Bank, 2015. *Decarbonizing Development: Three Steps to a Zero-Carbon Future*. World Bank, Washington, DC.

Worthington, R., 2015. *Depending on Renewable Energy: South Africa's Best Development Path*. 350 Africa. Available at http://350africa.org/files/2015/07/RE-Report_web.pdf (accessed 13 October 2017).

WWF, 2012. *National Development Plan Overlooks Environmental Imperative*. 20 August 2012. Available at www.wwf.org.za/?6660/ndp-and-environment (accessed 13 October 2017).

6 Transitioning South Africa's finance system towards sustainability

Chantal Naidoo

Introduction

South Africa is not a homogeneous country and varieties of sustainability transitions are evident across and within national, provincial and local levels of government, including differences amongst actors and institutions within the country (Death, 2015). The financial system plays an important role in navigating such differences and can support the emergence of new development pathways, yet policymakers generally overlook its strategic role in achieving sustainable outcomes (Jeucken, 2001; Naidoo *et al.*, 2014). On the other hand, the financial system has historically been unaware of the motivation and pressures of transitioning to more sustainable development pathways *and* oblivious to the key role it can fulfil in achieving this (Jeucken, 2001). To be fair, these views have advanced as more financial institutions recognise that greening finance opens new market opportunities (Ramiah and Gregoriou, 2016). But doubt still exists about the pace, rate and scale of change within the financial system to support sustainability transitions. Only time will tell whether current efforts will facilitate the process of sustainability transitions, yet time is something the world does not have (Schmitz, 2015). In the timeless words of William Shakespeare (1602):

> "if money goes before, all paths do lie open"

which implies that unless money is put towards the process of sustainability transitions, transitions will not materialise or at best, would not result in transformative changes.

This chapter briefly outlines the global context of financing sustainability transitions, presents insights from academic literature and offers a historical background to South Africa's financial system and its structural challenges. The chapter draws on three examples which provide useful insights into the early learnings of finance mechanisms seeking to improve access to finance for individuals and small firms wanting to participate in South Africa's sustainability transition. They include (i) The Green Fund which is managed by the Development Bank of Southern Africa (DBSA) and (ii) South African National

Biodiversity Institute's (SANBI) role as a financial intermediary of international environmental funds. The third example highlights a potential blindspot in South Africa's financial system, that of inadequate access to finance for women. The chapter concludes with reflections on the country's journey to date and proposals for further work.

The global context – past and present

Economists such as Schumpeter believed that the financial system has the potential to drive radical and transformative changes in the economy (Schumpeter, 1911/1939 cited in Mathews, 2015; O'Sullivan, 2005). But what is this financial system and how does it operate? In 1864, Walter Bagehot described it as an organisation of credit which allocates finance amongst those with excess finances to those who require it (Bagehot cited in Spratt, 2009). Over 150 years later, this description remains useful as a basic textbook description, but now needs to take into account the connections between national and international systems that organise such credit flows. Regulations and industry standards govern risk allocation, protect providers and users of finance and maintain the

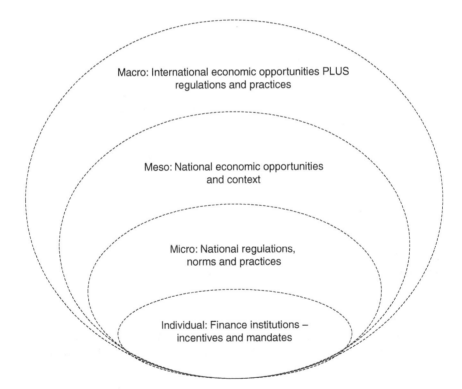

Figure 6.1 Nesting of financial institutions within national and international contexts.

Source: Author depiction.

stability of the financial system. Economic opportunities and performance determine the organisation and accessibility of credit. The guiding light of investment decisions by these individual financial institutions is maximising return and minimising risk. Such risks are largely measured against financial dimensions, that is, risk-adjusted rates of return per unit of lending or investment over a prescribed time period (Spratt, 2009). Figure 6.1 offers a view of the nesting of finance institutions within the micro, meso and macro context. While the nested positions influence the incentives and mandates of the finance institutions, it is important to recognise that these financial institutions have the power to significantly impact national and international economic and regulatory contexts, as the 2008 financial crisis demonstrated.

Environmental and social dimensions within the financial system were viewed as obstacles to investment in the early 1990s and therefore did not feature prominently as part of lending or investment decision-making (Jeucken, 2001). This view is changing as "green economy" and "green growth" paradigms are adopted as a response to global concerns of poor growth quality, loss of livelihoods and climate change. Seen in this light, these global shifts, as presented in earlier chapters of this book, represent new economic opportunities to create greener jobs and promote clean technologies (Stern, 2007; Death, 2014).

Sustainability transitions towards an inclusive economy are uncontested and common goals of multilateral processes led by the United Nations in recent years – in 2015 alone, the Paris Agreement on Climate Change, the Addis Ababa Action Agenda on Financing for Development and the Sustainable Development Goals 2015–2030 – were agreed upon. Embedded within these agreements is a central role for financial systems in achieving sustainable development and climate goals. Awareness efforts to "green" global and national financial systems, led by, amongst others, United Nations Environment and the G20 Green Finance Working Group, have escalated. "Green" finance is growing as a niche field, driven mainly by green and "climate-aligned" bond issuances – with US$895 billion issued by September 2017 (Climate Bonds Initiative, 2017). New "green" multilateral institutions such as the Green Climate Fund are growing in prominence while "green finance pacts" by insurers, pension funds, national and international development finance institutions are proliferating. Further evidence of the changing landscape is the 2017 Global Risks Report published by the World Economic Forum, which says failure to mitigate and adapt to climate change, the increased incidences of extreme weather events and water crises around the world are amongst the top five interconnected risks, linked to conflict and the migration of people (WEF, 2017a). Investment flows seems to be shifting too – as reported by Bloomberg New Energy Finance (BNEF), US$266 billion was invested in renewable energy in 2015, twice that of new coal investments for the same year (BNEF cited in WEF, 2017a).

There is much talk, some action – but is money flowing towards sustainability transitions at the scale and pace required? Let's explore – there is US$74 trillion managed by institutional investors globally, while only US$440 billion to

US$989 billion per year is needed to invest in sustainability transitions (UN, 2014). And only US$7 trillion per year is needed for climate smart investments (UN, 2015). The majority of required investment for sustainability transitions remains unfunded despite the availability of funds (Morel *et al.*, 2016). This funding gap may be attributed to poor investment incentives, unavailability of appropriate finance, low willingness to shift investment flows and insufficient public expenditure, or as some authors argue, despite finance being available, project pipelines are of poor investment quality (Foxon, 2015; Mazzucato, 2015; Volz *et al.*, 2015).

Efforts are currently focused on bridging the funding gap through niche financial products that crowds in new investors, especially the private sector and on divestment from fossil fuel industries. Niche "green financial instruments" create new asset classes which some authors argue are insufficient to impact the entire investment portfolio of asset managers (Mathews, 2015). Multilateral and bilateral development finance and specialist agencies also play an important role, especially in developing countries. Generally, however, most efforts lack a sense of "urgency" (Schmitz, 2015). Will the growing reality of economic, social and environmental breakdown in many countries shift the finance flows along the path of sustainability transitions?

Sustainability transitions and finance

The specific link between financial systems and sustainability transitions is not yet established in academic literature (O'Sullivan, 2005; Mazzucato, 2013; Mathews, 2015; Spratt, 2015). There are, however, studies which argue that well-functioning financial systems support economic development (Demirguc-Kunt and Levine, 2008 and Levine, 2005, both cited in Mohamed, 2014). Sustainability transitions however are about more than just economic development as environmental and social aspects are heightened priorities. In support of this distinction, Spratt (2015) argues that the financial system's response to sustainability transitions depends on the level of ambition of the green transformation process and the intensity of its social impacts, as illustrated in Table 6.1.

According to Spratt (2015), a "light green approach" focusing on sectoral reform (e.g. transport or energy) implies loan and equity for project financing with low interest in social impact. In comparison, "light green and red" and "dark green and red" approaches, such as those adopted by China, Ethiopia and Rwanda, require substantial restructuring of financial incentives and decision-making capabilities, new institutions and the inclusion of environmental and social risks as well as active divestment from fossil fuel industries. This is a useful framework to situate South Africa's sustainability transition process, which could be argued to fall within Spratt's (2015) "light green and red" quadrant. This positioning is based on the example of the renewable energy programme, which has a sectoral focus. This programme had social aspects that bidders needed to comply with, that is, emphasis on using local suppliers and

Table 6.1 Typologies of the intensity of green transformations and social impact

Intensity of social impact	Intensity of Green Transformation	
	Low	High
Low	**Light Green** Restructure of economic systems e.g. energy with zero/low interest in social issues – with "green growth" as a solution.	**Dark Green** Precautionary approach prioritising human quality of life, with low interest in social issues.
High	**Light Green & Red** Dominant approach to sustainable development in terms of income inequality and poverty with concern for environment.	**Dark Green & Red** Precautionary approach combined with interest in income distribution and wealth.

Source: Adapted from Spratt (2015).

manufacturers where possible, and the inclusion of previously disadvantaged communities as beneficiaries of the programme. The domestic financial system, as stated in this chapter, was able to support the majority of investment, including the participation of previously disadvantaged individuals and communities. Their support however has come under criticism as favouring larger investors at the expense of the programme's social objectives (Baker, 2015).

What types of finance are necessary to support sustainability transitions? The financial system is not homogeneous – it is made up of different actors that offer different types of finance and would interpret the new economic opportunities offered by sustainability transitions based on their risk–return perceptions. The implication of this is that the type of finance available to support sustainability transitions is dependent on the financial actors within that financial system (Spratt, 2015; Mazzucato and Semieniuk, 2018). We could argue that a particular "quality" of finance is necessary for sustainability transitions such as first, longer-term and more patient capital applied towards, for example, project development, early stage investment and capacity building (skills, policies); second, short-term funding in the form of working capital; and third, ensuring broad and diverse access to finance to facilitate the social aspects of the sustainability transition, especially for marginalised groups (Mazzucato, 2013; Spratt, 2015; Naidoo, 2018). Some aspects of sustainability transitions are difficult to finance, especially for developing countries such as the prototyping, research and development, and commercialisation of new technologies and concepts. In this regard, multilateral and bilateral development agencies – in partnership with government and the private sector, can help to finance technical assistance (Mazzucato, 2015).

During the "transition period" policymakers need to break down the practices and norms linked to the old system, while simultaneously nurturing new "greener" systems (Voß *et al.*, 2009). This is a key feature of transitions management, also discussed in Chapter 5 with reference to the need for system innovation while concomitantly undertaking system improvements. This destabilising "transition" period may place new demands on the financial system that challenge the "status quo" (Naidoo, 2018). Can the South African financial system respond to the demands of sustainability transitions?

The South African finance system – past and present

The foundation of South Africa's financial system was laid by its colonial and apartheid legacy, which created institutions and practices that served the ruling party interests of the time (Mohamed, 2014; Verhoef, 2009). Initially dominated by British-owned banks, the discovery of gold, diamonds and other precious minerals led to the emergence of imperial banks to support British business and settler interests (Mohamed, 2014). These mineral discoveries made South Africa an attractive destination for European capital and British institutional investors who sought assurance that their investments were secure (Kubicek, 1979; Mohamed, 2014). Five imperial banks entered South Africa in the nineteenth century – each bringing with them strong banking practices and norms developed in England to ensure the stability and protection of British investors (Jones, 1996). By the time the Union of South Africa was formed in 1910, these imperial banks dominated the banking sector. As the Afrikaner nationalist movements grew in strength, by 1948 new institutions had emerged, such as Sanlam and the Volkskas Bank, to support the business interests and households of the Afrikaners (Fine and Rustomjee, 1996; Mohamed, 2014;). Although banking deregulation since the mid-1980s aimed to reduce the concentration of the banking sector, it only served to liberalise the market operations. The 90 per cent of banking assets held by a few banks in 1910 is still the case in present day South Africa (Verhoef, 2009).

South Africa's financial system is viewed as a mature and well-regulated banking sector with deep capital markets guided by prudent and conservative regulation that meets international standards (Naidoo and Goldstuck, 2016a and 2016b). The banking sector has high levels of institutional concentration with six banks holding 90 per cent of banking assets and an insurance industry equally dominated by four large companies (OECD, 2017). Other non-bank lenders also play a role in allocating resources, including institutional investors, private equity firms, development finance institutions and the Public Investment Corporation. This depth of financial institutions and expertise supports South Africa's ranking as the most innovative financial system in the region (WEF, 2017b). The country has also made efforts to redress its apartheid legacy through the Financial Sector Charter, introduced in 2004, which supports increased access to finance for previously disadvantaged South Africans. Its content is seen as innovative but there are lessons to be extracted from the challenging process of the mainstreaming of social issues into the banking sector (Naidoo and Goldstuck, 2016a).

South Africa is, in principle, able to mobilise significant domestic resources for its sustainability transition. This is best demonstrated by the financing of the country's renewable energy programme, valued at R201.8 billion between 2011 and 2016, of which 76 per cent was funded by domestic investors and 24 per cent by foreign investors (IPP, 2017). South Africa has two major development finance institutions that support investment in industrial development and infrastructure. The Industrial Development Corporation committed R25 billion to financing green industries over a three-year period up to 2015 and the Development Bank of Southern Africa (DBSA) commited R20 to R30 billion over the same period for green energy projects. Since these commitments were made, both institutions have significantly contributed to South Africa's renewable energy investment programme.

Importantly, direct and indirect allocations in the national budget have played an important role in financing the country's sustainability transition. Preliminary work in 2013 by the National Treasury and DBSA suggests that between R14.7 billion and R18.7 billion were allocated towards environmental objectives within the national budget for 2012/2013, including allocations for climate, transport, water, sanitation and environmental protection (Hemraj, 2012 and Naidoo, 2012, both cited in Montmasson-Clair, 2013). Although South Africa benefits from official development assistance, this historically only accounts for 1 per cent of the government budget (OECD, 2011). In the context of international multilateral funds supporting environment and climate issues, South Africa has benefited from the Global Environment Facility, Clean Technology Fund, Adaptation Fund, and the Green Climate Fund.

Progress towards financing South Africa's sustainability transition

There are promising features within the South African financial system that support future investment in sustainable development and climate action. These include new investment principles introduced in 2011 under revisions to Regulation 28 of the Pensions Fund Act ("Regulation 28"). These revisions were motivated by the 2008 financial crisis and intended to encourage investors to shift from short to longer-term investment horizons. Amongst the revisions is the need for funds to understand the environmental, social and governance characteristics of all investments being made. Supporting Regulation 28 are industry guidelines which may be voluntarily adopted – the Code for Responsible Investing in South Africa (CRISA), which encourages institutional investors to develop sustainability policies and considerations in their investment analysis and activities. These soft regulatory and governance measures have raised awareness and enhanced reporting standards amongst investors, however capital allocations are still not shifting decisively towards sustainable alternatives (Naidoo and Goldstuck, 2016b).

The King III Code on Corporate Governance was adopted in March 2010 and required listed companies to integrate sustainability and financial reporting into a single annual report – reflecting companies' contributions to economic, social and environmental challenges in South Africa. Integrated financial and sustainability reporting by listed companies improves the transparency of listed companies' efforts and complements the efforts by the Johannesburg Stock Exchange's Social Responsibility Investment Index. This exchange was launched in 2004 to highlight companies that integrate a focus on environment, social and governance in their business operations. Active engagement in sustainable development and climate policy is facilitated through, amongst others, the Banking Association of South Africa and National Business Initiative. For example, the National Business Initiative, supported by a grant from The Green Fund, ran an action learning project bringing together policymakers, project developers and financiers to define and understand the variables involved in setting policy priorities for greening South Africa's economy (Nichols *et al.*, 2016).

From a policy perspective, the National Climate Change Response Policy (2011) commits to a series of eight actions to enhance participation and partnership within the financial system in South Africa (DEA, 2011). These actions were meant to be addressed over the short, medium and longer term and include (i) contributing to multilateral debates and reforms to secure funding for the region; (ii) attracting new sources of international assistance; (iii) creating tracking mechanisms for finance; (iv) forging domestic funding partnerships; and (v) designing a long-term national financing strategy to ensure a sustained transition. While some of these policy proposals are in progress, some are yet to be activated, in particular the longer-term financing issues (Montmasson-Clair, 2013; Mughogho, 2017).

What does South Africa's financial system need to support the sustainability transition process?

Observations from surveys amongst financial actors in South Africa conducted in 2007, 2011 and 2016 show that there has been a progressive shift in the understanding of environmental, social and governance factors within the financial system. The survey of 2007 aimed to understand the awareness levels amongst investment practitioners of environmental, social and governance considerations in their investment decision-making and to determine the future prospects for "responsible investment" in South Africa. The results showed that although most regarded environmental, social and governance factors as marginally material, this view was not reflected in their investment allocations. The barrier to investments cited at the time was lack of demand from their institutional and retail customers, which more legislation could potentially unlock (UN, 2007).

A 2011 survey involving the public and private financial institutions that informed the National Climate Change Response Policy (Van Zyl *et al.*, 2011) identified three critical barriers limiting investment in sustainability transitions. These were (i) the lack of a long-term policy framework and legislation which creates uncertainty for investors; (ii) a poor regulatory environment for approving and implementing untested technologies, which limits new investment and innovation; and (iii) the lack of consumer understanding of benefits of green/climate-friendly products and services. Financial stakeholders were also asked to identify what role they could play in the country's sustainability transition process. The survey showed that, in 2011, banks, insurers and development finance institutions in South Africa were aware of challenges of sustainable development and climate action, but were restricted in their ability to act voluntarily and required clear policy signals from government. The responses to this survey was high amongst the four major banks and the country's development institutions, yet the microfinance institutions did not participate. Their absence at the time reflects low recognition of the economic opportunities for small and medium-sized businesses in sustainability transitions. By comparison, a 2016 survey identifies a heightened consciousness amongst institutional investors and banks with suggestions from such investors to promote their engagement – these include (i) strengthening the fiduciary duty of financiers; (ii) packaging by government of green project pipelines and facilities; (iii) new models to quantify environmental and social risks; (iv) developing frameworks for lender liability; (v) instituting reforms for unlisted assets; and (vi) creating a common vision for a sustainable finance system (Naidoo and Goldstuck, 2016b).

The 2007, 2011 and 2016 surveys show a progression in understanding of investors from being marginally aware of the importance of environmental, social and governance factors (2007) to appreciating that existing investment practices are insufficient to promote sustainability transitions (2016). This positive trajectory may have been influenced by the investment experience of the Department of Energy's renewable energy programme and bodes well for the future.

What are the structural challenges to financing sustainability transitions in South Africa?

Despite these positive signals, there are still structural challenges within the financial system to overcome. South Africa has a concentrated banking sector (i.e. a few large banks) which generally means that firms (especially small and medium sized) have low access to financial services (Beck *et al.*, 2009). Therefore, broadening the country's access to finance should be a major priority (OECD, 2017). Failure to address this challenge implies inadequate access to finance for smaller firms and the risk that the sustainability transition benefits some but not all firms and individuals. South Africa also lacks, in its private banking sector, a market standard-bearer that focuses on access to finance for women. Positive developments to broaden access of finance are new online banks and crowdfunding platforms to support small and medium-sized businesses and entrepreneurs.

The banking sector is highly interconnected with non-banking lenders (i.e. "shadow banking") including informal saving schemes such as community banks and stokvels, which means that instability in one part of the system will impact all other lenders in the system (Kemp, 2017). While the non-bank lenders broaden financing sources and lower the cost of funding through increased competition amongst lenders, left unregulated the risk for financial instability remains high (Kemp, 2017). The imminent changes in regulation in the country, led by the Reserve Bank, may address these risks (OECD, 2017).

South African banks are criticised as operating on the same basis as those in developed countries – where they speculate on their financial assets to increase their income (i.e. 'financialisation') versus increasing lending volumes to deliver real economy outcomes (Mohamed, 2014). This raises a few questions – what role should South African banks play in advancing sustainability transitions in South Africa? To what extent can financialisation trends be reversed or regulated? The latter question may be addressed through imminent Reserve Bank regulations (OECD, 2017). There are innovative examples to draw from, showing that some banks are actively engaged in responding to government's long-term development goals. One such example is Nedbank which, since 2015, is piloting its Fairshare 2030 Programme. This initiative is designed to invest in the future of the environment, society and their business, targeting new lending of R6 billion from 2015 to 2030 towards long-term development goals and in sectors of relevance for sustainability transitions (Nedbank, 2016).

In summary, the extent to which the South African financial system, including its public finances, is fit for purpose to support sustainability transitions will determine the depth, scale and pace of the country's transition. Ongoing work by the National Treasury's Green Finance Working Group to assess sustainable finance in South Africa will help shape a vision on how the financial system in South Africa can evolve to achieve this transition. This will be an important development to watch. For the time being, a focus on broadening access to finance is an important priority.

Case studies: finance interventions to support South Africa's sustainability transitions

This section presents examples of financing mechanisms and institutional arrangements in South Africa that are supporting its process of sustainability transitions. The first case outlines the formation and early experiences of the national Green Fund, designed to catalyse investment in a "green economy". The second example describes SANBI's role in mobilising international finance mechanisms to promote climate resilience and social inclusivity, while the third example highlights the risk that women may be left behind in South Africa's sustainability transition as no significant efforts are being made towards their inclusion. The section concludes with reflections on each example in the context of South Africa's financial system.

Case study – The Green Fund: designed for "learning by doing"

The Green Economy Summit in May 2010 identified a need to demonstrate what is meant by "green economy". In response, the Department of Environmental

Affairs (DEA) issued a call to determine the level of public interest in "green projects" – the response was overwhelming with over 300 proponents offering ideas on renewable energy, energy efficiency, waste management, water, transport, natural resource management and the built environment. Followed by a series of focus groups in August 2010, interest in government-led "green economy programmes" was firmly established and the need for specific public budget allocations was expressed. In 2011, the national budget assigned R800 million to the DEA to establish a national Green Fund, subsequently increased to R1.195 billion for use up until 31 March 2019 (National Treasury, 2011). The DEA, the National Treasury and the DBSA worked together to design and operationalise The Green Fund by 2012.

Box 6.1 Learnings from South Africa's Green Fund

The establishment of a dedicated national Green Fund came at an opportune time in South Africa's history – it coincided with a period during which the DEA was advancing the implementation of green economy projects, which built upon legacy projects and event greening projects that emerged after the successful hosting of a low-carbon FIFA World Cup in 2010. The Green Fund was designed to promote investment through appropriate financial support and attract additional funders, particularly from the private sector, and international development assistance. It was also designed to offer policy feedback to inform government's future policies and programmes on the green economy, climate and sustainable development. The Fund also sought to support research, development and innovation, and capacity development. These objectives are reflected in the capital allocation of its three functional areas, being:

- *Green Investment*: 75 per cent for green projects and programmes, either as non-recoverable grants, recoverable grants or as concessional loans (up to 4 per cent less the market-based rate);
- *Capacity building*: 20 per cent for capacity building in green initiatives through grants; and
- *Policy and research development*: 5 per cent for policy and research development grants.

The target beneficiaries of The Green Fund are inclusive of small to medium-sized businesses, and policy and research institutions who responded to specific calls for proposal by The Green Fund. A total of 55 projects were approved across these functional areas: investment (31), capacity development (8) and research and development (16). Most of these projects are active, and several have been completed (mainly research and policy). The portfolio is valued at R679.8 million.

An unpublished impact evaluation, commissioned by the DEA, of ten of the investment projects currently under implementation, indicate that all projects contributed positively in pursuing the green economy agenda and demonstrating low-carbon development options (DEA, 2017). Development gains include approximately 24.5 tonnes of recyclables diverted from landfill and sold for re-use, 6,981 individuals being trained, 6,620 direct new jobs created and 21,230 hectares of land restored. These early results uphold the objectives of The Green Fund: to harness ideas, contribute to development in different parts of the country, encourage job creation, grow South Africa's green economy through experience and knowledge and identify replication opportunities through new financing partners.

The impact evaluation considered the degree of change before and after implementation of the projects. The ten projects predictably reflected a gap between expecations at approval when compared to delivery during implementation. The gap was due to the short timespan since implementation, low ability to monitor transformation and the implementation capacities of the proponents. Certain projects – despite challenging socio-economic contexts and implementation conditions have resulted in major shifts towards sustainability, that is, farming fish in the Karoo, creating a profession for shepherds, solar power supply to informal settlements and waste generation from abattoir waste. Amongst the success factors of these projects are that they "made economic, social and environmental" sense, received access to appropriate finance from The Green Fund, and saw committed project proponents and communities working together.

Further important impacts of The Green Fund identified by the impact study include:

- Job creation and capacity development, especially in communities where pilot projects led to localised economic diversification and where there were new opportunities for skills development and sector growth;
- Amplification of the awareness of a diversified "green" skills base, needed to support sustainability interventions across sectors and within industries, supporting industry bodies and strengthening institutional capacity.
- Development of new insights into the development of a domestic green economy, ranging from new market concepts to strategic assessments aimed at influencing policy and investment, bridging an important research funding gap.

According to the DEA, The Green Fund's future positioning needs to evolve from these early experiences. Priorities for change include (i) attracting external development partners and private investors, which was not possible due to its legal status as a programme within the Ministry for Environmental Affairs; (ii) "buying down" risk of national projects and securing an adequate return on its investment; (iii) creating a transparent governance structure focused on generating a strong pipeline of bankable projects, preferably at scale to attract potential investors; (iv) applying strong monitoring and evaluation systems; and finally, (v) diversifying its product and services to ensure future financial self-sustainability of The Green Fund (e.g. possibility of adding senior and subordinated loans and equity).

Source: Jenitha Badul and Michelle Layte

Reflections on The Green Fund's impact

The Green Fund shone light on a "blindspot" in the South African financial system that was not fully apparent in 2010 when the DEA issued its call for green economy projects and programmes. Such projects were not on the investment horizon of the major banks at the time. It is clear from the impact study that the majority of the projects supported by The Green Fund to date would not have been financed. The structural barriers to the South African financial system, mentioned above, offer insight into why this may have been the case. The higher concentrated banking sector means that medium and small projects in general have limited access to affordable finance; new "projects" have high opportunity costs which may mean higher risk profiles (untested technologies, new entrants with limited track record); and further, uncertainty on the returns that may be derived relative to "business as usual" projects. Taking these factors into account, the South African government, through its Green Fund, could be viewed as an "entrepreneur" (Mazzucato, 2013) – stimulating new green markets, offering appropriate finance, facilitating partnerships to unlock co-financing and promoting policy and research to better understand the green project requirements. The impact of entrepreneurial ventures is not usually visible in the short term – yet The Green Fund through its thematic programmes has demonstrated how to catalyse and create demand for green economy projects, promote the uptake of new and emerging technologies, and support research and development alongside capacity development. The longer-term benefits from The Green Fund's role in South Africa's sustainability transition will unfold as the projects mature and offer further learnings. The process of sustainability transitions is strongly focused on "learning by doing" (iterative, uncertain, testing new concepts and entrants/institutions). This means that both the successes and failures of The Green Fund are important for its learning and future positioning and also highlights the need to design metrics to measure impact over the short, medium and longer term.

Now that the initial funding period for The Green Fund is nearing its conclusion, is the financing support it provides still necessary? The Green Fund played a significant role in breaking ground in collaboration with certain private and other financing partners. It can build on these learnings to ensure that the sustainability transition gathers momentum. The effectiveness of the next phase of The Green Fund's contribution can be enhanced if the current and future needs of "green economy" projects and programmes are defined. This would ensure that The Green Fund is significantly distinguishable from other sources of funding in the country, and is well positioned to harness other international environment and climate funds, broadening access to the private sector – including small and medium-sized businesses.

Case study – SANBI: *a financial intermediary of international environment and climate mechanisms*

South Africa's annual adaptation investment and planning costs are estimated to be between US$3.8 billion and US$29.9 billion between 2021 and 2050 for water, forestry, energy, agriculture, biodiversity and disaster risk reduction (DEA, 2015). Some sectors requiring adaptation support such as energy, mining, public infrastructure and transport have not yet been costed. Although the demand for funds for resilience and adaptation efforts in South Africa is significant, the impact on poor and marginalised communities is not fully accounted for. Project development for adaptation and resilience can only happen at a community level, through participatory vulnerability assessments and co-developing associated response strategies. Projects are mainly community-led, requiring extensive stakeholder engagement and access to grants and technical assistance for implementation, as they do not yield immediate financial returns that can be serviced through debt or equity. These are amongst the issues being considered in the national adaptation strategy under development by the DEA.

As a national entity, SANBI supports the Department's adaptation efforts by focusing on projects in areas and communities where it is difficult for private finance to be engaged. SANBI has achieved this through accessing finance from various sources, including international environment and climate funds. Until recently, such funds were only accessible to developing countries through multilateral agencies such as the United Nations Development Programme or the World Bank. To access these funds directly, entities are required to undergo a rigorous due diligence process after which they are then "accredited" to serve as the financial intermediary of a particular fund. This example explores SANBI's experience as a national financial intermediary of the Adaptation Fund and Green Climate Fund, both of which offer technical assistance through concessional loans and grants to developing countries for climate and environment programmes.

Box 6.2 How a national financial intermediary enhances the impact of international funds

Although formally established in 2004, SANBI's origins date back to 1989. The institute was established to conserve and study South Africa's diverse fauna and flora, through research and policy support in partnership with other stakeholders. Since 2002, SANBI has been executing a project portfolio in excess of US$30 million, with the Global Environment Facility, United Nations Development Programme and the World Bank as intermediaries. These projects primarily focus on management, conservation and restoration of biodiversity, and the policy and regulatory systems necessary to support these efforts. The locations of the projects were mainly in underserviced and vulnerable rural locations. The experience gained from these projects built institutional capacity within SANBI to expand its project development and implementation roles. Such capacity prepared SANBI to successfully apply and be appointed as a national accredited entity of the Adaptation Fund (in 2011) and Green Climate Fund (in 2016) at the request of the Minister of Environment.

In setting up the Adaptation Fund, SANBI harnessed the institution's long traditions of extensive stakeholder engagement, participatory approaches to programme development, inclusive and diverse governance structures and transparent project prioritisation criteria. Proposals presented to the Adaptation Fund through SANBI would thus reflect the most urgent and pressing needs within the identified communities. SANBI also developed a unique investment framework for

Adaptation Fund projects. This framework adapts international funds for local use by embedding South Africa's national development objectives of job creation, gender, marginalised communities and geographic balance directly into investment criteria. A National Steering Committee supports SANBI's work programme. The investment framework was put into practice in developing SANBI's application to the Adaptation Fund – which led to the Fund successfully raising US$10 million to deliver local adaptation responses within the context of local government development priorities. The impact of this financial support is significant as it allows for mainstreaming climate change in the development programmes of the district municipalities where these projects are located. These impacts include:

- Building individual capacities of officials to practically integrate climate change into different sectors
- Catalysing partnerships amongst officials from different sectors and line departments that can identify and consider the multiple stressors influencing local level vulnerabilities
- Building high-level support to address climate change within municipal and service delivery programmes
- Providing an evidence base that shows how international funds are useful to support future local level interventions

SANBI was accredited to the Green Climate Fund in 2016, for grant-based projects of up to US$50 million. This level of accreditation is a major boost to financing adaptation interventions in South Africa, especially for those projects reliant upon grant funding. It increases SANBI's capacity to support adaptation and resilience five-fold, allowing it to develop a work programme more closely aligned to South Africa's national adaptation priorities.

SANBI is one of two financial intermediaries to the Green Climate Fund in South Africa, the other is the Development Bank of Southern Africa, which is also accredited to the Global Environment Facility. SANBI intends to focus only on the grant-based programmes, and will work synergistically with other financial intermediaries on projects requiring other forms of finance.

SANBI actively engages with a wider community of financial intermediaries from other developing countries to enhance developing country agency and capacity by exchanging common challenges and aspirations, tools and approaches.

Source: Mandy Barnett

Reflections on SANBI's experience as a national intermediary

International environment and climate funds such as the Green Climate Fund, Global Environment Facility and Adaptation Fund are useful to bridge funding gaps in the financial system. However, certain preconditions exist for such funding to be used effectively so that they have longer-term impacts, beyond the support of individual programmes. SANBI's process of engagement as a financial intermediary to international funds illustrates how such funds can be used more strategically. The deliberate planning, engagement and design processes it embarked on ensured that the national and local government prior-ities are embedded within the investment criteria of these funds. SANBI, as a national finance intermediary, effectively "localised" international funds, signifi-cantly enhancing the quality of the programmes and projects for which it sought finance. Poor quality project pipelines is cited as one of the reasons for funding gaps – SANBI is addressing this upfront through its investment framework, par-ticipatory community engagement, integration of development and climate, and transparent governance structures. These processes support the capacities neces-sary for a long-term sustainability transition. This strategic consideration of how to utilise international assistance within the national financial system is already increasing the effort, rigour and focus of South Africa's climate change response programme in anticipation of future investments. This should be extended to private finance institutions to develop a co-financing strategy so that public, private and international assistance can be effectively deployed towards funding the country's climate response strategies.

As a financial intermediary of international funds, SANBI should be guided by a clearly articulated vision for South Africa's sustainability transition. To enhance the effectiveness and impact of international finance though, South Africa would need to consider a few critical questions. The response to these questions can identify the range of programmes and projects necessary for its transition, costing and selection of ideal implementation partners:

- What are the future political, economic, social, technological, organisa-tional, legal, and environmental systems necessary for its sustainability transition?
- What types of institutions, arrangements and capacities are needed to create these systems?
- Who are the important actors in the future systems, and how can their capacity to participate be built?

Although South Africa has a mature and diverse financial system, it also has structural barriers and funding blindspots that threaten the financial inclusivity of its sustainability transition. While all forms of finance are not able to act in the same way, a financing strategy that articulates the optimal use of inter-national funds informed by the funding gaps in the national financial system would be very helpful. This would also benefit the private finance institutions in defining their own place in supporting the country's sustainability transition, and especially its adaptation and resilience efforts.

Case study – financial inclusion of women in sustainability transitions

Financial inclusion can be described as "a state in which all working age adults have effective access to credit, savings, payments and insurance from formal service providers" (AFI, 2015, p. 2). Effective access in this context means that such services should be delivered conveniently, responsibly and at an afford-able cost (CGAP, 2011). With over 80 per cent of its adult population holding an account at a formal financial institution (Fanta and Mutsonziwa, 2016), South Africa is considered to have a high degree of financial inclusion. Yet the numbers tell a different story – only 20 per cent of women have active bank accounts, 54 per cent are excluded from credit and 65 per cent are excluded from savings strands (Fanta and Mutsonziwa, 2016). In the case of men, only 40 per cent hold active bank accounts, 54 per cent are excluded from credit and 63 per cent excluded from savings strands. The numbers also show that financial institutions are not the major source of funding, especially for informal small and medium-sized enterprises; of the total 1,517 registered enterprises with sales under R1 million, over 44.6 per cent are run by women. Funding sources are mainly savings from their own resources (72 per cent) and limited support from non-bank lending through stokvels (Stats SA, 2013). Several reasons are cited why women face barriers in accessing finance for their businesses, including insecure land rights, discriminatory societal and custom-ary practices, and a lack of knowledge and the practices of financial institutions (AfDB, 2015).

Based on this background, what are the chances that women in South Africa will be able to actively participate in the new economic opportunities offered by the process of sustainability transitions? What implications does this have for a financially inclusive transition? This section of the chapter describes initiatives in South Africa that have emerged in response to the barriers faced by women in accessing finance through traditional banking channels.

Box 6.3 Actions to improve access to finance for women in South Africa

Financial institutions have practices that present barriers to the inclusion of women, according to the Alliance for Financial Inclusion. These barriers include (i) lack of gender-disaggregated data which means that gender-specific products and services are difficult to design, (ii) risk aversion by banks to lend to smaller enterprises (most commonly run by women), (iii) complexity of financial terms, and (iv) maladapted service delivery in terms of the interface between women and bank staff (AFI, 2015). The discussion below examines how these barriers are being responded to in the South African context:

  (i) *Lack of gender-disaggregated data and market response:* "First for Women" is a short-term insurance company established in 2004, developing products and services for women, including business insurance. The company applies a gender-lens to its business model based on empirical evidence that women are statistically-proven to be safer drivers than men, taking fewer risks, making claims less often than men and at lower claim values. The First for Women's business model supports findings in other countries, which shows that financial products and services can be tailored for women and women-led enterprises through gender-disaggregated data (GBA, 2014).

(ii) *Risk aversion of banks:* Small to medium-sized businesses have higher collateral (i.e. assets that can offset losses in the event of loan default) requirements due to perceived risks of higher business failure rates when compared
to larger enterprises. This creates a funding gap that non-bank lenders such
as Cooperative Financial Institutions can bridge by broadening access to
finance. Through a membership-based banking model, they offer loans to
members based on deposits received from members on flexible terms and at
lower interest rates than banks (Genesis, 2013). Despite relatively small
deposits of R233.8 million (CBDA, 2016) compared to R3,451.7 million
held by banks in February 2015 (SARB, 2015), they support an underserv-
iced market segment which requires smaller-sized loans.
(iii) *Complexity of financial terms:* Financial knowledge measured in terms of
"financial literacy" for women in South Africa was 57.2 per cent and 58.9 per
cent for men (OECD, 2013). In response, Sector Education Training Authorities have been created to raise awareness amongst consumers, and support
financial literacy training programmes funded by corporate payroll deduc-
tions, corporate social responsibility programmes and industry-level initiatives. While useful, these efforts are inadequate as certain aspects of financial
literacy are dependent on macro-economic factors, that is, the ability to exercise financial control over their affairs and future financial planning (Struwig
and Gordon, 2016). These aspects mean that current efforts are unlikely to
increase financial literacy levels amongst women and women-led enterprises.
(iv) *Maladapted financial service delivery:* The company, Business Partners is partly
owned by the South African government and supports women enterprises
through its Women in Business Fund. The service offering to women includes
no minimum contribution from its clients, access to a female investment
team to support the loan application process, information and networking
opportunities, access to a web-based library and electronic newsletters, mentorship, networking and seminars, and technical assistance grants. The
Women in Business Fund demonstrates the findings of the Global Banking
Alliance for Women, namely that women clients require accessible collateral
and unbiased loan decisions, linkages to buyers/markets, financial information and product understanding, and networking through peer-to-peer collaboration and mentoring (GBA, 2014).

Source: Malango Mughogho

Reflections on ensuring the financial inclusion of women

These examples show that the barriers faced by women in accessing finance are
partly being responded to within the South African financial system. Business
models have arisen in response to financing gaps and using gender-disaggregated
data to develop market-based strategies that ensure women are included in the
economy. The growth of Cooperative Financial Institutions and specialist funds
allows small and micro women-led businesses to participate in the economy,
while financial literacy efforts build knowledge and awareness. Amongst the
four major banks in South Africa, there are incubator programmes to support
women-led businesses, specialist women funds and hosting of annual events to

honour women in specific industries, while amongst the development finance institutions, the Industrial Development Corporation tripled its loan approvals to "women-empowered" businesses in 2017. These are encouraging foundations on which the financial inclusion of women in South Africa's sustainability transition can be built.

Females account for 51 per cent of South Africa's 56.5 million population at present (Stats SA, 2017), so ensuring that these efforts are scaled up to include women entrepreneurs in sustainability transitions, particularly those building small and micro enterprises, is critical. Some reflections would be necessary by the South African financial system and government: What can be done to increase access to appropriate finance for women to enable them to participate in the country's sustainability transition? What types of regulation and governance can be embedded within the banking and institutional funds to ensure representation of women in investment allocations? The responses to these questions will be important to ensure a financially inclusive transition that supports the participation of women and women-led enterprises.

Furthering progress

The extent to which the South African financial system, including its public finances, is fit for purpose to support sustainability transitions will determine the depth, scale and pace of the country's transition. South Africa has strong financial foundations due to a mature and sophisticated financial system with many useful features and initiatives that could promote the sustainability transition processes. New governance measures, regulatory requirements, policy responses and financing mechanisms have emerged from within government and the private sector as described in this chapter. There is a growing awareness and responsiveness amongst financial actors since 2007 to account for environmental, social and governance factors in their investment allocations. What is less certain is whether these raised awareness levels are translating to a redirection of finance flows. Despite the positive foundations, financial inclusion remains a concern, particularly ensuring that women and smaller businesses benefit from the new opportunities offered by sustainability transitions. Although the case studies demonstrate strong efforts through gender-informed products and services and The Green Fund, these efforts lack scale as they are not embedded within the financial system.

Finance institutions both act and are acted upon by international and national influences (see Figure 6.1 of this chapter). Theoretically, this implies that government actions should encourage other financial actors to participate in new economic areas. The chapter describes how The Green Fund pioneered access to finance for new green sectors, especially smaller businesses, and secured access to international assistance for rural adaptation interventions. In addition, government created dedicated institutional support for the renewable energy sector. In furthering progress, two questions arise here: first, what additional actions may be necessary by government to encourage a financially inclusive transition; and second, with government having laid the initial foundations, to what extent will private finance institutions organically respond to the (financing) needs of South Africa's sustainability transition? A frank conversation amongst the financial actors may be useful, based on existing learnings.

As a developing country, South Africa is eligible to access international climate and environment funds. Can these funds be strategically deployed to maximise their national relevance and impact? The SANBI case study provides a useful example of how this may be achieved. Aligning international assistance to bridge domestic funding gaps offers a useful example to build on in the development of a national financing strategy for sustainability transitions. This strategy should define roles for each of the financial actors within the financial system and identify the optimal use of international development funds to complement national sources. This was one of the objectives of the National Climate Change Response Policy (DEA, 2011) and remains relevant.

Further work is needed to correlate the financial needs of South Africa's sustainability transition process with the intensity and degree of transformation that the country is aiming for. This raises questions – is the South African financial system compatible with the government's vision and policies on sustainability transition? What needs to change in this system? Can it change? What would it take to change? These are areas for future research. Since South Africa is part of a globalised financial system, there are elements that depend on international developments, but the country should not tarry in doing whatever remains within the national realm of control.

This chapter reflects on a journey in progress, there is a long road of learning ahead of learning through uncertain and iterative processes that will test the mettle, responsiveness and resilience of the country's financial system and policymakers. It is a story that is still being written as with many other countries, time is a good teacher as long as we choose to learn.

Acknowledgements

I would like to gratefully acknowledge the case study contributions by Dr. Jenitha Badul, Dr. Mandy Barnett, Michelle Layte and Malango Mughogho.

References

AfDB, 2015. *Empowering African Women: An Agenda for Action*. Cote d'Ivoire: African Development Bank Group.

AFI, 2015. *Managing the Twin Responsibilities of Financial Inclusion and Financial Stability*. Alliance for Financial Inclusion, Issue 2.

Baker, L., 2015. The Evolving Role of Finance in South Africa's Renewable Energy Sector. *Geoforum*, Volume 64, pp. 146–156.

Beck, T., Demirguc-Kunt, A. and Peria, M., 2009. Bank Financing for SMEs: Evidence Across Countries and Ownership Types. *Journal of Financial Services Research*, Volume 39, Issue 1, pp. 35–54.

CBDA, 2016. *2016 Annual Report*. Cooperative Banks Development Agency. Pretoria.

CGAP, 2011. *Global Standard Setting Bodies and Financial Inclusion for the Poor*. Global Partnership for Financial Inclusion.

Climate Bonds Initiative, 2017. *Bonds and Climate Change: The State of the Market 2017*. Climate Bonds Initiative.

Death, C., 2015. Four Discourses of the Green Economy in the Global South. *Third World Quarterly*, Volume 36, Issue 12, pp. 2207–2224.

DEA (Department of Environmental Affairs), 2011. *National Climate Change Response Policy*. Pretoria: Department of Environmental Affairs.

DEA, 2015. *South Africa's Intended Nationally Determined Contributions*. Pretoria: Department of Environmental Affairs.

DEA, 2017. *Green Fund Impact Study Technical Report*. Department of Environmental Affairs. (unpublished).

Fanta, A.B. and Mutsonziwa, K., 2016. *Gender and Financial Inclusion: Analysis of Financial Inclusion of Women in the SADC Region*. FinMark Trust.

Fine, B. and Rustomjee, Z., 1996. *The Political Economy of South Africa: From Minerals-Energy Complex to Industrialisation*. Boulder, CO: Westview Press.

Foxon, T.J., 2015. Transition Pathways for a UK Low Carbon Electricity Future. *Energy Policy*, Volume 52, pp. 10–24.

GBA, 2014. *How Banks can Profit from the Multi-Trillion Female Economy*. Global Banking Alliance for Women.

Genesis, 2013. *Understanding Financial Cooperatives in South Africa, Malawi and Swaziland*. FinMark Trust.

IPP, 2017. *Independent Power Producers Procurement Programme (IPPP): An Overview as at 30 June 2017*. Department of Energy, National Treasury and Development Bank of Southern Africa. Pretoria.

Jeucken, M., 2001. *Sustainable Finance and Banking: The Financial Sector and the Future of the Planet*. Earthscan Publications Limited. London.

Jones, S., 1996. The Imperial Banks in South Africa 1861–1914. *South African Journal of Economic History. Special Issue 2*, Volume 11, pp. 21–54.

Kemp, E., 2017. *Measuring Shadow Banking Activities and Exploring its Interconnectedness with Banks in South Africa*. South African Reserve Bank Occasional Paper Series OP/17/01. Pretoria.

Kubicek, R.V., 1979. *Economic Imperialism in Theory and Practice. The Case of South African Gold Mining Finance, 1886–1914*. Durham, NC: Duke University Press.

Mathews, J.A., 2015. *Greening of Capitalism – How Asia is Driving the Next Great Transformation*. Stanford, CA: Stanford University Press.

Mazzucato, M., 2013. *The Entrepreneurial State: Debunking Public vs Private Sector Myths*. London: Anthem Press.

Mazzucato, M., 2015. The Green Entrepreneurial State. In Scoones, I., Leach, M. and Newell, P. (eds.), *The Politics of Green Transformations* (ch. 9). New York: Routledge.

Mazzucato, M. and Semieniuk, G., 2018. Financing Renewable Energy: Who is Financing What and Why it Matters. *Technological Forecasting and Social Change*, Volume 127, pp. 8–22.

Mohamed, S., 2014. Banking and Credit Markets. In Bhorat, H., Hirsch, A., Kanbur, R. and Ncube, M. (eds.), *The Oxford Companion to the Economics of South Africa* (ch. 20). London: Oxford University Press.

Montmasson-Clair, G., 2013. *Tracking Climate Finance Inflows to South Africa*. Discussion document presented to the Climate Change Expert Group Global Forum. March 2013. Paris.

Morel, P., Teschner, C., Rhode, W., Saumya, S., Veissid, A., Gubelt, C., Strauss, M., Le Boulay, G. and Worrell, L., 2016. *Global Capital Markets 2016: The Value Migration*.

Mughogho, M., 2017. *Financing the National Adaptation Strategy*. Department of Environmental Affairs (unpublished).

Naidoo, C., 2018. *Financing Sustainability Transitions – Business as Usual or New Demands of the Financial System?* Conference presentation, September.

Naidoo, S. and Goldstuck, A., 2016a. *The Experience of Governance Innovations in South Africa*. Geneva: United Nations Environment Programme.

Naidoo, S. and Goldstuck, A., 2016b. *Experience and Lessons from South Africa: An Initial Review*. Geneva: United Nations Environment Programme.

Naidoo, C., Jaramillo, M., Dimsdale, T. and Amin, A., 2014. *Strategic National Approaches to Climate Finance*. London: Third Generation Environmentalism.

National Treasury, 2011. *Estimates of National Expenditure 2011*. Pretoria: Government of South Africa.

Nedbank, 2016. *Supplementary Report to the Nedbank Group Integrated Report*. Johannesburg: Nedbank.

Nichols, S., Vermaak, M. and Moolla, Z., 2016. *The Power of Collective Action in Green Economy Planning*. National Business Initiative. Johannesburg.

OECD, 2011. *Aid Effectiveness 2011: Progress in implementing the Paris Declaration, Volume 11 Country Chapters*. Paris: OECD.

OECD, 2013. *Financial literacy and inclusion: results of OECD/INFE survey across countries and gender*. The Russia Financial Literacy and Education Trust Fund with OECD and World Bank.

OECD, 2017. *OECD Economic Survey: South Africa*. Paris: OECD.

O'Sullivan, M., 2005. Finance and Innovation. In Fagerberg, J., Mowery, D.C. and Nelson, R.R. (eds.), *The Oxford Handbook of Innovation* (ch. 6). Oxford: Oxford University Press.

Ramiah, V. and Gregoriou, G.N., 2016. *Handbook of Environmental and Sustainable Finance*. London: Elsevier.

SARB, 2015. *BA900 Returns as at 18 February 2015*. South African Reserve Bank.

Schmitz, H., 2015. Green Transformations: Is There a Fast Track? In Scoones, I., Leach, M. and Newell, P. (eds.), *The Politics of Green Transformations* (ch. 11). New York: Routledge.

Shakespeare, W., 1602. *The Merry Wives of Windsor*. Act 2 Scene 2.

Spratt, S., 2009. *Development Finance – Debates, Dogmas and New Directions*. Oxon: Routledge.

Spratt, S., 2015. Financing Green Transformations. In Scoones, I., Leach, M. and Newell, P. (eds.), *The Politics of Green Transformations* (ch. 10). New York: Routledge.

Stats SA, 2013. *Survey of Employers and the Self-employed*. Statistics South Africa. Pretoria.

Stats SA, 2017. *Women in Power: What do the Statistics Say?* Media release. Statistics South Africa. Pretoria.

Stern, N.H., 2007. *The Economics of Climate Change: The Stern Review*. Cambridge: Cambridge University Press.

Struwig, R.B. and Gordon, S., 2016. *Financial Literacy in South Africa: Results from the 2015 South African Attitudes Survey Round*. Human Sciences Research Council. Pretoria.

UN, 2007. *The State of Responsible Investment in South Africa*. UNEP Finance Initiative, African Task Force, Noah Financial Innovation and University of South Africa. Pretoria.

UN, 2014. *Human Development Report 2014*. United Nations Development Programme. New York.

UN, 2015. *UNCTAD: Investing in Sustainable Development Goals*. United Nations Conference on Trade and Development. New York.

Van Zyl, P., Redelinghuys, P., Schaffernorth, Z., Armine, I. and Lees, Z., 2011. *High Level Consultation with Finance Sector on Climate Change and Funding Mechanisms*. Department of Environmental Affairs. Pretoria.

Verhoef, G., 2009. Concentration and Competition: The Changing Landscape of the Banking Sector in South Africa 1970–2007. *South African Journal of Economic History*, Volume 24, Issue 2, pp. 157–197.

Volz, U., Bohnke, J., Eidt, V., Knierim, K., Richert, K. and Roeber, G., 2015. *Financing the Green Transformation – How to Make Green Finance Work in Indonesia*. Basingstoke: Houndmills.

Voβ, J.P., Smith, A. and Grin, J., 2009. Designing Long-term Policy: Rethinking Transition Management. *Policy Sciences*, Volume 42, Issue 4, pp. 275–302.

WEF (World Economic Forum), 2017a. *The Global Risk Report 2017*. 12th Edition. World Economic Forum. Geneva.

WEF, 2017b. *The Global Competitiveness Report 2017–2018*. World Economic Forum. Geneva.

7 The role of national systems of innovation in South Africa's sustainability transition

Shanna Nienaber

Introduction: positioning innovation systems within the context of sustainability transitions

This chapter considers the role of the South African National System of Innovation (NSI) in supporting a sustainable and just transition to a future that is able to balance human and environmental well-being. The premise of this chapter is that transitions occur within the context of a multilayered system of role players (actors) and drivers which involves institutions and policies, technologies and markets, and a host of practices, behaviours and values (Fakir, 2017). One of the core drivers in this multilayered system is science, technology, data, and research capabilities and networks (Cole, 2015; WRC *et al.*, 2015). Sustainable development research and technology options are thus important levers in sustainability transitions (Cassiolato *et al.*, 2003; Ockwell and Byrne, 2016).

Geels and Schot (2007) suggest that there are three interrelated aspects driving transitions that have implications for nurturing sustainability NSIs: socio-technical landscapes, socio-technical regimes and niche technologies (Geels and Schot, 2007; Fakir, 2017). The socio-technical landscape constitutes a variety of external social, cultural, environmental and economic drivers, which place pressure on a specific regime or "way of doing". Here the research community is key to articulating and understanding the different cultural, environmental and economic drivers that regimes need to respond to. Research also helps planning for the future by supporting activities such as biophysical and climate change modelling (Swilling *et al.*, 2015). The second level of analysis is the socio-technical regime, an established set of rules, norms and social structures expressed through institutions, regulations, specific technology or solution choices, and practices. Here the NSI is part of the institutional landscape that is expressed through a variety of organisations and research practices. Swilling *et al.* (2015) suggest that the research community produces a range of outputs that prepare for current circumstances, looking at more efficient and appropriate ways of managing current challenges. The third level refers to a set of niche technologies, which emerge as "safe spaces" for testing or exploring new practices, processes or technologies. These activities are expected to provide examples and disruptions that interact with changes in a regime and the wider landscape. The NSI is vital for this third aspect as it provides a pool of innovations to draw from, can be instrumental in setting up the innovation spaces for demonstrating and exploring new solutions, and is also key to driving institutional capability and skills to operate in emerging or niche areas.

This chapter provides an overview of some of the key conceptual issues needed to understand NSIs. It then shifts to describing South Africa's policy and institutional framework, which drives sustainability in the NSI. From there, and drawing from case studies, an aspiration for the future of a sustainability-oriented NSI is laid out. Due to the importance of public investment in catalysing a sustainability transition, and the importance of public for funding research and innovation, this chapter primarily focuses on the role of the public sector and publicly supported organisations in driving sustainability in the NSI.

Contextualising NSIs and science for impact

National systems of innovation and sustainable development

There is no uniform definition or description of an NSI, but it is possible to derive a core semantic (Guan and Chen, 2012; Wang *et al.*, 2012). In broad terms, an NSI refers to the national system of institutions and industries that produce knowledge, solutions and technologies across sectors (Altenburg and Pegels, 2012; Guan and Chen, 2012; Ockwell and Byrne, 2016). More specifically, Ockwell and Byrne (2016: 843) assert that an "NSI is made up of interconnected firms, (research) organisations and users all operating within a national institutional environment that supports the building and strengthening of skills, knowledge and experience, and further enhances the interconnectedness of such players". This occurs within a context of socio-technical factors and a range of national and international connections.

There are three implications of this broad NSI description. First, NSIs impact on a country's economic performance and are thus important in driving development in a country (Acs *et al.*, 2016). Second, NSIs have some level of goal orientation driving the various institutions and their outputs (Wang *et al.*, 2012). And third, the notion of a system implies that NSIs are not just about the production of knowledge and solutions, but also the intricate set of institutional dependencies, governance arrangements, and policies that enable research, development and innovation.

Having considered NSIs in general terms, it is necessary to reflect on sustainability-specific issues in NSIs. A sustainability transition requires mainstreaming of climate and environment considerations into wider developmental planning to transition societies and economies towards more sustainable development pathways. This demands that NSI institutions, activities and indicators are structured to be more sensitive to climate, environment and sustainability issues, and will require a powerful coalition of interests to drive the direction of state institutions, policy and action (Swilling *et al.*, 2015).

Sustainability-focused innovation is often a subset or specific focus area within wider NSIs and has not yet been elevated to a cross-cutting principle in most NSIs. It is often framed as a specialised and niche focus area requiring specific insight, training and skills to nurture new ideas. Within the broader thinking around NSIs, various authors (Altenburg and Pegels, 2012; Scott *et al.*, 2013; Swilling *et al.*, 2015) advocate a specific focus on green and sustainability issues, given the specific trajectories that green solutions have. This can happen through redirecting budgets to sustainability issues, setting up tax incentives and other processes. Mainstreaming sustainability work in national NSIs typically needs government assistance and a consistent long-term policy framework that factors environmental sustainability into economic decision-making (Altenburg and Pegels, 2012; Scott *et al.*, 2013; Swilling *et al.*, 2015). This is particularly important given that "green solutions" typically need to overcome market failures in terms of developing new technologies before there is clear commercial viability. Further, sustainability-related knowledge and solutions are being developed in response to societal challenges which require rapid response times, given the urgency of climate change, water challenges and other factors. Given that the research and development fields tend to be slow moving, this makes for a challenging management and planning space (Hübner *et al.*, 2000; Altenburg and Pegels, 2012). In addition to the specific trajectories that green innovation may have, a focus on climate innovation and the learning that happens amongst these individuals makes these actors valuable agents in influencing wider institutional networks (Ockwell and Byrne, 2016).

This chapter asserts that it is vital to explicitly prioritise sustainability research, development and innovation. This requires a cohort of skilled people, effective innovation institutions, well-resourced innovation activities and a well-articulated body of sustainability knowledge and solutions to achieve the systemic nudges to drive a wider sustainability transition.

Positioning the sustainability NSI for uptake

It is widely accepted that the activities and outputs of research, development and innovation (RDI) need to be accountable, not only to scientific peers but also to the relevant end users. This is a particularly important principle when public funding is used for RDI activities (Ely and Oxley, 2014; REF, 2017). This is important not only to ensure the responsible use of public money, but because policy design and implementation informed by robust evidence are likely to be more appropriate, cost effective, and justifiable (Strydom *et al.*, 2010). This reality has led to a discourse that touches on questions of the impact of research on policy, society, culture, the economy, environment or quality of life in groups that extend beyond academic circles. A number of common issues are cited in relation to science–policy uptake (Strydom *et al.*, 2010; Funke *et al.*, 2011; Funke and Nienaber, 2012):

- Policymakers, implementers and scientists work in very different institutions where they are driven by completely different cultures, goals and incentives;
- Science and policymaking lines of accountability, balance of power and interest differ depending on where the sources of funding are coming from, and who the responsible managers are;
- Communication and lack of engagement is a challenge. This relates to the identification and development of research topics, and the challenges of co-production, but also to the need for scientists to communicate their results amid uncertainty, and the ability of policymakers to apply this "uncertain" knowledge. Another factor affecting the quality of communication is the limited time and space for engagement with the research processes, particularly given that stakeholder engagement is often under-supported, both in terms of cost and time;
- Science, policy and implementation typically operate on very different time horizons. This can impact on the appropriateness of the timing of different findings and interventions;
- Capacity and institutional constraints in policy and implementation environments can impact on the ability of institutions to use the outputs of research and engage in the research process.

This suite of challenges has given rise to various research initiatives that focus on how institutions can orientate themselves for better brokering of knowledge and how scientists can better position themselves and their work for uptake. At an institutional level, the issue of knowledge brokering is typically the main focus (Godfrey *et al.*, 2010; Magnuszewski *et al.*, 2010; Wenger *et al.*, 2011). This is a process "in which intermediaries (knowledge brokers) link the producers and users of knowledge to strengthen the generation, dissemination and eventual use of that knowledge. Knowledge brokers help to ensure relevance and … (build) 'institutional bridges' between policymakers and researchers" (Godfrey *et al.*, 2010: 5). Knowledge brokering can broadly be understood in terms of, first, strategies for strategic relationship-building that enable better information transfer, and that interaction between the science and implementation (policy) domains is considered. Here the focus is on enhancing communication between scientists and implementers and positioning evidence to influence decision-making. Second, the framing, translation and interpretation of science enables an understanding that science in policy is a highly politicised process (Sheate and Partidario, 2009; Magnuszewski, 2010; Holmes and Lock, 2010).

Knowledge brokering actions take place in the context of networks and communities of people and institutions. Thus, collaboration is central to driving information flows, initiative linkages, joint problem-solving, and knowledge creation. Communities of practice and networks are thus social structures that go beyond individual skill sets and are spaces where learning and experience can be shared (Magnuszewski, 2010; Wenger *et al.*, 2011) – these can be regarded as the transition arenas in NSIs.

Taking solutions to the market

Where RDI activities produce a product or technology, a set of complexities emerge in taking the new solution to the market. The failure to commercialise research effectively has been termed the "innovation chasm" or "valley of death". In order to take research from the early testing (laboratory) stage to the market, where industry and enterprises will invest, larger-scale demonstrations are typically required to provide proof of concept and effectiveness (DST, 2008). This higher-level demonstration is usually costly (actual plants or technologies need to be built) and risky (there is no guarantee that the technology will work on a larger scale). It is a challenge to find an organisational structure and set of partnerships that can collectively absorb and share this risk.

The innovation chasm is not unique to South Africa. Many authors note a substantial "readiness gap" in moving research-derived solutions to the market (Rice *et al.*, 2002; Slater and Mohr, 2006; Arundel and Bordoy, 2008). Based on these insights it is clear that technology-specific brokering is key to addressing the innovation chasm. Similarly, there is a need for risk-taking and investment ring-fencing that extends beyond traditional research investments to drive many technology-derived innovations to the market. Various strategies can be used to support the transition of new technologies to the market including: conducting transition readiness assessments; assembling a transition team; establishing an oversight board; developing a transition plan; providing transition funding from corporate sources; laying the groundwork for a big market; and engaging senior management champions (Rice *et al.*, 2002).

The South African policy and institutional landscape relating to the sustainability NSI

The policy and institutional landscape of the sustainability NSI is complex. In many cases, elements of the institutional NSI and RDI are embedded in policies dealing with a wide range of sustainable development-related issues. Other times, there are specific policy interventions that focus on the NSI and RDI. A diverse range of government departments are the custodians of these documents, and have, at times, oversight of various RDI-related entities that drive the sustainability NSI. In principle, these departments are held together by constitutionally enshrined principles of cooperative governance. In practice, however, this and the host of aspirations enshrined in the policy documents, have proven difficult to achieve.

This section attempts to piece together some of the pivotal national legislation that creates the enabling mandate to drive a sustainability NSI in South Africa. This is not intended to be a complete policy scan and does not delve into the sub-national level where there are many examples of powerful shifts enabling transitions. Figure 7.1 maps out the main policies and strategies that create a mandate and focus for the South African sustainability NSI, and notes the key public RDI institutions and their line departments responding to the RDI aspects of the sustainability transition in South Africa.

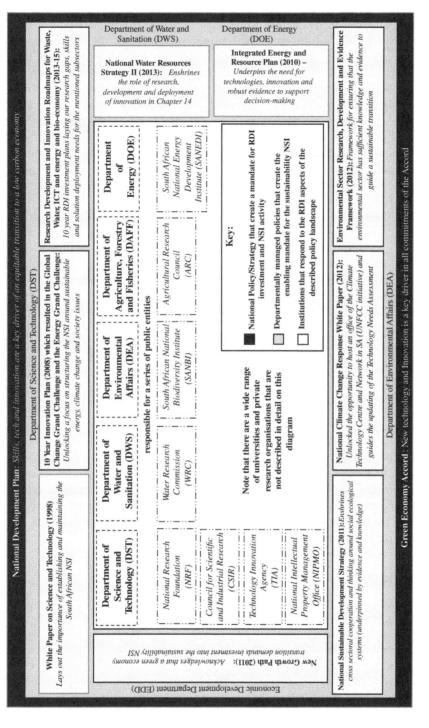

Figure 7.1 A summary of the sustainability-focused NSI in South Africa.

The Department of Science and Technology (DST), mandated through the White Paper on Science and Technology (1998) is the primary custodian of the overall NSI. Whilst the DST has primary oversight, there is a range of other government departments responsible for research entities in their domain of expertise. The DST drives the structure and investment into the sustainability space through a series of policies and strategies, which is then implemented through its network of RDI entities and partners (see Figure 7.1). At a high-level, the 2015/2016 Research and Development Survey pegged Gross Expenditure on Research and Development (GERD) (expressed as a percentage of Gross Domestic Product) at 0.8 per cent. Government investment makes up 44.6 per cent of this total (DST, 2017a) which emphasises the importance of the public sector in RDI. When focusing specifically on green RDI, it is noteworthy that South Africa is already investing heavily in this space. Of the R23.9 billion overall spend on research and development in 2012/2013, 28 per cent was spent on Green RDI putting the growth rate of investment into Green R&D at close to double that of the rate of growth of overall RDI investment (DST, 2016).

Despite a complex and maturing policy and institutional landscape driving the sustainability NSI in South Africa, there are a number of challenges that still hinder its impact. First, despite growing funding in this area, severe funding shortages remain – particularly in the later stages of the innovation cycle where costly demonstrations and scale up of solutions is imperative. There is inertia and lock-in of funding around specific green subsectors, which makes it challenging to reallocate resources to emerging areas such as solid waste RDI. Second, there is a range of cooperative governance and multi-institutional, multi-policy, multi-partner inefficiencies which result in duplication, a struggle to move solutions into practice, expenditure on solutions that do not have a "pull" from the market, and limited overall social and economic impact. This is discussed in the next section. Third, there is an ongoing need to legitimise and defend RDI expenditure in the face of numerous pressing national priorities. In many ways the traditional RDI impact indicators, to which institutions report, are not sufficient to tell the story of the impact of science on society. This speaks to the need to look at the impact indicators that are driving this system and how to shift this approach.

Envisioning a South African sustainability NSI: insights

Shifting towards an optimal sustainability NSI will require sensitivity to two main factors. The first is recognising that

> transitions inevitably involve difficult structural changes as the existing and often unsustainable systems are stabilised through various lock-in mechanisms, such as economics of scale, sunken investments, technological path dependence, infrastructure, behavioural patterns, preferences and user practices, competencies, favourable subsidies and regulations and vested

interests. These lock-in mechanisms create path dependence and make it difficult to dislodge existing systems.

(Fakir, 2017: 15)

Second, acknowledging that change needs to happen across a range of different institutions that operate in different spheres, scales and mandates.

The subsections and case studies below provide a high-level overview of the clusters of institutions that the authors saw as pivotal to driving this systemic change, including: research institutions (teams and projects), research funders, research policy organisations and sectoral institutions or non-traditional RDI role players.

Research institutions

Traditionally, the environmental sector has been dominated by a technical, expert-driven approach firmly rooted in scientific traditions that "have relied heavily on notions of objectivity, quantification, accuracy, linearity, and rationality" (Jacobs and Nienaber, 2011: 667). This has had a number of implications for sustainability in practice. It has given rise to a propensity to manage different aspects of the natural environment – in governance, legal and technical arenas and in institutional silos. It has also given rise to a wide array of domain-specific experts which run the risk of perpetuating separate realities of the sector (Dent, 2011; Jacobs and Nienaber, 2011).

While this deep technical knowledge and domain expertise remains important in understanding the complex issues associated with sustainable development, many of the challenges facing a sustainability transition require a more integrated and holistic vision. This implies that sustainability problems are nested in a complex set of cause-and-effect relationships that overlap across many scales and sectoral boundaries giving rise to a discourse around transdisciplinarity understood as a supra-discipline, methodology and way of seeing the world. There are two broad ways to understand transdisciplinarity. The first relates to taking concrete action to consider multiple scales when addressing a complex problem. The second, and more challenging interpretation of transdisciplinarity, requires adopting a unique positionality and approach to science that "calls on individuals to think through the limitations of binary, linear logic (rationalism) that is predominant in the scientific world (Cilliers, 1998, 2001; Max-Neef, 2005; Jacobs and Nienaber, 2011; Audouin *et al.*, 2013).

Based on these insights, transdisciplinary projects, approaches and positioning are fundamental to grappling with the complex issues that sustainability transitions demand. This has various implications for research institutions (including universities), teams and individuals working within universities, and the approach to specific research projects.

At the level of institutional management and structuring, research institutions are going to have to look at four key issues to prepare themselves for contributing to the future. The first is to achieve a balance between building deep disciplinary expertise and broader, cross-cutting multi, inter- and transdisciplinary research into organisational strategy (Jacobs and Nienaber, 2011). Currently the scales are tipped more in favour of enabling deep knowledge without creating sufficient space for more cross-cutting approaches. Second, universities and science councils need to support existing and, where needed, establish new research units that focus on nurturing transdisciplinarity. Third, university and science council leadership need to look carefully at incentives and performance indicators that enable transdisciplinary action. This requires careful consideration of publication and impact score expectations. It also demands that universities look closely at incentivising social engagement in a structured and sustained way (Wenger *et al.*, 2011; Clark *et al.*, 2016). Finally, there is a need to look at training and degrees that prepare students and current researchers for this changing future. Students require skill sets that go beyond deep technical expertise (Clark *et al.*, 2016) and which equip them to build networks in unfamiliar domains, manage deep and complex dialogues with diverse role players, and which enable a deep sectoral and social consciousness (Jacobs and Nienaber, 2011; Wenger *et al.*, 2011).

The research teams driving transdisciplinarity should incorporate a suite of methodologies, values and mechanisms. Further, this research approach should seek to account for interlinked levels of reality, different types and forms of information, different ways to disseminate or communicate knowledge, complexity, and grapple with context-specific and bounded knowledge challenges (Funke and Nienaber, 2010; Strydom *et al.*, 2010; Audouin *et al.*, 2011; Funke *et al.*, 2011; Glaser and Bates, 2011; Jacobs and Nienaber, 2011; Ely and Oxley, 2014).

Box 7.1 Case study: Rhodes University – promoting transdisciplinary research for sustainability

South African universities and science councils have a number of initiatives which demonstrate how research institutions can shift towards approaches that grapple with the multifaceted and complex nature of sustainability challenges. This case study examines Rhodes University, which has an evolving approach to transdisciplinary practice which it employs when approaching sustainability research.

The shift towards a more explicit commitment to transdisciplinarity took place in 2011 with the initiation of the Rhodes University Transdisciplinary Research Group in 2011. This, however, was embedded in a much longer critical reflection of what it takes to meaningfully contribute to the sustainability challenges that emerged in South Africa's democratic transition and also the fundamental issue of producing research that has relevance, impact and value in society (Rhodes, 2016, 2018). At Rhodes three core hubs form the central locus of transdisciplinary collaboration: Institute for Water Research (IWR), Environmental Learning Research Centre, as well as the Environmental Science Department. These core hubs also collaborate with other departments, focusing on different aspects of science, economics and management, and social sciences where co-supervision opportunities emerge through projects (Rhodes, 2016, 2018). This core group of transdisciplinary collaborators loosely coordinate themselves through working on specific research projects together, co-supervising students and engaging on a monthly basis in transdisciplinary research reflection and learning sessions (Rhodes, 2018). While there is a fairly large, loose team of transdisciplinary collaborators, there is a small group of two of three core thought leaders in this collaboration who hold together the vision which drives transdisciplinary research approaches. This is important to note as it often is key individuals within institutions who are the core change catalysts.

One of the key principles that unlocked this collaboration is a loose unity around a broad set of conceptual and theoretical framings, methodologies, data collection and data analysis methods. From the perspective of the conceptual and theoretical framings, critical realism, general critical complexity, social-ecological systems and Cultural Historical Activity Theory are some of the framings that have "united" collaborators. Methodologically, all collaborators have a commitment to transdisciplinarity, case study and mixed method research (Palmer and Munnik, 2017).

Over and above this broad methodological unity, the issue of doing research according to a common set of principles is vital. For the collaborators at Rhodes, nine key principles are internalised by all. These are

> to tolerate and even welcome discomfort and unresolved tensions ...; be sensitive to "aha" moments or insights, and note that irritation and conflict often signal moments of insight and a learning opportunity; engage with balanced generosity (listen and share); practice tolerance, build integrity and mutual trust; be sensitive to "arrivals" of both people and ideas; create and use reflective opportunities; manage discontinuities (people come and go, and arrangements change suddenly); sustain enquiry (keep going when it is tough) and be conscious that everyone involved in the process is a whole, multi-dimensional person, with the potential to engage with their whole self and many ways of knowing.
>
> (Palmer *et al.*, 2015: 1)

At an institutional level there are a number of key enabling factors that support this kind of work. Staff career development and promotion rests on three key pillars: teaching, research and community engagement. Community engagement is also encouraged by an award called the Vice Chancellor Community Engagement Award. Having a key performance area that focuses on the scholarship of engaged learning is important as it encourages researchers to embed themselves within a specific place, community and set of social change processes. This is fundamental to achieving social change and is a feature that is distinct in all transdisciplinary research projects and activities of the research teams described above.

Rhodes University has also enabled a flexible approach to defining which faculty students will graduate from. For example, in the case of the IWR, students participating in their research projects would typically be supervised or co-supervised by someone at the IWR as well as a supervisor in a faculty that best suits the prior educational experience of the student and the main theoretical focus of the topic. If the bulk of the student's work has a natural science basis, they can graduate through IWR. If the bulk of the work has a management or social science contribution the student may graduate from Management Sciences or elsewhere (Rhodes, 2018). This flexible approach gives students the space to find their focus and interest in a topic, and is key to supporting a student to achieving a transdisciplinary output. It is also important to note that not all research that an institute like IWR or a department like Environmental Sciences does, would be considered transdisciplinary. Depending on the type of project a student is supporting and what their interests and affinities are, students may grapple with a "deep disciplinary" topic or a more cross-cutting transdisciplinary method and output. This balance and flexibility is also important in achieving a balance between deep disciplinary knowledge and wider, more cross-cutting transdisciplinary research.

Despite this progress to institutionally enable transdisciplinary research and action, there are still a number of challenges in overcoming wider disciplinary silos. One of the major barriers to transdisciplinary research outputs remains the publication incentive that is part of the academic career progress ladder. Academics are subsidised for each paper they publish. The challenge with transdisciplinary outputs is that they are typically highly collaborative which means that multiple authors are involved and the papers take longer to produce, given the complexity of issues being covered. This means that the number of publication outputs is typically lower and the author subsidy is shared between many people. This trade-off between meeting traditional research output targets and committing to transdisciplinary research outputs continues to hinder this space.

Notably, the Rhodes transdisciplinary research group is an important forum for training, grooming and reflection by this community of practice. The research group meets monthly to discuss methods, paradigms and principles and is attended by students and senior academics. This is also a space for project teams to come together and reflect on what they are learning and unpack where they are facing challenges. This research group has also developed a transdisciplinary training course (Rhodes University, 2016; Palmer and Munnik, 2017).

Research, development and innovation funding organisations

RDI funders have a major role to play in driving the sustainability NSI by prioritising sustainability research, and designing and implementing funding mechanisms that enable long-term thinking and change. They also ensure that innovation system discontinuities are addressed, and support the interface between research and uptake. Each of these is considered in the section below.

In South Africa there is a range of generalist (for example the National Research Foundation and Technology Innovation Agency) and more specialist public research funding organisations (for example the Water Research Commission). Sustainability is thus approached and prioritised differently. For the generalist organisations that fund research across a range of scientific fields, it is imperative to manage organisational strategy and associated budgets in such a way that cross-cutting sustainability issues are given sufficient space and budget on the organisational agenda. Part of this balancing act is to ensure that the majority of RDI activities contribute, in some way, to sustainability and that there are also specific green RDI activities being supported. For organisations that focus on specific subsectors of sustainability, the challenge is to operate in a way that avoids the deepening of silos within the sustainability discourse. Notably, the prioritisation of sustainability-focused RDI is not only a matter for internal organisational strategy, but also needs to be a key agenda point for research institutions seeking funding.

Designing and implementing long-term funding mechanisms that unlock sustainable change is the second issue under discussion here. Developing an appropriate mix of funding mechanisms is critical. For example, trade-offs need to be made on how much funding will be awarded to technical knowledge activities in relation to wider, more systemic and transdisciplinary initiatives (Jacobs and Nienaber, 2011). Similarly, trade-offs need to be made between investing in short-term research that gives fairly rapid results and longer, more substantive research investments into complex and evolving issues (Palmer and Munnik, 2017). Another trade-off is between investments into technical hardware, technologies and tangible solutions in relation to funding research into the social dynamics around knowledge localisation, governance and social change (Ockwell and Byrne, 2016). Getting this right requires skilled fund managers who are not just general programme managers, but rather individuals who understand key trends, shifts and opportunities in their respective areas of expertise.

A third key issue for research funders is to ensure that innovation system discontinuities are addressed by supporting the interface between research and uptake. The first opportunity to consider here is the need for RDI funding institutions to be sensitive and responsive to windows of opportunity where RDI can affect change (Palmer and Munnik, 2017). These opportunities come in many forms, such as policy reform processes, an environmental crisis or disaster that provides spaces for new solutions, or the opportunity to embed new practices into community support organisations at the grass-roots level. Another key action is to invest in mechanisms and instruments that facilitate brokering within the system of innovation. Such interventions are particularly powerful if they are positioned to broker change in typical "sticking points" or "innovation chasms" in the RDI community. Ockwell and Byrne (2016) put forward a brokering mechanism model that they refer to as climate relevant innovation system builders (CRIBs). They look at the importance of these mechanisms in matching the right solutions and technologies to the most pressing national priorities. The CRIB model ultimately describes lean brokering units, positioned in appropriate, existing institutions. These can be government departments or entities or in a variety of local organisations (depending on specific focus or need). CRIBS focus on strategic facilitation by linking up relevant national actors, targeting and coordinating project and programme-level interventions to maximise the benefits to NSIs; synergising national priorities with emerging solutions; facilitating the matchmaking of national and international capabilities to insert and localise appropriate solutions and mediating participatory processes to formulate action plans for specific innovation opportunities (Ockwell and Byrne, 2016).

Box 7.2 Case study: The Water Technologies Demonstration Programme (WADER): a technology demonstration innovation intermediary

WADER is hosted at the Water Research Commission (WRC), a South African public entity established under the Water Research Act of 1971. The WRC is mandated to promote coordination, cooperation and communication in the areas of water research and development, through identifying RDI needs and priorities, stimulating and funding water-related RDI and supporting the effective transfer of knowledge, solutions and technologies (RSA, 1971). The WRC is thus an example of a specialist funding organisation.

Although the WRC reports to the Department of Water and Sanitation (DWS), it has a long-standing relationship with the Department of Science and Technology (DST) given their joint interest in RDI. In 2014, a window of opportunity emerged to address a long-standing innovation gap in the water sector in terms of scaling water technologies up, testing and demonstrating technologies, and in so doing sufficiently "de-risking" new solutions to enable public and private sector partners to implement emerging solutions.

The window of opportunity emerged as the DST and WRC were jointly developing a Water RDI Roadmap, described in the next case study, to guide the next decade in water RDI investment and solution deployment. Simultaneously, the DWS began a process of looking at how to evaluate appropriate technologies for the water sector. This window of opportunity and converging interests led to a sector engagement process, convened by the DST, that gave rise to the Water Technologies Demonstration Programme (WADER) – a mechanism which brokers a key gap or challenge in the system of innovation.

WADER is working towards fulfilling its niche in supporting the upscaling and deployment of water-related technologies to the market. It is thus an innovation intermediary that pulls together the applied research and development and pre-commercialisation stages of the water innovation continuum. Put differently, WADER is an example of a brokering/CRIB mechanism described above. It fulfils this function by:

- Issuing a series of water technology innovation calls as well as an ongoing scouting process for solutions that need demonstration to shift them forward;
- Demonstrating technologies in partnership with municipalities and technologies and independently assessing their performance in the field in order to check if technical performance standards are met at scale;
- Providing matchmaking and networking support to water innovators and municipalities in terms of finding sites for tech demonstration, leveraging of resources and support for demonstrations, exposing partners to solutions and possible markets;
- Developing partnerships that enable greater learning about emerging technology options, demonstration funding and opening of markets for new technologies;
- Providing basic technology advisory services to support innovators and government to manage the myriad solutions on the market under conditions where there is limited institutional capacity to assess technology appropriateness, maturity and viability; and

- Acting as an institutional repository for technology learning and assessment to minimise unnecessary duplication in different parts of the country (WADER, 2018).

The WADER mechanism is not without its challenges. The sustainability of funding for technology demonstrations remains a challenge with few municipalities able to free up budgets for unsolicited demonstration projects. Transitioning from a demonstration facility to a full-scale facility is also difficult. Further, building the right partnerships, which do not just look at the technology itself, but consider the technology in the context of setting up a viable business, is needed.

Time will tell whether this intervention is able to systemically shift the number of new innovations being implemented in practice, but the cross-sector and partnership-based learning that has already taken place in the first three years of implementation has been valuable in starting to address the water technology innovation chasm. WADER also presents an interesting model for other subsectors of the environmental sector.

Research policy organisations

Literature on NSIs is not highly explicit about the role of organisations which oversee the high-level coordination of the NSI. This observation is supported by Edquist (2001) who notes that innovation and NSI theorising largely lacks a focus on the role of the state in determining innovation policy and strategy. Indeed, there seems to be a debate about whether or not this high-level institutional coordination is actually constructive or not (Edquist, 2001; Geels, 2004; Woolthuis *et al.*, 2005). This being said, many countries do have national departments that are responsible for setting the strategic NSI strategy for a country, nurturing a long-term systematised focus on key issues and structuring the NSI along the entire research to market value chain. In South Africa, the primary institution mandated to drive this area of work is the DST, guided by the White Paper on Science and Technology (DACST, 1996).

Having an arm of the state, in this case a national ministry, that exclusively focuses on the coordination of innovation policy and institutions (and in particular driving a sustainability agenda within the wider NSI), is critical. Based on institutional and organisational theory, institutions are understood as key in driving economic behaviours, impacts and performance through a system of laws, rules and standards of behaviour (Edquist, 2001; Geels, 2004; Woolthuis *et al.*, 2005). In any broad institutional setting, including sustainability NSIs, there are "hard aspects" to institutions that formalise rules, put organisations and mandates in place, regulate intellectual property and manage incentives and risks. There are also "soft" aspects to institutions that guide social norms and values, culture, the willingness to share resources with other actors, the entrepreneurial spirit within organisations, tendencies to trust, risk averseness, etc. (Woolthuis *et al.*, 2005). This combination of hard and soft factors is key to hindering or stimulating innovation and thus needs dedicated capacity and focus from a mandated state department to understand and influence these complex dynamics.

There are three particular issues that state departments guiding innovation policy need to manage and be aware of when shifting an NSI to enable greater sustainability. The first is to understand that the existing rules, incentives and indicators in the system guide perception and behaviour. This means that any changes to the rules come up against deeply embedded perceptions. Second, the various soft and hard institutions involved in innovation play out within powerful networks that normalise certain patterns and values and behaviours. Change thus needs to be planned in the context of a network. Finally, socio-technical systems all have powerful material artefacts (e.g. where resources are allocated) that are nurtured by the rules and networks (Geels, 2004; Hansen *et al.*, in press). Making changes to this material system, especially when reallocation of resources is involved, requires careful and innovative approaches.

Box 7.3 Case study: RDI Roadmaps and Portfolio Management Units (PMUs) of the DST

The DST has adopted an approach of developing RDI Roadmaps as a way of planning RDI investments, activities, and partnerships over a ten-year period. These roadmaps mark a shift in RDI planning by which the policy department designs a long-term investment plan aligned to its theory of change. This translates into planning with a significant emphasis on how a solution or idea would be deployed in practice.

Significantly, these roadmaps are not DST operational plans, but are positioned as sector-wide interventions that are co-developed to guide a range of different public and private actors to focus their strategies, investment and activity planning. This is important, given the highly complex institutional, policy and stakeholder landscape that invariably interacts within a specific subsector. In 2015, two roadmaps that are key drivers in the sustainability space were completed, focusing on the solid waste and water-sanitation sectors.

Given the need to ensure sector-wide alignment and co-investment, the roadmap development process follows a carefully structured co-development and collective legitimisation process. The key aspects include: the identification of multiple needs and the articulation of interventions that would respond to these needs. From there, a sense-making process kicks in where needs and interventions are jointly clustered. This then unlocks the ability to look at defining objectives, performance measures and desired impacts and what the RDI response must be. In parallel to this, a capability mapping process takes place to determine the capacity to respond to the needs. The defining features of this roadmap development process are collective and iterative sense-making, extensive involvement from a diverse set of organisations and an orientation towards the needs of the user in order to respond to demand-driven investments (DST and CSIR, 2015; WRC *et al.*, 2015).

In order to start the process of operationalising the roadmaps, the DST is exploring the mechanism of placing Portfolio Management Units (PMUs) into sector institutions. The purpose of the PMUs is to support the implementation process through partnership development, inputs to proposals to leverage resources for the plans, project management as well as systematic monitoring and evaluation of RDI activities in the subsector. In this regard, the PMU structure is a similar model to the CRIBS promoted by Ockwell and Byrne (2016).

Some of the early success of this roadmap approach in the water and waste sectors is more systematic water and waste RDI ecosystem tracking, a range of cross-departmental policy and strategy synergies emerging, a growing suite of partnerships driving different aspects of research, skills development and innovation deployment and, particularly in the waste sector, a positive response from industry, which is seeking the clear and focused strategy that a roadmap approach provides. Given the ten-year horizon on these plans, time will tell whether systemic shifts will occur that could enable greater uptake and use of RDI-derived solutions.

Drawing non-traditional sectoral institutions into RDI

In the innovation literature, there has been an enormous amount of work on the role of the "firm" and private sector in shifting innovations to the market. However, just as there is very little literature grappling with the role of a national department managing a countries innovation strategy (Edquist 2001), there is also a gap around the role of other government departments and public entities in contributing to the national RDI landscape. A reflection of this institutional and organisational complexity is key to fully unpacking the public sector NSI.

In South Africa, the DST is responsible for overall NSI coordination. However, there are also a number of other national departments that influence the NSI in various ways. This may occur when national departments are custodians of public research entities or think-tanks. For example, the Department of Water and Sanitation is the custodian of the Water Research Commission. Other times, national, provincial and local government directly commission their own research. An example here would be the annual research call issued by the Department of Environmental Affairs' Natural Resources Management programme. Similarly, utilities, municipalities and various public departments may engage in innovation cycle activities such as technology demonstration, testing and validating.

Government institutions are often responsible for policy formulation, laying out the rules of the game that enable the procurement and uptake of new innovations, and putting in place incentives that stimulate innovation. In principle, this range of institutional and organisational actions, interactions and processes should be coordinated through cooperative governance. In practice however, this does not happen uniformly. Organisations who do not view themselves as traditional NSI role players have limited capacity to articulate their RDI strategy and approach and their attention is more focused on a range of implementation processes.

In driving a sustainability transition it is important for all branches of government to prioritise RDI activities as part of the overall contribution to sustainability. Non-traditional RDI institutions such as municipalities, utilities and specialist government departments are vital in testing late-stage innovations for the market, developing skilled personnel to adopt new innovations, and building the incentives and rule systems that allow the adoption and "pull" for sustainable solutions. The case below illustrates this well.

Box 7.4 Case study: The Ntabelanga-Lalini Ecological Infrastructure Project (NLEIP): research for impact

In 2014 the Department of Environmental Affairs (DEA) launched the Ntabelanga-Lalini Ecological Infrastructure Project (NLEIP) initiative, which aims to rehabilitate and improve land management practices in the sub-catchment impacting on the Umzimvubu Water Project (UWP). The UWP will result in the building of two large dams for potable water, hydro-electric power and irrigation. The proposed locations of the dams are not ideal due to the high levels of suspended sediment that moves through this catchment, which will impact on the holding capacity and lifespan of the dams. To this end the NLEIP initiative aims to support UWP by restoring and repairing the ecological infrastructure in the eight years leading up to the building of the dams and aims to support local community livelihoods by securing greater access to ecosystem services (Fabricius *et al.*, 2016; Botha *et al.*, 2017).

There is an implementation and a research component to this initiative. The actual land management and restoration processes are being managed by the DEA, with support from the Expanded Public Works Programme – a national public employment programme. Here a range of teams will be working on invasive alien plant clearing; land and wetland rehabilitation; and appropriate fire and grazing management through the Working for Ecosystems, Working for Water, and Working on Fire programmes. These activities are intended to effectively reduce the sediment load that will move into the planned dams. All of these implementation activities need to be guided by complex biophysical understanding of the landscape, sediment movement, water flows, landscape and biodiversity health. These interventions also interact with a complex governance and social landscape affecting the livelihoods of a range of different communities. This is where the research community was drawn in. The DEA has invested in an eight-year research programme that will guide the restoration implementation, planning and management activities in the catchment. This is being led by a network of universities, institutes and other partners (Fabricius *et al.*, 2016; Botha *et al.*, 2017).

Insights drawn from this case illustrate how public departments, which do not traditionally operate in the NSI space, can play a pioneering role in supporting and engaging with the sustainability NSI. First, the DEA has brought on a number of partners who are co-funding research projects with them including the DST and the Water Research Commission. Second, extensive time was spent on co-developing an NLEIP research and development strategy along with a framework that guides action and activity in the research and implementation space. This has been pivotal in ensuring a common approach, a transdisciplinary orientation and co-learning between the different organisations involved. Third, research coordination is happening through a series of university-run nodes or communities of practice, focusing on different topics such as governance, sediments, livelihoods and so on. This is proving to be powerful in presenting opportunities for co-learning between researchers, implementation teams, communities and government departments.

Conclusions

This chapter has argued that an NSI which has an explicit mandate and focus on sustainability issues is a key driver in a sustainability transition for South Africa. We have also suggested that substantial state investment into a sustainability NSI helps to de-risk co-investment in new innovations and test market opportunities for solutions. For this reason, this chapter has largely focused on public institutions and entities and their role in the sustainability NSI.

The fundamental challenge in the NSI to provide more support and even drive sustainability transitions is the need to reorient the system of NSI institutions towards adopting sustainability within their paradigm of operation (and thought). This is also key to dealing with the discontinuities between institutions that hinder the movement of innovations to the market, or make the uptake and use of new knowledge ineffective.

Transitions needs to happen at multiple levels within the NSI, including within research institutions, at the level of funding institutions, and at the level of departments that set the strategy for the NSI. Further, all public departments and entities (even those that do not traditionally see themselves as NSI role players) have a role to play in supporting the sustainability NSI. This complex coordination and collaboration is key to the country's transition to an inclusive, just and sustainable future.

Acknowledgements

Deepest thanks to Dr Najma Mohamed for her insightful edits and recommendations for this chapter. Thanks also to Dr Henry Roman of the Department of Science and Technology for his thought and input to the thinking around the structure of this chapter.

References

Acs, Z.J., Audretsch, D.B., Lehmann, E.E. and Licht, G. 2016. National Systems of Innovation, *Journal of Technology Transfer*, 42(5), 997–1008.
Altenburg, T. and Pegels, A. 2012. Sustainability-oriented Innovation Systems: Managing the Green Transformation, *Innovation and Development*, 2(1), 5–22.
Arundel, A. and Bordoy, C. 2008. *Developing Internationally Comparable Indicators for the Commercialization of Publicly-funded Research*. United Nations University UNU-MERIT Working Paper Series, #2008–075.
Audouin, M., Preiser, R., Nienaber, S., Downsborough, L., Lanz, J. and Mavengahama, S. 2013. Exploring the implications of critical complexity for the study of social-ecological systems, *Ecology and Society*, 18(3), 12.
Botha, L., Rosenberg, E., Biggs, H.M., Kotschy, K. and Conde-Aller, L. 2017. *Ntablenga-Lalini Ecological Infrastructure Project: Participatory Monitoring, Evaluation and Reflection and Learning Framework*. Department of Environmental Affairs, Cape Town.
Cassiolato, J., Lastres, H. and Maciel, M. 2003. *Systems of Innovation and Development: Evidence from Brazil*. Edward Elgar, Cheltenham.

Cilliers, P. 1998. *Complexity and Postmodernism: Understanding Complex Systems.* Routledge, London, New York.

Cilliers, P. 2001. Boundaries, Hierarchies and Networks in Complex Systems, *International Journal of Innovation Management,* 5(2), 135–147.

Clark, W.C., van Kerkhoff, L., Lebel, L. and Gallopin, G.C. 2016. Crafting Usable Knowledge for Sustainable Development, *Colloquium Perspective,* 17, 4570–4578.

Cole, M. 2015. Is South Africa Operating in a Safe and Just Space? Using the Doughnut Model to Explore Environmental Sustainability and Social Justice. *Oxfam Research Reports.* Oxfam, Oxford.

Dent, M. 2011. Personal communication, 24 September 2011. Senior Lecturer, School of Environmental Sciences, University of KwaZulu-Natal, Pietermaritzburg.

Department of Arts, Culture, Science and Technology (DACST). 1996. *White Paper on Science and Technology: Preparing for the 21st Century.* Republic of South Africa, Pretoria.

DST. 2008. *Ten Year Innovation Plan.* DST, Pretoria.

DST. 2016. *Establishing a Baseline for Green Economy Research and Developments Investments as of January 2011.* Republic of South Africa, Pretoria.

DST. 2017a. *South African National Survey of Research and Experimental Development: Statistical Report 2015/16.* Republic of South Africa, Pretoria.

DST and CSIR. 2015. *Waste Research, Development and Innovation Roadmap.* CSIR, Pretoria.

Edquist, C. 2001. *The Systems of Innovation Approach and Innovation Policy: An Account of the State of the Art,* DRUID Conference Paper. TEMA: Aalborg.

Ely, A. and Oxley, N. 2014. *STEPS Centre Research: Our Approach to Impact.* Working Paper. Social, Technological and Environmental Pathways to Sustainability Centre (STEPS), Sussex.

Fabricius, C., Biggs, H. and Powell, M. 2016. *Research Investment Strategy: Ntabelanga and Lalini Ecological Infrastructure Project.* Department of Environmental Affairs, Cape Town.

Fakir, S. 2017. Transition Realism: The Implications of Rent Seeking to Achieve South Africa's Low Carbon Technology Ambition. *World Wildlife Fund Report.* WWF: Cape Town.

Funke, N. and Nienaber, S. 2012. Promoting Uptake and Use of Conservation Science in South Africa by Government, *Water SA,* 38(1), 105–113.

Funke, N., Nienaber, S. and Henwood, R. 2011. Scientists as Lobbyists? How Science Can Make its Voice Heard in the South African Policymaking Arena, *Journal of Public Affairs,* 10(1002).

Geels, F.W. 2004. From Sectoral Systems of Innovation to Socio-Technical Systems: Insights About Dynamics and Change from Sociology and Institutional Theory, *Research Policy,* 33, 897–920.

Geels, F.W. and Schot, J. 2007. Typology of Sociotechnical Transition Pathways, *Research Policy,* 36, 399–417.

Glaser, G. and Bates, P. 2011. *Enhancing Science-Policy Links for Global Sustainability.* International Council for Science, Paris.

Godfrey, L., Funke, N. and Mbizvo, C. 2010. Bridging the Science–Policy Interface: A New Era for South African Research and the Role of Knowledge Brokering, *South African Journal of Science,* 106(5/6).

Guan, J. and Chen, K. 2012. Modelling the relative efficiency of National Innovation Systems, *Research Policy,* 41, 102–115.

Hansen, U.E., Romijn, H., Kamp, L.M. and Klerx, L. In press. Sustainability Transitions in Developing Countries: Stocktaking, New Contributions and a Research Agenda, *Environmental Science and Policy*.

Holmes, J. and Locke, J. 2010. Generating Evidence for Marine Fisheries Policy and Management, *Marine Policy*, 34, 29–35.

Hübner, K., Nill, J. and Rickert, C. 2000. *Greening of the Innovation System? Opportunities and Obstacles for a Path Change Towards Sustainability: The Case of Germany.* Discussion Paper 47/00. Institut für Ökologische Wirtschaftsforschung, Germany.

Jacobs, I. and Nienaber, S. 2011. Water Without Borders: Transboundary Water Governance and the Role of the "Transdisciplinary Individual" in Southern Africa, *Water SA*, 37(5), 665–678.

Magnuszewski, P., Sodomkova, K., Slob A., Muro, M., Sendzimir, J. and Pahl-Wostl, C. 2010. *Report on Conceptual Framework for Science-Policy Barriers and Bridges.* PSI Connect: Delft.

Max-Neef, M.A. 2005. Foundations of Transdisciplinarity. *Ecological Economics*, 53, 5–16.

Ockwell, D. and Byrne, R. 2016. Improving Technology Transfer Through National Systems of Innovation: Climate Relevant Innovation-System Builders (CRIBs), *Climate Policy*, 16(7), 836–854.

Palmer, C.G. and Munnik, V. 2017. *Practising Adaptive IWRM: Integrated Water Resources Management in South Africa: Towards a New Paradigm.* Water Research Commission, Pretoria.

Palmer, C.G., Biggs, R. and Cumming, G. 2015. Applied Research for Enhancing Human Well-Being and Environmental Stewardship: Using Complexity Thinking in Southern Africa. *Ecology and Society*, 20, 1.

Rice, M.P., Leifer, R. and O'Connor, G.C. 2002. Commercializing Discontinuous Innovations: Bridging the Gap from Discontinuous Innovation Project to Operations. *IEEE Transactions on Engineering Management*, 49(4), 330–340.

REF (Research Excellence Framework). 2017. Initial Decision on the Research Excellence Framework 2021. Available at www.ref.ac.uk/media/ref,2021/downloads/REF2017_01.pdf (accessed 22 January 2018).

Rhodes University. 2016. *Transdisciplinary Research Exploratory Training Workshop for Postgraduate Scholars.* Rhodes University: Grahamstown.

Rhodes University. 2018. *Personal Correspondence with the Director of the Unilever Centre for Environmental Water Quality*, 27 January 2018. Rhodes University, Grahamstown.

RSA. 1971. *Water Research Act*, Number 34 of 1971. Pretoria, South Africa.

Scott, A., McFarland, W. and Seth, P. 2013. *Research and Evidence on Green Growth.* Overseas Development Institute, United Kingdom.

Sheate, W.R. and Partidario, M.R. 2009. Strategic Approaches and Assessment Techniques – Potential For Knowledge Brokerage Towards Sustainability, *Environmental Impact Assessment Review*, 30(4), 278–288.

Slater, S.F. and Mohr, J.J. 2006. Successful Development and Commercialization of Technological Innovation: Insights Based on Strategy Type. *The Journal of Product Innovation Management*, 23, 26–33.

Strydom, W.S., Funke, N., Nienaber, S., Nortje, K. and Steyn, M. 2010. Evidence Based Policymaking: A Review, *South African Journal of Science*, 106(5/6), 1–9.

Swilling, M., Musango, J. and Wakeford, J. 2015. Developmental States and Sustainability Transitions: Prospects of a Just Transition in South Africa, *Journal of Environmental Policy & Planning*, 18(5), 650–672.

WADER. 2018. *Water Technologies Demonstration Programme Service Offering*. Available at http://wader.org.za (accessed 20 February 2018).

Wang, Y., Vanhaverbeke, W. and Roijakkers, N. 2012. Exploring the Impact of Open Innovation in National Systems of Innovation – A Theoretical Analysis, *Technological Forecasting and Social Change*, 79, 419–428.

Wenger, E., Trayner, B. and de Laat, M. 2011. Promoting and Assessing Value Creation in Communities and Networks: A Conceptual Framework. *Rapport 18*. Ruud de Moor Centreum: Open Universiteit, Germany.

Woolthuis, R.K., Lankhuizen, M. and Gilsing, V. 2005. A System Failure Framework for Innovation Policy Design. *Technovation*, 25, 609–619.

WRC, DWS and DST. 2015. *South Africa's Water Research, Development and Innovation (RDI) Roadmap: 2015–2025 Roadmap*. Water Research Commission, Pretoria.

8 Green skills

Transformative niches for greening work

Presha Ramsarup, Eureta Rosenberg,
Heila Lotz-Sisitka and Nicola Jenkin

Introduction

As the need for transitions to sustainability becomes more widely recognised, so too does the importance of investing in green skills. To shift towards sustainability, we require more than awareness. We need to practically and conceptually change "business as usual" in social and economic activities in general, and in work and workplaces across sectors and industries.

This chapter will focus on the skills needed in a society *en route* to sustainability and in particular, on the skills needed in workplaces aiming to contribute to, and benefit from, a socially just, environmentally sustainable or "green" development path (NDP, 2012). It contends that to understand the skills and capabilities needed to support the transition to a greener economy and more sustainable society, we need to understand a range of necessary work and occupational changes at three analytical levels, which are transitioning work, transitioning industry and sector, and transitioning society. Using a multi-level perspective on transitioning, put forward by socio-technical transition theorists (Geels, 2010; Rotmans and Kemp, 2003), the chapter highlights skills determination and skills development as important mechanisms to enable sustainability transitions. It also positions green skills as potential transformative niches within the transitions framework presented in this book.

Geels (2002, 2010) claims that learning that can accelerate transitions takes place at the level of niches within multi-level systems. While we support that contention, we argue here that attention must be given to learning processes and skills development at both a practical niche level where sustainability and green work is practised, and at the regime level where skills planning takes place. Without such attention, such learning will at best be neglected, and at worst retarded, with significant implications for transitions to sustainability. This has been evident in South Africa, where green skills planning and emergence was identified as being substantively re-active rather than pro-active (DEA, 2010; ILO, 2010; Ramsarup, 2017b). This has implications for the transformation of sectors, as well as sustainability and green economy praxis. Transitions theorists interested in learning tend to focus on the need for, or processes of learning or focusing on learning processes as mechanisms that accelerate transitions (Geels and Kemp, 2012), while few *consider those system processes that support learning, such as adequate or transformative skills planning*, brought into focus in this chapter.

The chapter advances the need for a "transformative" methodology that is able to provide a nuanced view of skills planning across different levels to support greening of work. It further aims to demonstrate a conceptual framework for skills planning, while in the process sharing findings from a series of occupationally directed green skills studies, with a more in-depth look at one such study in the chemicals (surface coatings or paints) sector.

We conclude that a multi-levelled, transitioning systems model is useful for framing green skills research (looking at both skills systems and work systems), and also that investing in green skills (GS) (and GS research) can be important niches that can (together with landscape-level pressures) enable regime-level changes in the skills system and in economic sectors.

To make our discussion in this chapter more accessible, we use the terminology of "greening work" and "green skills", recognising the limitations of these terms. We understand "greening work" to mean the integration of sustainability practices into traditional work practices, and "green skills" to mean skills for sustainability.

The importance and the challenge of determining green skills needs

Investing in the development of skills and capabilities for sustainability is an important requirement in supporting sustainability transitions. Nobel Laureate economist North (n.d.) argues that systems transitions are enabled by changes in the "knowledge stocks" held by organisations and societies. Research, conceptual development, education and formal training are means of changing flawed or inadequate knowledge to relevant knowledge that will support sustainability and enable green work.

Various skills strategies in South Africa, including the Environmental Sector Skills Plan (DEA, 2010), the Biodiversity Human Capital Development Strategy (HSRC, 2009) and the National Skills Development Strategy (DHET, 2011), which briefly refers to green skills as a funding priority, reflect the importance of planning for skills to support sustainability. However, coordinated uptake has been fragmented.

Recent studies have focused on the numbers of green jobs that can be created in South Africa at large-scale aggregate levels (e.g. Maia *et al.*, 2011; Ramsarup, 2017a, 2017b). The green jobs projection narrative remains an aspirational one, but does not create meaning for employers and provides little insight into how workplaces and actual work can transition into becoming greener or more sustainable. Furthermore, aggregate green jobs narratives have a tendency to see green jobs as a "one size fits all". As argued elsewhere in this book (Chapter 4) green jobs are not homogeneous. Therefore, they require differentiated skills strategies. Changes in education and training offerings, whether in institutions or in workplaces, must be informed by an understanding of the necessary learning needs. How do we systematically identify and plan for skills in sustainability transitions?

Agreeing on concepts and their scope is an important start. Despite various attempts at unifying definitions, the concept of green skills is a notoriously fuzzy concept. In one of the more widely used definitions, the OECD defines green skills as the "knowledge, abilities, values and attributes needed to live in, develop, and support a sustainable and resource efficient society", with the expansion that

> green skills can be defined as the skills needed by the workforce, in all sectors and at all levels, in order to help the adaptation of the products, services and processes to the changes due to climate change and to environmental requirements and regulations.
>
> (OECD/Cedefop, 2014: 18)

Another useful definition from the Australian Green Skills Agreement, states that green skills are "the technical skills, knowledge, values and attitudes needed in the workforce to develop and support sustainable social, economic and environmental outcomes in business, industry and the community" (Australian Green Skills Agreement, 2009: 3).

Thus, for work systems to transform from "business as usual" to environmental sustainability, employers and employees need to change the way they work, or shift to new forms of work. New knowledge, skills and competencies are essential to transition towards sustainability, but anticipating, identifying and understanding the demand for these skills has been somewhat ad hoc, reactive and completely inadequate in relation to the need.

Internationally, several studies (OECD/Cedefop, 2014; Dalziel, 2011) have articulated the difficulty in defining and measuring green skills at an aggregate level. The challenges include the dependence of this constructed concept on its context, and the fact that green skills are intangible and tend to be disruptive of current visible practices. Dalziel further noted that a demand-led approach (generally led from the market) to green skills has not worked because employers are often unable to effectively articulate their skill needs to skills planning and delivery bodies. Employers may lack a futures perspective on skills needs, particularly if their industries feature path dependence and lock-ins. However, Rafferty and Yu (2009), in the Green Jobs in Australia Report, found that "where significant progress has been made in green skilling – leadership has been shared between employers and unions" (p. 60), which raises the importance of employers as potential niche actors. This chapter will demonstrate some of the complexities related to employers and other niche actors and how these create difficulties for coherently articulating demand for skills, in relation to a case study of the South African paint industry.

Globally, as countries embark on greener development paths, research is starting to surface challenges related to the supply and demand of green skills.

A study across seven European Union countries (Cedefop, 2012, see also Cedefop, 2010 for good foundational reading) showed patterns in systemic sustainability transitions:

> ... The green economy significantly *affects labour demand, education, skills, occupations* and the geographical distribution of jobs and workers. Yet we know little about how this trend affects the demand for skills and the provision of education and training.... Uncertainty about environmental regulations and policies makes it difficult to anticipate skill needs; multiple entry routes and insufficient recognition of skills acquired through non-formal or informal learning tend to deter workers from transferring to green jobs; learning providers are not sufficiently active in anticipating demand and are discouraged by uncertain and diverse employer needs ... the aim should be to *improve recognition of green skills*, making it easier for people to apply them to new jobs, new workplaces or new regions.
>
> (Cedefop, 2012: 1, own emphasis)

Furthermore Rademaekers *et al.* (2015) state that in developing countries, skills development plays a crucial role to support transitions to a green economy by seizing the potential opportunities green growth or more sustainable development could present. Their study also found that there is "insufficient understanding and addressing of greening skills in developing countries" (Rademaekers *et al.*, 2015: 31).

In South Africa, despite rapid and expanding commitment to a green economy at a political and policy level, Ramsarup (2017b: 298) argued that despite good intent, there is

> very little evidence of skills planning for green skills entrenched within the current skills planning mechanisms and systemic frameworks and certainly not at different levels of skill ... thus support for green skills "seems to appear everywhere and is actually nowhere"!

Ramsarup also found fragmented patterns of green skills surfacing as an emerging area of skills development in South Africa.

In such contexts, we argue, one needs transformative research that is generative of new practices, not research that will simply reinforce the current skills and occupational sectors' rules and practices (Rosenberg *et al.*, 2016a)

Methodology

The methodological work outlined in this chapter draws on research undertaken in the national Green Skills Project,[1] which undertook six sector studies to understand the skills implications of greening work. The studies were undertaken in a diversity of economic sectors.

The six studies addressed the need of universities and Sector Education and Training Authorities (SETAs) to know where best to invest in green skills planning. Thus Rosenberg *et al.* (2015) determined green skills needed for coal mining; Ward *et al.* (2016) studied skills needed to support sustainable procurement practices in government; Cobban *et al.* (2016) focused on skills needed for climate smart agriculture in the Western Cape; and Ward *et al.* (2016) are completing a study on green skills in the petroleum industry, commissioned by the Chemicals Industry SETA (CHIETA). This chapter will draw for illustration purposes on another occupationally directed study commissioned by the CHIETA, conducted by Jenkin *et al.* (2016) on a chemicals subsector called surface coatings, focusing on decorative and automotive paints.

The "skills demand determination" methodology developed and used in the green skills studies involved the following data collection and analytic tools:

- A contextual driver analysis
- An extended value chain analysis
- "Hotspotting" to identify the best places to intervene in the system
- Occupational mapping and actor analysis
- Job analysis and skills identification (and in some studies, skills provider identification).

The studies in the national Green Skills Project listed above, were undertaken to understand the skills implications of greening work, and to pilot a suitable methodology that would encourage a generative, transformative approach. All were conceptualised within a wider transitioning framework, taking account of factors at the niche, regime and landscape levels and the connections between them, within a laminated system methodology, described below.

Reconfiguring a multi-level approach to analysing skills for green work

Drawing on a multi-level transitioning framework and perspective, this section provides theoretical and explanatory tools to look at greening work through an interplay at three analytical levels:[2]

- LANDSCAPE LEVEL: *The transitioning society*. Landscape-level pressures on industries and sectors towards new production and consumption patterns start to orientate society towards sustainable development and a green economy. The macro-economic and systemic drivers, which impact on social, political and economic systems, are central to analysis.
- REGIME LEVEL: *The transitioning sector and nature of work*. Operating norms and practices within a regime (which could be a sector or work area) begin to shift, requiring the exploration of the lock-ins that hold dominant practices in place. An analysis of changing value positions and the disruptive norms and practices that could address potential lock-ins, occurs at this level.

- NICHE LEVEL: *The transitioning work, workplace and worker.* Transitions in the nature of work, work systems and workplace practices provide evidence of the opportunities for transformative praxis. The unit of analysis at the niche level is the type of work, workplace practices and the worker, whose occupational tasks, knowledge, competencies and job are changing.

These three levels are not ontological descriptions of reality, but rather broad analytical and heuristic concepts that illustrate the complex nature and dynamics of the change inherent in the transition to a sustainable society (Geels, 2010). The relation between the levels must be viewed as a "nested hierarchy".

The *landscape* acts as a peripheral structure in which the regime and niches interact, thus necessitating an understanding of the contextual drivers influencing and shaping the sector. Geels (2010) emphasises that there is no single cause or driver, rather processes from multiple dimensions that link up at different levels and reinforce each other to initiate change. Thus, the contextual driver analysis drew on political and legal drivers that may influence green skills demand; economic drivers affecting the industry; social drivers (such as labour issues and historical inequalities, with historical elements given a stronger focus than would have been the case in a standard Porter field scan); technological drivers; and finally environmental drivers that may influence skills demand. Landscape-level analysis illustrates the pressures that are potential drivers to destabilise the regime. This comprehensive driver analysis also provides the basis for envisioning the future system and the potential directions where skills will be needed to green work.

Regimes can be interpreted as either a rule set or a system. Geels and Kemp (2012) argue that the Multi-level Perspective (MLP) does not prescribe how broad or narrow the concept of regime should be and should be directed by the object of analysis. Thus to analyse the regime structure and the interplay of transition actors the green skills studies drew on a value chain analysis which consisted of mapping the value chain and looking for opportunities to extend it. Typical value chains are also locked into traditional conceptions of consumption and production with regime actors sharing common beliefs and being blind to developments outside the current scope of value chain activity.

Geels (2010) and Geels and Kemp (2012) explain how *niches* are particularly productive spaces for change as this is where people gather, struggle and learn together how to make the changes necessary for sustainability transitions. In the green skills studies, we sought to define the skills needed to support and enable the transitions, arguing that green skills are the enabling mechanism in facilitating such learning, and reflect the growth of organisational knowledge necessary for sustainability transitions (North, n.d.). Hence this represents an important leverage for niche innovation and the impetus for regime change.

In the next section, we use one of the six Green Skills studies, the paint study conducted by Jenkin *et al.* (2016) to illustrate the dimensions of skills planning that come into focus if one works with a multi-levelled transitioning systems perspective to guide methodological work.

Case study of green skills for the paint sector: interplay of landscape, regime and niche

This section presents some of the observations within the paint case study.

Contextual driver analysis

While a contextual driver analysis is similar to a PESTLE Field Analysis (looking at Political, Economic, Social, Technological, Environmental and Legal drivers), it proved important to consider the interplay between macro- and meso-level drivers.

Macro-level drivers affecting the paint industry included international legislation, such as the international standards for lead paint (which has shifted to reducing the amount of lead previously allowed). Although this legislation applies in South Africa as elsewhere, we found that it affects only those companies operating in-country, but which have international head offices. Thus, this driver did not affect some local companies, who continue to produce lead-based paints (more cheaply) because local enforcement of the lead-content was poor. Thus, an interplay between macro- (landscape) level drivers, and meso-level contextual factors, became evident. Macro-level drivers impacted differently on different companies – a factor that would have been missed if one or other of the levels in the system had been ignored.

Extended value chain analysis

A typical value chain in industry handbooks is presented as linear (see e.g. Jenkin *et al.*, 2016: 36). Industry interviews and site visits indicated that, in fact, some recycling does take place during paint production as a cost-saving exercise. Jenkin *et al.* (2016) pointed out that post-consumer collection and re-use of leftover paint (e.g. for low-cost housing or charities) can extend the value chain. However, it was only when additional layers of the value chain were recognised, that additional priority skills needs were identified. In Figure 8.1 below, four streams of activity were overlaid onto the linear representation of the value chain.

By extending the scope of their analysis (based on the drivers identified in the contextual review) to cover the regulatory functions, Jenkin *et al.* (2016) noticed that environmental health officers/inspectors played a critical role in the value chain of the paint industry, and that the scarcity of this skill at the municipal level, could well contribute to the impact of poor regulation in the industry.

Regulation is not typically seen as "adding value" to the core business, but if chemical pollution becomes so excessive that it impacts health or aesthetics (leading to brand damage), it detracts from a company's value-add and becomes detrimental for business. The example of poor regulation of lead-based paints in South Africa, demonstrated in this case study, shows that better regulation would eventually make better business sense, not necessarily to individual companies but to the industry and society as a whole.

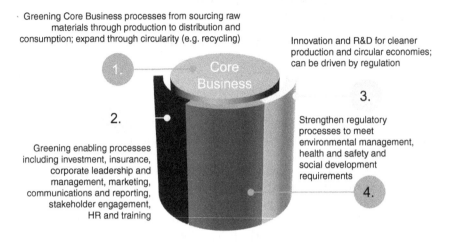

Greening Core Business processes from sourcing raw materials through production to distribution and consumption; expand through circularity (e.g. recycling)

1. Core Business

Innovation and R&D for cleaner production and circular economies; can be driven by regulation

3.

2.

Greening enabling processes including investment, insurance, corporate leadership and management, marketing, communications and reporting, stakeholder engagement, HR and training

Strengthen regulatory processes to meet environmental management, health and safety and social development requirements

4.

Figure 8.1 Expanding current linear value chains to surface greening possibilities.

Research, development and innovation (RDI) is increasingly recognised as a vital part of industry value chains. Regulation and innovation can have a mutually supportive relationship – stronger enforcement can drive innovation. Thus, countries where legislation is stronger seem to be taking the lead with innovation in the chemicals industry, for example in the production of new bio-polymers, or bio-remediation. In this study, scarcity and economic drivers in the form of intermittent power supplies were driving the automotive spray-paint manufacturers to search for new production processes that would use less electricity; with this came the need for new skills not only in new plant and machine design but also in plant operation and maintenance. Employers could readily identify these "immediate future" skills, but none of the employers interviewed were taking a longer-term perspective where industrial processes could be completely revised (such as producing paint from bio-polymers rather than mined materials, which could be an example of a regenerative economy and potentially, a cyclical economy).

"Hotspotting" to identify best places to intervene and for actor analysis

Most green skills studies seem to conclude that "green skills are needed everywhere": from the painter and his supervisor who must know how to apply paint so that it lasts, to the brand manager who needs to know how to promote eco-friendly paints, and the chemists and engineers who need to design new plants. This is, of course, not helpful when deciding where best to invest in skills in the system.

The paint study utilised a prioritisation "filter" for choosing "environmental hotspots" or strategic places in the system for introducing green skills: this consisted of a set of lenses used to determine where there were opportunities in the value chain to achieve environmental, economic and other social benefits (like the reduction of waste, job creation, improved compliance, or better working conditions), and where the levers to bring about this change would include the development of skills. Thus, a "hotspot tool" is a matrix that estimates social, economic, and environmental benefits and weighs them up against each other. For example, investing in entry-level painters' skills has certain socio-economic benefits, but investing in chemical engineers' design skills could shift a system as a whole. It has become apparent, however, that while the skills system tends to prioritise either one or the other, within the system at industry level, actors work in occupational networks – engineers, technicians, supervisors and workers are connected in activity systems and if they are not all skilled in a systematic manner, the system is affected.

The Green Skills paint study showed that the actors who need to be skilled as a collective, rather than as (or in addition to) individual specialist groups, also span sectors. An example again is the core business of the regulatory functions in the extended value chain of paint manufacturing, where local Government shares a responsibility for water quality with the national Department of Water and Sanitation; and for paint safety, with the national Department of Health – along with the shared responsibility of the chemicals industry.

Occupational mapping, job analysis and skills identification

In the current skills frameworks in South Africa, which uses occupations as a key defining category for skills planning and skills development (DHET, 2010), a core component of good skills planning is the effective use of the Organising Framework for Occupations (OFO) (Ramsarup, 2017a, 2017b). The OFO is a coded occupational system and is the Department of Higher Education and Training's key tool for identifying, reporting and monitoring skills demand and supply in the South African labour market at regime level. It shapes significantly the practice of skills planning and provisioning at niche level in the skills systems, for example the types of courses and qualifications available, as outlined in Ramsarup (2017b) and Lotz-Sisitka and Ramsarup (2017).

Occupational mapping for this project took place in two phases:

- Phase one – involved an initial assessment of literature and occupational information-derived OFO and O*NET (international benchmarking) was mapped to the emerging greening issues in the specific value chains that were uncovered at the workplace and sector level.
- Phase two – the key occupational tasks and related job titles linked to greening (emerging from the workplace and associated value chains in the sector studies) were mapped to the OFO at regime level. For these identified occupations, a detailed occupational profile was developed illustrating the potential greening options.

In the Green Skills paint study, development of a more nuanced idea of the dimensions of skills that need to be addressed when looking at greening work and hence occupations, was adopted. Two frameworks were utilised.

The first of these is a more nuanced typology used to examine the scope of green work which includes focusing on (1) core green jobs, which are specially defined as green jobs from a purpose, product and process point of view; (2) emerging specialisation in existing occupations where some specialisation in green skills is required to support sustainability-oriented changes in the workplace, if not all the time; and (3) jobs not traditionally regarded as green but which have latent potential for supporting sustainability and sustainable value. This typology was adapted from ILO (2011) to enable it to align with occupational work within the OFO and to provide concrete links into the system of occupational framing and skills development.

The second of these is a framework to look more deeply into skills specialisation within an occupation. Thus, to inform the development of the occupational profiles in the paint study, Greenwood's (2008, cited in ILO, 2011) articulation of four areas used to review skills specialisation in an occupation was used, namely: (1) the field of knowledge required; (2) the tools and machinery used; (3) the materials worked on or with; and (4) the kind of goods and services produced (ILO, 2011).

Drawing on these two frameworks, the study was able to develop a more nuanced view of the dimensions of occupational change that needed to be considered with respect to greening occupations within the paint sector against each identified hotspot occupation. Table 8.1 reflects the dynamics between niche-level organisational job shifts observed in the workplace, and the regime structuring of the occupation and occupational tasks. This then provides the means of linking niche-level insights to the broader political project of linking the specific green skill need identified in the workplace, to the more widely framed occupational frameworks which are significant to regime change dynamics when shaped by the landscape-level influences explained above. "Occupational tables" (see Table 8.1 below, an example of the Environmental Health Officer) detailed what occupational changes and skills were needed, directly linked to occupations in the workplace, and the OFO. The Environmental Health Officer is already a listed occupation in the OFO; but now with recommendations on how the occupation can be "greened" based on insights gained from the study.

Furthermore, at the regime level, green skill transitioning is also dependent on the co-evolution of the occupational and skills system. Hence the representation of the jobs, skills system and provisioning, and the framing of occupational tasks within the OFO, all need to be viewed from a transitions angle. Ramsarup (2017b) detailed the lock-ins within the skills system in South Africa and the extent to which the OFO determines skills provisioning resources. The characteristics of existing regimes set the preconditions for the development of new transition pathways, hence existing framings of work, of occupations, job descriptions and occupational tasks set the framework for how greening should

Table 8.1 Example of an occupational table

Occupation Name: Environmental Health Officer

OFO major group (code)	OFO sub-major group (code)	OFO unit group (code)	OFO occupation code
Professionals 2	Health Professionals 22	Environmental and Occupational Health and Hygiene Professionals	226301

Segment of the value chain	Skills band (high/intermediate/low)[1]
Regulation	High
Occupation description and purpose	Develops, enforces and evaluates environmental health policies, programmes and strategies to improve health outcomes and oversees the implementation and monitoring of environmental health legislation. (needs to integrate Lead Regulations, 2001 from Health Act)
Greening the occupation recommendations	Field of knowledge: • Monitors, evaluates and then regulates the effects of lead-based paint production and use, and the wastewater by-product on people and the environment. • Draws up the legislative framework for lead-based paints, and then for the disposal of paint-based waste water. • Monitors regulations for lead-based paint which are separated to managing people's exposure to lead once paint has been applied, and manages the exposure of those working with lead in factory production processes. • Monitors all premises (private and public) to ensure compliance with applicable health requirements, and minimisation of any detrimental environmental health risks to give effect to the principles of Agenda 21 and the "Healthy Cities" approach (external to factory function). Tools & technology: • Monitoring tools and procedures • Exposure to airborne lead; Assessment of potential exposure; Air monitoring; Control of exposure to Lead. *The evidence collected suggests that there is critical need for both an external and internal role function of EHOs (within and out of factory). The role of supporting EHOs through the Department of Health, is to build capacity in Environmental Health Practitioners for conducting inspections and, or environmental health investigations, to ensure reduction in conditions that constitute a health hazard (e.g. lead).*

be envisioned. Without mechanisms to destabilise the regime and the upscaling of potential niche experiments within the skills system overall, the regime will tend towards lock-in where it maintains and reproduces its internal dynamics. This would result in an OFO which fails to take adequate account of green work, the greening of occupations (Ramsarup, 2017b) or the extended value chain of associated occupations, as was illustrated in the intersectionality of environment and health in compliance skills. The power of the current regime to maintain the status quo would be maintained, and any future actions or actors linked to green work would be constrained by the existing rules and current regime practices, including those in the skills system and those in the workplace. The manner in which these interface (or not), would also be impacted.

Pivotal to the idea of lock-in is that innovative systems follow specific paths that are often difficult and costly to escape. As such, they tend to persist within an organisation resulting in continued use of "dated" knowledge, skills and business models or technologies (North, n.d.). In the Green Skills paint study with its lens on green skills in technical and engineering occupations, it was also suggested to bring back retirees (and their skills) as consultants. One potential problem with this is the "recycling" of "old" knowledge and ways, reducing the possibility of bringing in "new" knowledge and potential for significant changes or innovations, unless the retirees were at the forefront of the field, bringing in new knowledge of technical and other innovations (e.g. how to avoid the use of lead in paint). It was also noted that when the organisations hired or promoted from within, for example, when a sales person was moved to the role of a Safety, Health and Environmental Quality Officer or manager, at times the environmental knowledge base within the sector was being compromised.

Figure 8.2, which draws on the MLP work of Geels, illustrates the various conceptual tools used in the paint study, and attempts to surface the possibilities for transformative praxis for greening work and surfacing the green skills needs through empirical work at the different levels noted above. This coherent methodology provides a vantage point to explore a multi-level view of green skills needs, thus strengthening demand analysis beyond the level of niche only. The diagram shows that the following processes were considered for skills demand analysis at the three levels.

Synthesis of findings from the multi-level analysis in the paint study

Using the MLP as a guide and the methodologies as outlined above, the paint study (Jenkin *et al.*, 2016) identified those occupations that were core to environmental and social sustainability within paint companies. More than this, it also identified how different jobs are *related to each other* in the enabling of a "green" or sustainability-oriented value chain in the paint sector. For example, the health and safety officer's green work capabilities were significantly influenced by the compliance officer's abilities to successfully monitor regulations related to lead in paint (or not) as outlined in the example above. This shows

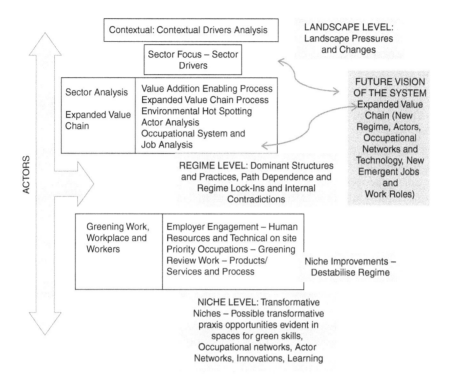

Figure 8.2 A multi-level methodology to understand the greening of work.

that there is need to develop such relational analyses in value chain work to enable social and environmental change in the implementation of associated roles and functions across individual occupations.

The study also surfaced the key knowledge areas required for successful sustainability practices in the paint sector (e.g. adequate knowledge of the health impacts of lead), and provided starting points for mapping out the need for critical learning processes for and between niche actors.

Pinpointing the types of learning processes that need to be prioritised within niches has also been emphasised by Geels and Kemp (2012) as critical processes within niches. Actors involved in the introduction of a new energy efficient automotive spray-paint plant need technical skills to design, produce and use new processes and equipment, but also transformative skills for envisaging something that has not yet been there before, or was dramatically different from "how we've always done it", and relational skills to bring others along in the process. The green skills studies all demonstrated that, in workplaces, people work best when they work together, both in their own workplace, and with others in different workplaces that intersect with theirs. This is particularly important when one system within interconnected systems plans to change.

Thus, learning needs might be best determined (and often also developed) within such functioning teams (see also Rosenberg *et al.*, 2016a).

The analytical work in the paint study linked to occupations, raised further evidence of the following key observations:

- The greening of specialist environmental roles was difficult to determine currently, and would probably need a more in-depth study, especially if all three categories of existing green jobs, greening of existing jobs, and latent potential for greening work are to be adequately analysed;
- The majority of green skills interventions require greening of current occupations, and the support of skills development that can foster more sustainable practices (what people do in jobs and the knowledge, skills and attributes), needs to be approached within a systemic approach in the workplace and within the value chain (i.e. it does not help much if only one person is implementing sustainability practices);
- There are three focal areas that provide opportunities to enrich and increase workforce capability to support a more sustainable paint industry: risk, regulation and innovation. These are also systemically linked;
- Environmental roles were characterised by institutional collaboration between different job roles (mentioned above);
- Evidence of underpinning skills and knowledge of greening required linked roles across related occupations (mentioned above, and also discussed further below); and
- The integration of sustainability practices appeared to prompt elements of multi-disciplinary practice, thus driving improved utilisation of skills in workplaces.

These findings, outlined above, all relate to the interrelated nature of green skills development across occupations, in multi-disciplinary formations and across niche and regime levels, and pointed to the need to develop a more sophisticated framing of occupations, outside of the typical framework of "single occupation" which is the dominant way of referring to occupations in the National Skills Development System and the OFO.

We use the concept of *occupational networks*, to make this relational dynamic of green skills occupations more visible for skills planning. Here the Green Skills paint study highlighted three occupational *networks* evident in the paint workplaces; these networks reflect a group of occupations with related roles. One occupational network, is represented below:

Safety, Health, Environment and Quality (SHEQ):

- *SHEQ Practitioner*
- *Sustainability Manager*
- *Environmental Officer*
- *EHO*
- *Health & Safety Manager or Officer*

To more fully develop an occupational network analysis, job titles from workplaces were collated and then mapped to relevant occupations on the OFO. Green skills needs were then analysed and presented to reflect needs across occupational roles in the network. It was not our intention to blur occupational boundaries but to reflect them as elements of multi-disciplinary practice that drive institutional collaboration within workplaces, necessary for sustainability transitions, with specific reference to sustainability at the niche level, where the level of knowledge and insight is still developing and being transferred within local practices. The occupational networks thus reflect the emergence of shifts in workplace occupational practices, that is, at niche level. The importance of maintaining and supporting occupational networks will enable the further greening of skills over time, and strengthen niche-level innovation, with higher levels of potential to effect regime change.

Observations on the occupational networks further reflect *the ways in which* the "stock of knowledge" in organisations and wider systems shift, a key feature of (social) learning, which North (n.d., quoted by Fakir, 2017) describes as an essential part of systemic transitioning.

These occupational networks therefore reflect important niches of creative activity in the skills system that have emerged and have systematically integrated sustainability practices across and between their traditional occupational practices. Nastar (2014) highlights the idea of *transition arenas*, which are networks of regime and niche actors in which the transition management takes place. These networks, according to Nastar (2014), stimulate the formation of coalitions of actors and networks to create alternative pathways of practice and to make sustainability transitions occur and hence set off processes to transform the regime. The observations linked to occupational networks, as framed in the paint study, has further resonance with Nastar's work. It offers an approach to study local occupational practices and associated green skills needs in context and to further illustrate that transitioning processes sometimes involve horizontal circulation (i.e. are not always vertical in nature).

These can be triggers for transformation, though horizontal development of niches often assists in building the vision of the niche which can gain momentum over time as the vision becomes more precise and broadly accepted. The Green Skills studies seem to point towards giving more attention to these occupational networks in skills planning as, over time, they may well become the backbone of workplace sustainability learning processes. It would also be interesting to examine this phenomenon historically in workplaces and sectors where sustainability transitions are already more substantively advanced, for further insight into occupational networks as units of analysis for green skills research and planning in a transition systems framework. This points, also, to the fact that it might well be a mistake to characterise all transitions as vertical whose sole purpose is to engage regime change. Given the importance of regime-level system elements such as the OFO, it would seem that, in green skills research and planning, there is need to give attention to horizontal processes within the niche-level transitioning processes *as well as* the links between these and regime-level changes. Geels and Kemp (2012) promote the support of networks as they provide the social and resource base for niche innovations, but these on their own may not be adequate to effect skills system changes within a pro-active orientation. This was also noted by the DEA (2010) and Lotz-Sisitka *et al.* (2013) who motivated for and established a national research programme, which addressed the lack of coherent engagement and coherence between niche-level innovations in the environmentally oriented skills system, and regime-level policy instruments (see also Ramsarup, 2017a, 2017b).

As can be seen from the paint study, the MLP framework, together with more sector-specific analytical tools which probe the dynamics of the MLP focusing in more depth on skills and occupations, facilitate a detailed under-standing of the specific lock-in mechanisms that support the current regime, as well as those potential mechanisms needed for advancing niche transformation. This provides a platform for concrete possibilities for green skills planning and development that can shift green skills planning from a re-active to a more pro-active modality, and which can also facilitate both niche-level and regime-level change. This, in turn, can also strengthen occupational networks which pro-motes future niche development.

Implications for understanding skills development for greening work within a sustainability transition

Following on from the study reported on above, this section briefly explores the implications for the co-evolution of the education and training system and systems of work in transitions, to show how related elements integral to joined-up implementation can support better planning for skills development and environmental learning.

As can be seen from the paint study discussed above (and also in the other five Green Skills studies), a multi-level perspective was able to highlight coher-ent iterations of possibilities and opportunities for greening skills and the con-current capability needs for education and training.

The methodological framework developed has illustrated the interplay of the landscape, regimes and niches, and the dynamics between niche-regimes, which helped to identify lock-ins in the paint industry. It highlighted the power and potential of focusing on transitioning arenas, in this case "occupational net-works" which foreground the relationality of green work, specialist green skills and green occupations.

The analytical work also showed that environmental roles were characterised by institutional collaboration between different job roles. Evidence of the green skills and knowledge required to support transitions highlights the need to link roles across related occupations and elements of multi-disciplinary practice driving improved utilisation of skills within workplaces. This points to the importance of conceptualising and carefully framing relational units of analysis for green skills research and planning. To accelerate sustainability transitions, collaboration between government agencies responsible for environment and education is essential to building green skills transitioning systems. This requires organised and managed networks and groupings of government, employers, workers and providers of training and education across industry to facilitate the exchange of information.

To understand the skills and capabilities needed to support the transition to a greener economy, it is necessary to examine the (co-)evolution of at least two systems and their inherent systemic elements: the work system (jobs; occupations; patterns of production and consumption in industries and economies) and the skills system, which also has a role in the framing of work. This requires a reconceptualisation of how the transitioning system/s are conceived and provisioned for. Figure 8.3 illustrates this.

Deepening the MLP systems framework, the concept of overlapping transitioning systems within education and work (Figure 8.3) provides a new framing for conceptualising and studying skills and skills needs. It views the individual who requires training as situated within multiple work and education-related systems. The broader social-ecological context is one in which unwanted chemicals are building up in the planet's water bodies and atmosphere and in a society where lobby groups, concerned citizens, scientists, etc. are calling for industry to take responsibility for their products and their disposal, through regulation, or direct pressure on workplaces to transform, perhaps through industry players, which then aim to influence employers. The state (as a subset of society), responding to the need for transformation to environmental

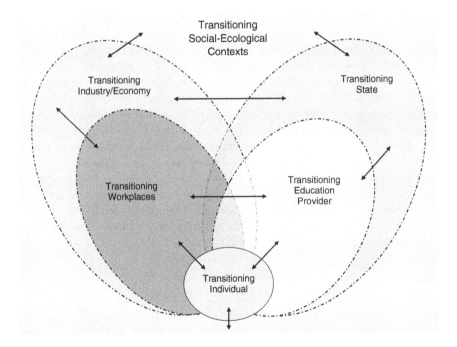

Figure 8.3 Overlapping transitioning systems relevant to green skills.

sustainability, provides (or fails to provide) regulatory mechanisms. Within the transitioning state is the education system, including education providers and skills development agencies. The Green Skills studies have demonstrated how these systems overlap, and that they need to be aligned at multiple levels illustrating that well-aligned pockets of transformation hold the potential to put pressure in and on systems that are slow to transform.

Conclusion

This chapter offers the possibility of foregrounding skills planning and development into wider transitioning systems research. As noted in the introduction, most transitions literature recognises the importance of learning in transitions, but few studies consider the underlying and surrounding system dynamics that make learning possible, especially from an occupational/skills development system perspective. This chapter has sought to offer this contribution to sustainability transitions-thinking, and to the skills development and planning literature in South Africa.

The framework, as illustrated and discussed, allows for multi-level analysis that connects macro and micro levels of greening work which provides an example of how the greening of work, so central to transitioning societies, can be empirically analysed in non-reductionist ways, and in ways that shift skills development and planning from a re-active to a pro-active modality with the power to influence regime-level or skills system elements and processes. In the current context, where these system elements have huge implications for the framing and allocation of resources for skills planning, such a contribution is significant for the development of systemic transitions.

Overall, the chapter shows the co-evolution of both work systems and associated education and training as central to green skill transitions, highlighting these as relational processes that require more complex units of analysis in skills system research than the individual occupation, or narrowly inscribed definitions of "green jobs", "green work", or "green skills". These insights provide a useful lens for understanding transformative possibilities for green skills development emergent from workplaces, offering significant seeds for systemic change, especially if seen in light of the fact that the greening of work, and the creation of green occupations, is required in *all sectors of society*, and *across all value chains* in the system of production and consumption, including also the public good sector where the country's resources are under the stewardship of public sector employees.

Notes

1 The Green Skills Project is a project of the National Environmental Sector Skills Planning Forum, which is funded by the DBSA under The Green Fund. Its purpose is to coordinate and undertake research into green skills system development. Partners involved in the programme are Rhodes University, the University of Witwatersrand, the University of Cape Town and a range of other sector partners See http://greenskills.co.za.

2 In this chapter three analytical levels are presented to align with the MLP of Geels *et al.* However, these analytical levels can be further disaggregated for more in-depth study of transitioning for skills planning using Bhaskar's laminated system framework, as explained and presented in Ramsarup, 2017a; Ramsarup and Lotz-Sisitka, 2017) but this analysis was beyond the scope of this chapter.

References

Australian Green Skills Agreement. 2009. Council of Australian Governments: Green Skills Agreement: An Agreement Between the Australian Government and the State and Territory Governments. Barton, Australian Capital Territory: Council of Australian Governments.

Cedefop, European Centre for the Development of Vocational Training. 2010. Future Skills Needs for the Green Economy. Research Paper. Luxembourg: Publications Office of the European Union.

Cedefop. 2012. Research Paper, No. 24. Green Skills and Environmental Awareness in Vocational Education and Training: Synthesis report. Publications Office of the European Union: Luxembourg.

Cobban, L. and Visser, Z. 2017. Green Skills for Climate-Smart Agriculture. A Case Study of Poultry, Winter Grains and Deciduous Fruit Value Chains in the Western Cape. Grahamstown: Rhodes University.

Dalziel, P. 2011. *Skills Development in the Green Economy. In Climate Change, Employment and Local Development in Sydney, Australia. OECD Local Economic and Employment Development (LEED)* Working Papers, ISN: 2079–4797. Available at http://dx.doi.org/10.1787/20794797 (accessed 16 April 2016).

DEA (Department of Environmental Affairs). 2010. *Environmental Sector Skills Plan for South Africa.* Pretoria: DEA.

Department of Higher Education and Training (DHET). 2010. *The Organising Framework for Occupations (OFO).* Pretoria: DHET.

Fakir, S. 2017. *Transition Realism: The Implications of Rent-seeking to Achieve South Africa's Low-carbon Technology Ambition.* Cape Town: WWF-SA.

Geels, F.W. 2002. Technological Transitions as Evolutionary Reconfiguration Processes: A Multi-level Perspective and a Case Study. *Research Policy*, 31, 1257–1274.

Geels, F.W. 2010. Ontologies, Socio-Technical Transitions (to Sustainability), and the Multi-level Perspective. *Research Policy*, 39(4), 495–510.

Geels, F.W. and Kemp, R. 2012. The Multi-level Perspective as a New Perspective for Studying Socio-Technical Transitions. Automobility in Transition. In Geels, F.W., Kemp, R., Dudley, G. and Lyons, G. (eds.), *A Socio-Technical Analysis of Sustainable Transport*, pp. 49–79. London: Routledge.

Geels, F.W. and Schot, J. 2007. Typology of Sociotechnical Transition Pathways. *Research Policy*, 36, 399–417.

Human Sciences Research Council (HSRC). 2009. *Guidelines towards a Human Capital Development Strategy in the Biodiversity Sector.* Research report. Lewis Foundation and the South African National Biodiversity Institute (SANBI). Pretoria: HSRC.

ILO (International Labour Organization). 2010. *Skills for Green Jobs in South Africa. Unedited Background Country Study.* ILO Skills and Employability Department. Available at www.ilo.org/skills/what/projects/lang-en/WCMS_115959/index.htm (accessed 30 November 2010).

ILO (2011). *Skills for Green Jobs: A Global View*. Synthesis Report based on 21 Country Studies. Geneva: ILO, Skills and Employability Department, Job Creation and Enterprise Development Department.

Jenkin, N., Molebatsi, P., Ramsarup, P. and Rosenberg, E. 2016. Green skills in the South African Surface Coatings Sector: A Focus on Paint. Grahamstown: Rhodes University and CHIETA.

Lotz-Sisitka, H. and Ramsarup, P. 2017. Introduction: Researching Sustainable Development Learning Pathways as Educational and Occupational Progression. *SAQA Research Bulletin. Researching Sustainable Development Learning Pathways as Educational and Occupational Progression*. Pretoria: South African Qualifications Authority (SAQA).

Lotz-Sisitka, H., Ramsarup, P., Gumede, M., Togo, M. and Rosenberg, E. 2013. Green Skills Development in South Africa. System Perspectives for the Shaping of Learning Pathway Possibilities for Sustainable Development, the Green Economy and Climate Resilient Development. Unpublished discussion paper. Grahamstown: Rhodes University.

Maia, J., Giordano, T., Kelder, N., Bardien, G., Bodie, M., Du Plooy, P., Jafta, X., Jarms, D., Kruger-Cloete, E., Kuhn, G, Lepelle, R., Makaulule, L., Mosoma, K., Neoh, S., Netshtomboni, N., Ngozo, T. and Swanepoel, J. 2011. *Green Jobs: An Estimate of the Direct Employment Potential of a Greening South African Economy*. Pretoria: Industrial Development Corporation, Development Bank of Southern Africa, Trade and Industrial Policy Strategies.

Nastar, M, 2014. Navigating Troubled Waters: An Analysis of How Urban Water Regimes in the Urban South Reproduce Inequality. Unpublished PhD thesis. London: University of Sussex.

National Planning Commission. 2012. *The National Development Plan. Vision for 2030*. Cape Town.

North, D.C. (n.d.) Five Propositions about Institutional Change. Available at www. econwpa.repec.org (accessed 8 January 2018).

OECD/Cedefop. 2014. Greener Skills and Jobs. Paris: OECD Publishing. doi.org/ 10.1787/9789264208704-en.

Rademaekers, K., Svatikova, K. and Yearwood, J. 2015. *Facilitating Green Skills and Jobs in Developing Countries*. Technical Report No. 9. Paris: Agence Française de Development.

Ramsarup, P. 2017a. A Critical Realist Dialectical Understanding of Learning Pathways Associated with Two Scarce Skill Environmental Occupations Within a Transitioning Systems Frame. PhD thesis. Grahamstown: Rhodes University.

Ramsarup, P. 2017b. Systems Elements Influencing the Emergence of Learning Pathways from a Green Skills Perspective. *SAQA Research Bulletin. Researching Sustainable Development Learning Pathways as Educational and Occupational Progression*. Pretoria: South African Qualifications Authority (SAQA).

Ramsarup, P. and Lotz-Sisitka, H. 2017. An Expanded Methodological View on Learning Pathways as Educational and Occupational Progression: A Laminated Systems Perspective. *SAQA Research Bulletin. Researching Sustainable Development Learning Pathways as Educational and Occupational Progression*. Pretoria: South African Qualifications Authority (SAQA).

Rosenberg, E., Lotz-Sisitka, H.B., Ramsarup, P., Togo, M. and Mphinyane, A. 2015. *Green Skills for the Mining Sector. Technical Report on Research for the Mining Qualifications Authority*. Grahamstown: Rhodes University and MQA.

Rosenberg, E., Ramsarup, P. Gumede, S. and Lotz-Sisitka, H. 2016a. Building Capacity for Green, Just and Sustainable Futures: A New Knowledge Field Requiring Transformative Research Methodology. *South African Journal of Education*, 65, 95–122.

Rosenberg, E., Rosenberg, G., Ramsarup, P. and H. Lotz-Sisitka, H. 2016b. *Green Economy Learning Assessment South Africa: Critical Competencies for Driving a Green Transition*. Pretoria: DEA, DHET and UNITAR.

Rotmans, J. and Kemp, R. 2003. *Managing Societal Transitions: Dilemmas and Uncertainties*. *The Dutch Energy Case Study*. OECD Workshop on the Benefits of Climate Policy: Improving Information for Policy Makers. Paris: OECD.

Rotmans, J., Kemp, R. and Van Asselt, M. 2001. More Evolution than Revolution: Transition Management in Public Policy. *Foresight* 3(1), pp. 0.15–0.31.

South Africa. Department of Higher Education and Training (DHET). 2011. *National Skills Development Strategy III*. Pretoria. Available at www.skillsportal.co.za (accessed 14 April 2016).

Ward, M., Jenkin, N., Rosenberg, E. and Ramsarup, P. 2016. *Occupationally Directed Skills Development for Green Public Supply Chain Management*. Grahamstown: Rhodes University and PSETA.

9 Creating partnerships to sustain value

Chantal Ramcharan-Kotze and Johan Olivier

> ...26. We recognize that sustainable development requires a long-term perspective and broad-based participation in policy formulation, decision-making and implementation at all levels. As social partners, we will continue to work for stable partnerships with all major groups, respecting the independent, important roles of each of them.
>
> (World Summit on Sustainable Development (WSSD),
> 26 August–4 September 2002, Johannesburg Declaration)

Sixteen years on from the World Summit on Sustainable Development (WSSD, 2002), growing population sizes, resource constraints and increasing levels of poverty that are being experienced globally, call into question our ability as a generation to improve the quality of life for the most marginalised communities, specifically in developing economies. From a sustainable development (SD) perspective – scholars, practitioners, business leaders, civil society and policymakers alike have touted strategic partnerships as being a key enabler for navigating the complex contexts that we operate and in which we live. Sustainable Development Goal 17 (SDG17), in view of the ambitious task towards SDG implementation, requires a revitalisation of global partnerships to improve challenges in developmental finance, technology, data, capacity building, trade, policy and institutional coherence. At the national and local level – the locus of SDG implementation, partnerships will be at the heart of achieving truly inclusive transitions towards sustainability.

But what does this mean? Partnerships are initiated by the existence or anticipated emergence of mutual interests and dependencies with parties that span institutional or sectoral boundaries (Ansell and Gash, 2007; Kivleniece and Quelin, 2012). Whether we are aiming for a green economy, a circular economy or overall sustainable development, the ability of society to respond speedily and responsibly to change, whilst adapting and growing value, is what matters most to shareholders, communities and investors. The concepts of "risk" "opportunity" and "livelihoods" are commonly used concepts across public, civil and private sectors. Unfortunately, the ease of addressing risks without affecting other strategic areas has become increasingly difficult due to the complex and integrated nature of social, environmental, economic and governance factors. In developing frameworks for modelling the complexity of sustainability transitions that adopt probabilistic, integrative, inclusive and adaptive approaches, Peter and Swilling (2014) highlight the need to go beyond the "parts" and "mechanisms" and gain a deeper understanding of the interdependencies that exist in systems. What does this mean for the partnerships that are required to drive and implement such transitions if we are still mostly embedded in linear systems?

Creative, innovative institutional arrangements are required to bridge knowledge, resource and capability gaps that exist within, and across salient actors (Streck, 2004; Porter and Kramer, 2011). Partnerships for sustainable development go beyond standard stakeholder relations – they are multi-dimensional pathways of engagement, co-development and converged commitment (Lozano, 2007).

The post-apartheid South African context provides fertile grounds and opportunity to test, explore and learn about partnership development. The process of negotiating a transition to a democratic state is possibly the most relevant and significant example of collaboration across racial, economic, political and psychological boundaries towards co-creating a pathway to redress the oppression of apartheid on the majority of the nation. Whilst we have a long way to go in addressing the triple challenges of poverty, inequality, unemployment and linked alternativee institutional arrangements (Akanbi, 2016), empowering black South Africans, improving access to services, and improving livelihoods still requires courageous leadership and collaborative approaches (Hellman and Schankerman, 2000; Bernstein *et al.*, 2014).

> "What is urgently needed is systematic action by government, in partnership with other social partners, to increase the scale and pace of our interventions.… We need more focus and collaboration. We need to mobilise more resources, use the resources we do have more effectively, and eliminate all forms of wastage and rent-seeking.… This is a time to prioritise the cries of the marginalised and the poor through policies and actions that promote sustainable and inclusive economic growth, effective redistributive measures and ethical management of public resources," stated President Cyril Ramaphosa at the Black Business Council.
>
> (*Daily Maverick*, 2017)

Partnership visions and sustainability transitions

The Simplicity Institute platform provides a contrary perspective to that of various sustainability scholars, stating that sustainability means focusing on creating new consumption cultures, governance structures that promote simpler ways of living and new systems of production.

A comparison of ideologies and theories on the role that partnerships play in creating value helps one reflect on the appropriateness of the systems that we are embedded in. It is clear that the understanding of value is disparate across policymakers, business and civil society actors. Furthermore, both policymakers and business practitioners are challenged by a lack of knowledge assets to measure the effective implementation of hybrid arrangements (Villani *et al.*, 2017). Various scholars and social actors are calling for a review of economic systems and the notion of value (Porter and Kramer, 2011; Bridoux and Stoelhorst, 2014). When considering governance structures and partnerships, we often rely on assumptions as to what the other party considers valuable and is willing to commit to. There exists an unequal understanding of value that often times is the primary factor derailing many partnership efforts, specifically in a developmental context. Sustainable development in itself is evolutionary and requires perpetual change that cannot always be planned for (Bossel, 1999). Adding to this complexity, is ensuring "just transitions" where inclusivity, externalities, labour-intensive industrialisation, redistribution of power and resources, and economic democracy remain central (Schmitz and Scoones, 2015). Ensuring that all of the above factors come into play requires a broad range of engagements and trusted multi-sector and multi-institutional relationships.

Cross-boundary engagements such as those between business, government and civil society are often seen and perceived as opposing forces where compromise and appeasement are expected (Selsky and Parker, 2005). The contributions of Porter and Kramer (2011) go beyond the neo-classical approach in their conceptualisation of shared value, whereby the creation of economic value can be achieved alongside the creation of societal value. By resetting capitalistic boundaries and linking success to societal improvement, new opportunities, efficiencies, differentiators and markets open up. Figure 9.1 reflects on the paradigm shift and boundary crossing that is needed in support of just transitions.

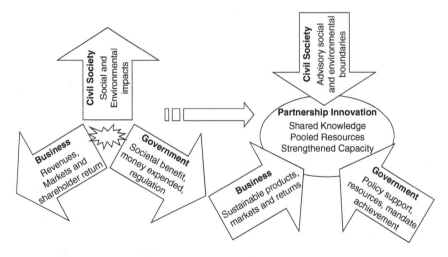

Figure 9.1 Transitioning to collaborative models of partnership engagement.
Source: Ramcharan-Kotze (2017).

By embracing the fact that institutions are nested within interdependent systems, both complexity and stakeholder theorists provide alternative views for use by practitioners when considering a broader and more holistic approach to value creation (Hart, 1995; Gray, 2006; Nidumolu *et al.*, 2014).

Improved service delivery, changes in systems that result in improved livelihoods, job opportunities, and education and skills development, are all examples of societal value. Often overlooked are factors that include the capacity to maintain cultural practices, access to key natural resources, status in the community and even contributing to developmental processes. Some are tangible and others less so (Bowman and Ambrosini, 2000, 2010). However, each has its place and importance depending on the stakeholders and contexts within which initiatives are designed and implemented.

SDG 17 states that a socially inclusive approach is required to mobilise, unlock and redirect efforts and investments. Without a clear understanding and appreciation for the intricacies and nuances of partnerships and the concept of value it will be impossible to review and monitor frameworks, regulations and develop incentive structures. The following sections provide insight into partnerships from the world of practitioners. This is followed by learnings, challenges and recommendations based on a consolidation of inputs layered over theoretical contributions.

Partnership value to government and civil society stakeholders

Partnerships in public administration are often referred to as cooperative governance. In South Africa, the Ministry of Cooperative Governance and Traditional Affairs (COGTA) is driven by a vision to ensure a "functional and developmental local government system that delivers on its Constitutional and legislative mandates within a system of cooperative governance" (COGTA, 2018).

However, the new hybrid arrangements that are being formed across sectors and institutions, are shifting strategy, policymaking and managerial modes. Collaborative governance goes beyond mere cooperation between stakeholders, especially in complex contexts (Kivleniece and Quelin, 2012). Collaborative governance brings public and private stakeholders together in collective forums with public agencies to engage in consensus-oriented decision-making (Ansell and Gash, 2007: 543).

Development theory suggests that frameworks and worldviews need to be changed when considering the investment in transitioning emerging economies and understanding the factors and experiences that constitute value to society (Alistair *et al.*, 2007). The following sections have been developed with inputs from the actors involved through in-depth interviews and provide a deep dive into a set of partnerships premised on value creation which addresses social and environmental justice. These cases and practitioner views span a range of partnership approaches and structures between the public, private and civil society actors.

Public–Non-Profit partnership: twinning social justice and biodiversity conservation

Partnerships such as the development and implementation of the 20-year Biodiversity Human Capital Development Strategy (BHCDS), between the South African National Biodiversity Institute (SANBI) and The Lewis Foundation, is such a case in point. Understanding the global rise to safeguard natural ecosystems to respond to climate change, food and water security, amongst others, the Lewis Foundation took the ambitious decision to provide catalytic funding to strategically develop higher-level biodiversity skills and capabilities in South Africa. Working with SANBI, the mandated national agency, and the Human Sciences Research Council (HSRC), it took two years to undertake the research that ultimately informed the development of a national strategy, and bring key players around the table to provide their critical inputs and buy-in to the programme of action that would support its subsequent implementation.

The GreenMatter programme was established in 2011 and a focused team with cross-disciplinary skills was brought on board and hosted by the Lewis Foundation. GreenMatter has, since 2010, supported approximately 90 postgraduate students, engaged over 18 universities, supported over 900 interns through the Groen Sebenza project, and developed multiple career, mentoring and interactive toolkits and apps (GreenMatter, 2017). Within five years of implementation GreenMatter transitioned into a stand-alone legal entity to ensure neutrality and programme sustainability. Key to this partnership was the strong engagement process with multi-sector actors and decision makers who would have to ensure successful outcomes by 2030. These included biodiversity, conservation, academia, national, provincial and local government stakeholders, research agencies, civil society organisations and labour unions, to name but a few.

What was most unique about the BHCDS and GreenMatter was that at its core, whilst responding to biodiversity skills, it equally aimed to change the legacy of apartheid that excluded black South Africans from the conservation sector. By combining and embedding equity, social justice, skills development and biodiversity management – SANBI and the Lewis Foundation have provided pathways of learning and impact to slowly shift a national system. It required depth of engagement, joint commitment, flexibility, the ability to draw on each other's networks, and most importantly, a shared vision to transform the sector in more ways than one.

> "The joint working of 'GreenMatter' has allowed us to unpack the problem into do-able chunks, including running a major job creation initiative…. I am very excited and proud that we are chipping away at this long-standing problem through the work of GreenMatter. It shows that working together is the best and most efficient and effective way to solve the compelling human challenges of the day," stated Dr Tanya Abrahamse.
> Previous CEO of SANBI, GreenMatter 3 Year Report 2013

Public-public-private partnerships: improving the "flow" of gender
equity through enterprise development in the water sector

With water security being amongst the top three global risks highlighted by the
World Economic Forum (WEF, 2017), the Department of Water and Sanitation
(DWS) in South Africa has been under significant pressure to respond to
improved water and sanitation services and the equitable allocation of scarce
water resources where the historical land and linked utility provision was prioritised to serve predominantly white population groups. The South African
constitution now provides for free basic water access to all (25 litres per person
per day).

As part of their transformation and infrastructure development targets, the
DWS together with the Water Research Commission (WRC), conceptualised
the Women in Water Empowerment Programme (WWEP), aimed to improve
the low levels of women participation in the water sector. The programme not
only aimed to support the professional development of female water specialists, it
focused largely on increasing the number of women-owned and -managed water
enterprises. However, the budget constraints within the DWS did not provide
for total inclusion of the approximately 90 women entrepreneurs and, seven
months into the three-year programme, the majority were still unmatched with
projects. Instead of waiting for the tide to turn, the WRC as the implementing
agent, began negotiating with private sector construction, engineering and
environmental services firms to support the incubation of the selected women
entrepreneurs. It took months to on-board partners and discuss partnership
modalities, contracting and expected deliverables. From what started out as being
a simple Public-Public Partnership, evolved into a Public-Public-Private Partnership that is still navigating its way through legislative and structural factors.

> Women are a watershed in society and the rest of us are downstream bene-
> ficiaries. We need to transform our sector to optimize this relationship and
> when firms … stand up to support this, we are heading in the right
> direction.
>
> Dhesigen Naidoo, Chief Executive Officer of the Water Research
> Commission, Infrastructure News, 2017

During the case interviews, Ms Virginia Malose, WWEP Programme Lead,
stated,

> Working with some of our private sector partners has highlighted that the
> value of transformation resides equally in the private sector and it is not all
> about profits, but also staying true to their values of sustainability. As the
> public sector, it was also our own recognition that we are not the be all and
> end all for these entrepreneurs. We need to understand that there exists a
> system of partners that can help these women. And the private sector has
> the capacity to deliver on time, with less red tape constraints.

Public-public partnership: responding to contextual dynamics and emerging issues facing cities

The South African Cities Network (SACN), established as a non-profit organisation in 2002, is a network of South African metros and partners that encourages the exchange of information, experience and best practices on urban development and city management. Its mission is to promote good governance, analyse strategic issues, and share knowledge across different actors to support city governance. Its efforts are aimed directly at city and local governments and indirectly to benefit city dwellers and national government.

Additional partners joined the Board of the SACN, typically represented by their relevant Deputy Ministers, such as the Departments of Cooperative Governance, Human Settlements, Transport, Public Works, Rural Development and Land Reform and the Local Government Association (SALGA). The partnership extends towards the inclusion of funders and international partners. The NPO formation ensured that the partnership programme was financially sustainable, included political and administrative influence and was based on a solid co-ownership approach. The 2015 SACN review showed that it was able to support peer-learning, generate new knowledge, and advocate for the urban agenda whilst maintaining political leadership. The partnership equally benefited from the coherence of a very firm and unwavering strategic plan, maintained by a small agile team, led by a dynamic Chief Executive Officer. The SACN has deliberately weaned itself off donor funding and enabled its members to "own" the cities agenda.

What makes the SACN visionary, is its pre-existence to the global and national call for city networks in response to sustainable development. Successes through this partnership platform include its ability to shape and influence national processes and platforms as well as create robust communities of practice in the spirit of innovation. Critical success factors for the SACN was its ability to effectively partner in the space of mutual benefit and maintain its support network in a "new politic".

> We had to ensure a basis for legitimacy in the cities space. This was aided by our ability as a team to maintain some level of professional independence and be principled when we needed to manage multiple actors and expectations.
>
> Dr Geci Karuri-Sebina, Executive Manager: Programmes,
> South African Cities Network

Value to industry and business

Organisations that bridge public–private collaboration

There are a number of organisations that exist to bridge policy, national strategies and on-the-ground implementation, which often assume non-governmental and non-profit institutional arrangements. These organisation's roles are often over-looked, while they can be regarded as "the glue that enables collaboration".

> We have had significant learnings related to the value that a bridging role plays. As a neutral party, we are able to ask tough, direct questions that neither our public nor private sector partners may be willing to vocalize. Being a facilitator of learning that has shifted private sector strategies and public sector approaches to policy has probably been the most impactful work we have experienced as value emanating from the partnerships in which we have been involved.
>
> Yolan Friedmann, CEO of the Endangered Wildlife Trust (EWT)

As hybrid associations and partnerships become the norm, the role of bridging organisations and the requisite need for related capabilities is sure to grow. This is indicated in Table 9.1 and in the Recommendations.

Public-private partnership: access to natural resources and planning for a positive post-mining legacy

As part of its integrated approach to sustainability, the De Beers Group of Companies (DBCM) places community engagement and well-being at the heart of its operations and social, labour and environmental planning. The majority of the firm's freshwater usage occurs in arid or semi-arid regions of southern Africa, particularly at its Venetia operations in Limpopo Province. Equally, the Venetia operations impact on land ownership, biodiversity, transfrontier conservation and operates within a national heritage site. In the late nineties the firm entered into a contractual agreement with public and non-profit agencies, contributing ZAR10 million towards the Peace Parks Foundation for the purchase of 5,000 km² of land to be managed by the South African National Parks (SAN-Parks). The new park was named Vhembe Dongola National Park and later renamed to Mapungubwe National Park, recognising the area's cultural heritage and national significance.

The operation in Venetia and protected areas, for conservation purposes, has been a highly contested subject. In addition to agricultural practices and ownership rights, water abstraction for the open pit mine was high on the agenda. The DBCM built a dam (4.5 mil m³ of water and mine reserves) to service both the Mapungubwe reserve and support the extensive water requirements of its mining operations as part of its 99-year lease to SANParks. Operational efficiencies, social licence to operate and careful closure planning drove the need to establish constructive partnerships with local authorities, communities and public agencies.

Venetia teams are currently working hand-in-hand with SANParks and local authorities to ensure that an effective handover of the asset is possible at some time into the futurem sustaining the water requirements of the park.

Bilateral and implementation partnerships: bringing dignity to the masses

Access to water and sanitation is a constitutional right in South Africa. However, within Sub-Saharan Africa there are 695 million Africans without sanitation access (WHO citing JMP, 2015). Those interviewed stated that systems are fraught with linear design models, resource inefficiencies, infrastructure backlogs, managing segregation legacies, and investment in inappropriate technologies and solution lock-ins. These factors pose a number of health, livelihood and economic issues for mostly poor communities.

The Bill and Melinda Gates Foundation (BMGF) partnered with the Department of Science and Technology (DST) in South Africa to explore the problem and possible approaches to developing a programme that could fast-track new generation sanitation solutions to African and global markets. Having implemented a number of research, development and innovation projects focused on sanitation, the Water Research Commission (WRC) was identified as the implementing partner and, together with the Gates Foundations and DST, shares the vision for "equal access to sanitation for all". As research, development and innovation (RDI) champions, the DST and WRC have initiated the foundations for a sanitation evolution in South Africa. Since 2012, the partnership has been central to transitioning the dialogue, debates, policies and innovations within a sustainable development framework.

> The partnership with the Gates Foundation and DST, amongst other efforts, has enabled us to access global networks and platforms from which we have been able to bring back learnings to South Africa and influence national policy and industrial planning to include disruptive innovations … we have much to do. Quoting my CEO, Dhesigen Naidoo, we are dealing with a 21st century problem, using 20th century technology whilst expecting a 19th century workforce to deliver.
>
> Jay Bhagwan, Executive Manager of the Water Research Commission

> Being the bridge between local and international partners, and managing the developmental agenda is quite challenging. However, working in a government department that allows one to experiment is so beneficial and critical for advancing science, innovation and technology in Africa. The implementation process has been an insightful process despite a number of unanticipated delays. We have gained from a deeper understanding of capabilities and where they start and stop, and how to smartly involve a breadth of implementation partners at various stages in the process.
>
> Chief Director Nonhlanhla Mkhise, Innovation for Inclusive Development, Department of Science and Technology

A number of key learnings were shared by the sanitation partners that included:

- the value in agreeing upfront to learn by doing in an unexplored domain;
- supporting each other as each partner brought to the table different strengths and areas of influence;
- having patience and persevering as not everyone is optimistic when they cannot see the visionary picture being painted;
- "… slaying many dragons" in relation to lessons on what it takes to shift entrenched technical and institutional models that do not allow for innovation and new processes.

These learnings, together with recommendations and challenges put forward by case respondents, have been incorporated in later sections of this chapter.

Multi-sector partnerships – developing a sustainable futures pipeline of entrepreneurs

The global sustainability agenda is reliant in part, on emerging enterprises that are capable of developing sustainable products and services. Entrepreneurs who are able to conceptualise and market innovations that minimise environmental impacts, improve livelihoods and contribute positively towards the growth of economies, are critical drivers of a greener economy. GreenMatter and the Young Water Professionals Network of South Africa (YWP-ZA) came together in 2013 due to the shared identification of the entrepreneurial skills gap that existed in the biodiversity and water sectors in South Africa.

"Imvelisi", signifying business and nature, was conceptualised after engaging a number of mainstream incubators who shared their experience as to the slow rate of "green entrepreneurs" accessing enterprise development, entrepreneurship programmes and incubators. The pre-incubation, or what is referred to as the ideation phase of the entrepreneurial journey, plays a significant role in establishing good foundations for success, which was not a clear focus area in South Africa at the time. The ability of young people to transition potential scientific innovations into effective business models and market solutions, was also lacking. Black and female entrepreneurs were equally not getting through the system and benefiting from the national incubator, small business and industrialisation instruments that exist.

The DST took a bold step to provide seed funding for three bootcamps between 2015 and 2017 and supported close to 120 aspiring entrepreneurs. The Imvelisi vision and spirit attracted a number of mentorship, specialist and incubator partners from the public and private sector, who volunteered their time and subsequently supported select entrepreneurs into the next stage of their business journeys.

Clear focus areas that benefit youth, black entrepreneurs, and niche, emerging green economy markets, provided the DST with a wonderful opportunity to partner on the Imvelisi initiative. The principles of partnership that were embedded in the programme did not aim to compete, but complement the efforts of other sector partners. This was extremely powerful overall and in leveraging resources to further support entrepreneurs who would otherwise never have had the opportunity to travel, create relationships beyond their towns, and grow their skills base.

Dr Henry Roman, Acting Chief Director, Department of Science and Technology

The social impact of Imvelisi supported 120 young enviropreneurs, but resource constraints limited a specific focus on women and youth much needed in South Africa. The emergence of new pre-incubation and ideation support platforms for green entrepreneurs has since increased, proving that scaffolding support is required to extend the pool of black, youth and women-led enterprises in South Africa, due to the historical legacies of apartheid and the persistent high unemployment amongst women and youth highlighted in this book.

Public-private-academic partnerships: towards competitive advantage through a triple helix model

The Technology and Human Resources for Industry Programme (THRIP) is a flagship Department of Trade and Industry (the dti) programme, managed by the National Research Foundation (NRF). Its overall aim is to support an increase in high-level technical skills required by industry, bringing together the best researchers, academics and industry experts with a 50:50 grant incentive. It was focused on private firms undertaking science, engineering and technology (SET) research, in collaboration with educational institutions to improve the participating firms' technological needs.

THRIP was a crucial partnership instrument with an important expectation to bridge the gaps between poor human resource development and the changing world of work within the South African context. Multi-sector and multi-institutional knowledge transfer, technology advancement and capacity building are central to THRIP.

There is a joint willingness to do research and development that could be innovative for the industry. Both parties benefit: both with regards to research and development and financially.

Industry project partner, Working Partnerships: HSRC Publication (2003)

A study undertaken by the HSRC in 2003 revealed a number of partnership efficiency indicators that supported the partnerships (HSRC, 2003). These included regular meetings and face-to-face contact between partners, frequency of communication in general, sharing of Intellectual Property Rights (IPR) and an increase in publications. Industry partner feedback suggested that firms invested significant time and resources in ensuring collaborative relationships and open lines of communication. Overall the project partnerships facilitated through THRIP generated value for both industry and higher education institutions. However, 2012/13 annual reports shared what was considered as high expectations resulting in unmet targets – establishment of small, medium and micro enterprises (SMMEs), publications, black grant holders and researchers, in particular, females (HSRC, 2003).

Similar industry–academia partnerships such as the Innovation Fund, international support programmes (e.g. Newton Fund's Industry–Academia Partnership Programme), and the Unilever–University of Witwatersrand-Chemical and Industries Education and Training Authority partnership, amongst others suggests that while there remain challenges in managing partnerships and ensuring tangible value, these hybrid modes of working do create value for those involved.

A consolidated view of value creation

Crossing sectoral and institutional boundaries towards building partnerships is challenging in itself. The fields of sustainability, strategy and partnership development provide opportunities to assist policymakers and business practitioners with the opportunity to improve our general understanding of implementation and value. However, the ability to measure what you need to manage remains the number one priority for most. Table 9.1 provides a list of case indicators highlighted by case respondents as a foundation towards addressing this challenge, and extends the view on shared value.

Barriers and challenges related to partnership development and impact

Every coin has a flip side and partnerships are no different. It is often the unique benefits of what such engagements bring that, if not managed or expected, create challenges and barriers to progress. Those shared by the actors in partnerships profiled in this chapter provide a view for partnership practitioners that could inform the various stages of partnership management.

Diversity in perspectives

Diverse perspectives bring to the table new options and ideas. However, at some point decisions need to be taken to advance the purpose of the partnership. Diversity can create a barrier to achieving consensus if not managed well. Formalised public-private partnerships (PPPs) tend to have a mediating platform or body that can move ideas to decisions. Unfortunately, informal partnerships neither plan for nor develop principles and processes that can guide such bottlenecks upfront.

Table 9.1 Case indicators of value creation through partnerships

---

Cast indicators of value creation for government and civil society partners

Social Value	• Improved service delivery to citizens • Change in policies, laws and systems, improving livelihoods and responding to social justice
Economic Value	• Shared resources to achieve a shared vision (financial, human and infrastructure) • Additional financial resources to extend impact • Ability to crowdfund through members
Intellectual Value	• New skills and process learnings • Shared and new knowledge generation • New approaches to sustainability
Governance Value	• Positive change in collaborative dynamics between cross-sectoral stakeholders • New governance models for future collaboration • Ways to build and maintain legitimacy

Case indicators of value to industry, business and international partners

Intellectual Value	• New standards development contributing towards a competitive advantage • Access to specialist expertise that resides in the public sector • Access to local context specific expertise that resides in development countries • Improved understanding of policy, regulatory, licensing requirements and processes • Learning how to navigate foreign contexts, systems with institutional gaps • Extending innovation scanning and opportunities
Economic Value	• Aids in responses to UN compacts, international principles and global best practice • Advises risk management and compliance responses and approaches
Environmental Value	• Provides access to natural resources • Improved management and planning for environmental and social externalities
Governance Value	• Improved governance platforms to engage the public sector • Improved understanding of public governance in multiple contexts

Case indicators of value to industry/business partners when partnering with research institutions/agencies

Social Value	• Effective development of skills and expertise that can be employed by the company • Improving equity targets within firms
Intellectual Value	• Access to research • Access to research expertise • Co-development of monitoring programmes • Opening up previously closed innovation processes

Table 9.1 Continued

Economic	• Cost effective development of industry specific skills and expertise • Advancing technology and linked services • Developing service growth areas in SA that were previously brought in by international partners • Indirect link to profitability
Environmental	• New sustainability solutions that can be further developed and improved on

Source: Author.

Linear approaches to development and partnerships for sustainability

Case stakeholders highlighted the disconnect between partners' acknowledgement of the complexity of reaching sustainability goals and the application of project and programme tools, measurement and reporting approaches which adopt a linear implementation model with very little room for flexibility. This did not align with:

- the multi-actor context with varying degrees of strategic influence during different phases of the partnership;
- project management versus programme management;
- frustrations with rigid programme management approaches applied within an exploratory context;
- downplaying the importance of process outcomes; and
- considering purely traditional financial indicators of success.

Process value vs impact

Having highlighted the importance of process outcomes and value, it is also stated that merely basing the success of a partnership on the "feel good" aspects of collaboration often hides the fact that the intended objectives and desired impact were not, or were only partially, achieved. Indicators of success need to move beyond the number of partnership meetings held, funding leveraged or platforms available. Following the principles of the theory of change – monitoring, evaluation and learning should constantly be looking for systemic changes such as increased levels of employment, improved operational efficiencies, retention of skills, trends in the influence of engagements on shaping institutional strategies and priorities, improved ecosystem health, amongst others.

Partnership behaviours and mental models

Following on from the barriers and challenges stated in relation to linear approaches to partnerships, the actors involved often demonstrate behaviours and hold assumptions that contradict the purpose of the partnership. At times, partners are not open to testing and adjusting their worldviews in light of new information and discussions. This often becomes problematic in the selection of projects, leveraging and allocation of funding, and maintaining trust in the partnership process. Basically, the implications of "not walking the talk" comes up strongly amongst the challenges shared.

Power and relational dynamics

Most case stakeholders shared their views on the power dynamics that played out during partnership processes, specifically by funding partners. Implementation and strategic partners are often reminded of the role of the financial contributions to the partnership, with this used to shape agendas. In response to this, certain partners in a number of cases made the decision to co-fund to a degree in order to level the playing fields. However, some shared that this did not necessarily resolve the problem, but merely shifted the narrative of who takes the lead in certain phases.

Identifying and managing dependencies

Mapping dependencies is often a poorly managed and prioritised activity during partnering initiation phases. Partnership actors are faced with challenges that crop up early in the implementation phases. The effort to consider scenarios and being transparent and open to new activities, processes and interventions, is not a popular strategising agenda item in partnerships as assumptions are made that partners have control over aspects within their sectors, countries or organisations.

Preparing for length and depth of engagement

Collaboration for complex issues, unlike coordinated short-term activities, proves to be lengthy and time-consuming by those involved. The upfront processes of co-development, broadening engagement, bringing on additional capacity and embedding principles of partnership take time and have in most cases been underestimated or not even addressed – resulting in failed partnerships and resource inefficiencies.

Working with conflicting objectives

Upon the initiation of partnerships, most actors noted a period of mutual agreement and the need to demonstrate that the partnership is on the right path. Following this phase, the realisation that each partner does have different objectives and varying expectations, comes to the fore. The ability to merge the common vision with diverse objectives is a common challenge for partners and practitioners who are called on to facilitate collaborative, yet impactful processes.

Underestimation of time, capacity and financial resources

All case stakeholders raised the concern of not planning for sufficient time allocations, the financial and human resources required to undertake the commitment that was made. How partnerships are developed and managed remains a sticking point that has created mistrust, along with legitimacy and financial risks for implementing partners. Organisations were often keen to partner, but were neither realistic nor aware of the internal capacity and capabilities required to respond effectively to its partnership roles and responsibilities.

Political context and uncertainty

Many partnerships were established to deal with political and regulatory uncertainty. Yet, when faced with emerging political dynamics which are beyond the known red tape and time delays, such as the discourse on state capture, partners have been left deeply concerned about partnership vision and achievements. Trust and the ability to be transparent has become difficult to achieve when one is questioning the associations, reputational and financial risks to which organisations are being exposed through partnerships. Lack of ownership of initiatives and their outcomes has emerged as an indicator of the effects of political uncertainty. Society is beginning to question public and private investment and, increasingly, partnerships are losing legitimacy due to either association or participation in poor governance and unethical practices.

Concluding recommendations

Partnerships evolve and often take on a life of their own that requires intuitive and adaptive management which is able to equally evolve and transform within the partnership process. Building partnering capabilities such as relational competencies within and across organisations is a critical component that every organisation, institution or agency should be investing in, in a world of increasing interdependencies and decreasing resource bases.

Working with others who have undertaken similar processes, albeit in other sectors, as learnings are transferable, can result in beneficial innovation in partnerships. Linked to this is identifying and on-boarding appropriate leadership and advisory partners that form part of a flexible governance structure that morphs as the needs of the partnership change. And it will. Partnerships should always start small before transitioning into longer-term, high investment strategies, programmes and clusters. It allows partners to improve the understanding of how each partner works, where expertise lies and what is possible in terms of expected value and impact.

Partners bring various tangible and intangible strengths to partnerships. The ability to influence, use one's mandate and engage communities due to legitimacy or knowledge power bases are as powerful as financial resources in achieving success. It is important to also be open to ending engagements and partnerships that do not lend themselves to the vision agreed to. In certain contexts, partnerships or specific models are not always the answer to the problem or challenge at hand.

The recommendations suggest that through partnerships one should always be flexible. The spin-off value from partnerships that work can have ramifications for communities and beneficiaries from a social perspective that are not always quantifiable through traditional models of value creation. Explore and innovate. However, ensure that decisions are taken and priorities are identified in order to realise broad societal impact.

Innovative hybrid associations are fast becoming approaches and mechanisms through which organisations, institutions and their actors are required co-generate value and perform. It is hoped that, through this chapter, practitioners and policymakers are able to better strategise, plan for and operationalise their partnerships to advance a more sustainable vision.

References

Akanbi, O.A. (2016). Addressing Africa's Triple Challenges: To What Extent do Physical and Institutional Infrastructures Matter? Inaugural lecture. Department of Economics, University of South Africa.

Ansell, C. and Gash, A. (2007). Collaborative Governance in Theory and Practice. *Journal of Public Administration Research*. Advance access publication, 18, 543–571, doi: 10.1093/jopart/mum032.

Bernstein, A., de Kadt, J., Roodt, M. and Schirmer, S. (2014). South Africa and the Pursuit of Inclusive Growth. *Democracy Works Country Report, Centre for Development and Enterprise*.

Bossel, H. (1999). Indicators for Sustainable Development: Theory, Method and Application. International Institute for Sustainable Development. ISBN 1-895536-13-8.

Bowman, C. and Ambrosini, V. (2000). Value Creation versus Value Capture: Towards a Coherent Definition of Value in Strategy. *British Journal of Management*, 11, 1–15.

Bowman, C. and Ambrosini, V. (2010). How Value is Created, Captured and Destroyed. *European Business Review*, 22 (5), 479–495, doi: 10.1108/09655341011068903.

Bridoux, F. and Stoelhorst, J.W. (2014). Microfoundations for Stakeholder Theory: Managing Stakeholders with Heterogeneous Motives. *Strategic Management Journal*, 35, 107–125, doi: 10.1002/smj.2089.

COGTA (Ministry of Cooperative Affairs and Traditional Affairs) (2018). Available at www.cogta.gov.za/?page_id=253 (accessed February 2018).

Daily Maverick (April 2017). Op-Ed: Radical economic transformation should be about building a more equal society. Cyril Ramaphosa South Africa 19 April 2017. Available at www.dailymaverick.co.za/article/2017-04-19-op-ed-radical-economic-transformation-should-be-about-building-a-more-equal-society/#.WngfDOeYPb1 (accessed 19 December 2017).

Gray, R. (2006). Social, Environmental and Sustainability Reporting and Organisational Value Creation? Whose Value? Whose Creation? *Accounting, Auditing & Accountability Journal*, 19 (6), 793–819, doi: 10.1108/09513570610709872.

GreenMatter (2017). Our Impact. Available at www.greenmatterza.com/our-impact.html (accessed 19 December 2017).

GreenMatter 3 Year Report (2013). Publication of SANBI and the Lewis Foundation.

Hart, S.L. (1995). A Natural Resource-based View of the Firm. *Academy of Management*, 20 (4).

Hellman, J. and Schankerman, M. (2000). Intervention, Corruption and Capture. The Nexus Between Enterprises and the State. *Economics of Transition*, 8 (3), 545–576.

Human Sciences Research Council (2003). Working Partnerships: Higher Education, Industry and Innovation: Government Incentivisation of Higher Education-Industry Research Partnerships in South Africa: An Audit of THRIP and the Innovation Fund. Available at www.hsrc.ac.za/en/research-outputs/view/848 (accessed September 2017).

Infrastructure news (2017). Greater Support for Water Sector's Female Entrepreneurs. Available at www.infrastructurene.ws/2017/06/26/greater-support-for-water-sectors-female-entrepreneurs/ (accessed November 2017).

Kivleniece, I. and Quelin, B.V. (2012). Creating and Capturing Value in Public-Private Ties: A Private Actor's Perspective. *Academy of Management Review*, 37 (2), 272–299, doi: 10.5465/amr.2011.0004.

Lozano, R. (2007). Collaboration as a Pathway for Sustainability. *Sustainable Development*, 15, 370–381, doi: 10.1002/sd.322.

Nidumolu, R., Ellison, J., Whalen, J. and Billman, E. (2014). The Collaboration Imperative. *Harvard Business Review*, 92 (4).

Peter, C. and Swilling, M. (2014). Linking Complexity and Sustainability Theories: Implications for Modeling Sustainability Transitions. *Sustainability*, 6, 1594–1622. doi:10.3390/su6031594.

Porter, M.E. and Kramer, M.R. (2011). The Big Idea: Creating Shared Value, *Harvard Business Review*, Boston, MA.

Schmitz, H. and Scoones, I. (2015). Accelerating Sustainability: Why Political Economy Matters. *Institute of Development Studies*. STEPS Centre.

Selsky, J.W. and Parker, B. (2005). Cross-Sector Partnerships to Address Social Issues: Challenges to Theory and Practice. *Journal of Management*, 31 (6).

Simplicity Institute. Envisioning a Prosperous Descent. Available at http://simplicity institute.org/ (accessed September 2017).

Streck, C. (2004). New Partnerships in Global Environmental Policy: The Clean Development Mechanism. *The Journal of Environment & Development*, 13, 295–322.

Sustainable Development Goal 17. Available at www.un.org/sustainabledevelopment/globalpartnerships/ (accessed 23 January 2018).

Villani, E., Greco, L. and Phillips, N. (2017). Understanding Value Creation in Public-Private Partnerships: A Comparative Case Study. *Journal of Management Studies*, 54 (6), 876–905.

Water Research Commission. Available at www.wrc.org.za (accessed September 2017).

World Economic Forum (WEF) (2017). The Global Risks Report. Available at www.weforum.org/reports/the-global-risks-report-2017 (accessed January 2017).

World Health Organization (WHO). Key facts from Joint Monitoring Programme (JMP) 2015 Report. Available at www.who.int/water_sanitation_health/monitoring/jmp-2015-key-facts/en/ (accessed February 2018).

World Summit on Sustainable Development, (2002). Available at www.dhs.gov.za/sites/default/files/legislation/The_Johannesburg_Declaration.pdf (accessed September 2017).

10 Inclusive sustainability transitions

Najma Mohamed

A new dawn

A multitude of challenges from corruption to stagnant economic growth has seen dramatic political changes in South Africa in 2018. Following the resignation of President Jacob Zuma after nine years in office, the appointment of Cyril Ramaphosa as the country's President on 15 February 2018 heralded the "dawn of a new era" in a country beset with governance challenges. In his State of the Nation address, the incumbent president committed to "accelerate progress in building an equitable society" and to turn the tide of corruption, which has crippled state institutions (The Presidency, 2018). His address touched on many of the critical socio-economic issues that were raised by various authors in this book – unemployment, inequality and stagnant economic growth. His message was one of revitalising the economy through innovation- and investment-led growth, employment and transformation.

Jobs, corruption, land reform, inequality and youth unemployment featured strongly in the President's address, highlighting the persistent socio-economic and governance challenges facing the country. He also provided a broad outline for achieving economic revitalisation, focusing on industries, such as mining and infrastructure as well as agriculture, which he termed "sunrise" industries, to stimulate economic growth and create jobs. While the visionary address was lauded in the country for its emphasis on ethical leadership, integrity and "public in service", it brought into sharp focus much of what this book laments – a failure to recognise that in addressing pressing socio-economic challenges, South Africa could simultaneously respond to the consequences of a changing climate and environmental degradation. As Greenpeace publicly noted in response to the President's address, "If the president is serious about job creation, he would ensure that the barriers to renewable energy are removed immediately, instead of declaring that the mining industry – which is in terminal decline – is a 'sunrise industry'" (Alfreds, 2018). What the President's address clearly illustrates is the work that needs to be done to address the economic growth paradigm, centred on the minerals energy complex, which still occupies a central place in policy planning while "the future of the climate (and all of us on this planet) makes a return of growth politically and socially unacceptable" (Fioramonti, 2017: 12).

As the country emerges from a difficult political era, policy- and decision makers have to take forward and deepen the promising start in transitioning towards a just, low-carbon and resource-efficient economy. Beyond the international commitments, which the country has entered into, such as the Paris Agreement and the adoption of the Sustainable Development Goals, South Africa has put in place a policy and political vision for a just transition. South Africa's transition to a low-carbon economy features prominently in the long-term development vision for the country, and is an integral part of the country's national climate change response strategy.

Diverse approaches towards sustainability transitions characterise the contributions to this book. Some assert that incrementalist discourses and interventions towards achieving green economic transformation are failing to respond to the critical social, economic and environmental challenges facing the country. Cumulative shifts, it is argued, which do not address the structural factors and vested interests which impede transitions to more sustainable pathways, will not achieve the transformational change required to deliver social and environmental outcomes. Others hold that transformative niches – in finance, innovation, partnership and skills development, could trigger systemic transitions by impacting both on vertical and horizontal regime- and landscape-level change to reconfigure the system-level structures hindering South Africa's transition to sustainability. The reflections in this book as a whole, however, affirm that in spite of South Africa's growing landscape of sustainability policies, projects and programmes, sustainable development has not been sufficiently mainstreamed in economic policymaking. In other words, despite the existence of transition visions, sustainable development narratives – of the green growth, green economy and green transformation varieties, are still largely marginal – in fact niche, to the core of the South African development narrative.

While reference to sustainable development, environmental sustainability or climate change was virtually absent in the 2018 State of Nation Address, a strong emphasis on radical socio-economic transformation affirms the centrality of justice and equity in the country's development narrative. Death (2014: 19) notes that "there is little sign that there is sufficient will or capacity to radically transform the South African economy in a more environmentally sustainable direction". Does this illustrate the assertion throughout this book that sustainability (including climate change) remains marginal to economic policymaking? Or is it indicative of the need for social and environmental justice activists to coalesce their campaigns to craft a society-led call for transitions to more sustainable development pathways? South Africa's transition goal is effectively one of "ensuring environmental sustainability and an equitable transition to a low-carbon economy". What is needed is to draw together the myriad of innovations which point to the viability of a just transition to make the case that, instead of a green economy being framed as a subset of economic activity, development pathways, have, of necessity, to centralise social *and* environmental justice in "a climate-altered world".

This chapter first draws out the key insights outlined in this book to distil some of the emerging characteristics and promising pathways of South Africa's sustainability transition, and then highlights some glaring blind spots impacting on social inclusivity. It then outlines inroads to reorient the dominant "growth" discourse – green growth included – which has thus far failed to deliver on equity and justice, both in terms of the environment and society in South Africa.

South Africa's sustainability transition

Promising pathways

As outlined in Chapter 5, the transition pathway in South Africa is still largely at the predevelopment stage and a far way off from the long-term, multi-level and cross-sectoral visioning, planning and design which should characterise (transformative) transition planning. Subsequent transition phases – termed take-off, breakthrough and stabilisation (Rotmans *et al.*, 2001), indicate to the system shifts and structural change, which South Africa's transition pathway has yet to deliver. The promising shifts – in new models of thinking, concepts and practice, transition planning, vulnerability analysis, partnerships for sustainability and transformative niches, could provide some impetus to take the country's transition pathway towards take-off, but this will require, foremost, that the development goals for the country include a strong commitment to achieving social *and* environmental outcomes.

The innovative models, concepts and frameworks – including the programmes, projects and partnerships discussed in this book – point to the representations of sustainability transitions in practice. The innovations that seek to deliver multiple outcomes exist across sectors, in energy, waste, construction, water and agriculture and have been well-documented (ESMAP, 2012; UNECA, 2015; PAGE, 2017). South Africa's innovation-led green growth strategy – outlined in Chapter 2, supports economic growth via investment in green industries and technologies. This has formed a major component of the country's transition vision as recent works attest (Assaf, 2014; Nicholls *et al.*, 2016). For instance, a recent analysis of South Africa's green economy landscape identified close to 1000 active "green economy" initiatives in the country, affirming that "technological innovation towards low-carbon and resource-efficient technologies has had significant uptake in South Africa" (PAGE, 2017: 75). However, this technocentric approach should be balanced with people- and sustainability-centred innovation, which is central to a just transition, but often does not garner the same level of support and investment that technological solutions do.

Fioramonti (2017: 200–201), in outlining the need to identify and adopt appropriate enabling *and* empowering technologies to achieve greater social and environmental well-being, cautions against technofixes inherent to the green growth paradigm, stating that, "even if we could fix all our environmental problems thanks to some formidable technology … we would have traffic jams of electric cars, stressed workers drinking safe water, broken communities with nice parks and poor people breathing clean air". Thus, several chapters in this book call into question the technocentric and market-based green growth paradigm – led by government and the corporate constituency, promoting instead a transition paradigm which could shift the South African discourse closer towards green transformation, with an explicit focus on "social justice, equity and redistribution" (Death, 2014) and one in which the voices of civil society become more prominent. More on the latter later.

Taking sustainability innovations, both technological and non-technological, to scale and putting them towards delivering both social and environmental outcomes, which addresses the country's key problems of poverty, unemployment and inequality, is imperative. "That these must become the core focus of innovation strategy and policy and be of relevance to the poor, rather than the elite, cannot be overemphasized" (Hart *et al.*, 2012: 32). South Africa's National System of Innovation (NSI), discussed in Chapter 7, denotes social innovation and innovation for development as an approach where "appropriate technologies or interventions that can address the challenge of the poor" (DST, 2012: 135), are prioritised. The Green Fund, the country's environmental funding mechanism discussed in Chapter 6, also adopts a broad interpretation of innovations which it would consider supporting – technology, business model, institutional arrangements or financing. Skills development in South Africa seeks to build both entry-level and high-level skills – a balance much needed in the country's fractured skills structure.

The innovative frameworks presented in this book also challenge the application of central concepts – such as green jobs and green skills, which drive transition dialogues globally. International drivers, including the recent multilateral agreements on climate change and sustainable development, have been notable in shaping South Africa's transition discourse. Similarly, concepts such as green jobs and green skills have been employed successfully in catalysing conversations and (some) actions on sustainability transitions. However, transitions management needs to go to the heart of the systems it seeks to change. Of particular note is the fact that these concepts and attendant frameworks should speak to economy-wide transitions and seek to impact (or at least catalyse) structural and system reforms. The frameworks presented in this book present nuanced and contextualised analyses which make the argument that "all sectors have a role to play in transitioning the South African economy to sustainability" and that there is a wide array of "skills and capabilities needed to support the transition to a greener economy".

The National Development Plan (NDP) acknowledges the importance of transition planning – but as noted throughout this book, this has not materialised at the pace, scale and depth needed. Efforts at long-term planning in energy transitions, however, have been notable, given the centrality of shifting to cleaner forms of energy and the implementation of energy efficiency measures in South Africa. Yet this has also revealed the vested interests and lock-in, which have to be addressed if the country is serious about decreasing its dependence on coal-based energy. Similar efforts have to be applied to understanding and planning for transitions in other key sectors. This has already begun at the sub-national level where provinces, cities and towns have developed transition plans and strategies in charting pathways towards sustainability. As the ILO (2015: 4) states, "[m]anaged well, transitions to environmentally and socially sustainable economies can become a strong driver of job creation, job upgrading, social justice and poverty eradication".

The vulnerability lens, which was outlined in the chapter on climate change, effectively shapes the thinking behind this book. The socio-economic context of South Africa, and the need to find a "safe and just" operating space (Cole, 2015) which links current and future climate risks and environmental well-being to socio-economic vulnerability, epitomises the just transitions approach adopted not only in this book, but in the policy vision of South Africa. This, as has been argued, reflects the post-apartheid sustainable development policy vision, which should be foundational to the country's sustainability transitions.

Early efforts at sustainable development policymaking "focused on socio-economic restructuring and empowering the disadvantaged through careful governance and institutional changes towards a more socially and environmentally just society". The shift towards managerialists and technocratic governance has fallen short of the emancipatory policy visions that held great promise in developing an environmental paradigm, which linked environment and development concerns to citizen empowerment and participation. Through the notion of vulnerability – the systems and actors most likely to be affected by the impacts of climate change and environmental degradation can be identified, ensuring that "future national and local development transition pathways and actions" align with the country's vision of radical socio-economic transformation. Further, vulnerability analysis has to move beyond "static and one-off assessments, with a heavy focus on poverty reduction" towards an understanding of "human capabilities, agency and change", highlighting the emancipatory potential of interventions which seek to achieve both equity and sustainability. There is growing evidence of grass-roots innovations which not only present models of community-driven environmental management of energy, waste and biodiversity, for instance (Conway, 2015; Douwes, 2015; Hlahla *et al.*, 2016), but also contribute towards building the foundations of participatory democracy – citizen engagement.

While several chapters in the book highlight the weakness and lack of collaborative and cooperative governance structures to facilitate the type of cross-sectoral and economy-wide policy planning and actions required in sustainability transitions, the centrality of partnerships for sustainability transitions is elaborated in the chapters dealing with research, development and innovation (RDI) and partnership development. The partnerships, which promote transdisciplinary research approaches and methods, or develop and implement water and waste RDI roadmaps for the country, have significantly impacted on furthering transitions-thinking and practice. In the wide-ranging partnerships presented in Chapter 9, the authors demonstrate the possibility of value creation amongst multiple stakeholders – governments, non-governmental organisations, companies, communities and universities which build on "mutual interests and dependencies" and which "span institutional or sectoral boundaries". Partnerships which facilitate progress towards transitions are thus vital in building pathways which can, if needed, operate in varieties of transition arenas, drawing upon local, regional and global networks.

Finally, the existence of transformative niches which can act as disruptors of systems – effecting both vertical- (regime and landscape) and horizontal-level changes – has been illustrated, notably in the chapters on skills, innovation and finance systems in South Africa. The impact of the catalytic renewable energy programme in South Africa – both on the utility-scale and embedded generation models of renewable energy, demonstrates the potential of transformative niches to effect both regime- and landscape-level changes. However, other than extensive work on the country's energy transition pathway, very little work explores the transition arenas and actor networks, which are the social base for much of the niche innovations in other sectors. Recent contributions "mapping" the sustainability transition landscape in South Africa, the *Green Economy Inventory for South Africa* (PAGE, 2017: 14), shows that "all key sectors in South Africa's economy and all provinces are active in or associated with the green economy in some way", and that there are key sectors driving this transition (UNEP, 2013). These mapping exercises also reveal that the pace of transition pathways varies considerably, and that greater impetus is needed in some sectors to stimulate transitions. Energy, transport and agriculture featured as key sectors in which sustainability transitions are actively being pursued (PAGE, 2017). This was highlighted in earlier work as well (UNEP, 2013; Green Fund, 2014). If transition pathways in South Africa are to harness these transformative niches to effect system and economy-wide change, then these disruptors will have to be identified and supported *across* economic sectors.

This analysis also has to be extended to the policy level – which is rich in transformative mechanisms, frameworks and tools – promoting renewable energy and energy efficiency, ecomobility, sustainable agriculture, biodiversity investment and cleaner production, which could be employed as disruptors of systems or catalysts to push against the vested interests and structural barriers which hinder a transformative transition pathway. However, a critical factor in enabling a just transition in South Africa is to build "strong social consensus on the goal and pathways to sustainability" (ILO, 2015: 5) requiring that social dialogue and citizen engagement drives sustainability transitions. This has been largely absent in South Africa's current transition pathway and is the subject of the next section.

Missing voices?

The NDP acknowledges that,

> [i]n many respects, South Africa has an active and vocal citizenry, but an unintended outcome of government actions has been to reduce the incentive for citizens to be direct participants in their own development.... Robust public discourse and a culture of peaceful protest will contribute to a deeper understanding of the challenges facing communities and reinforce accountability amongst elected officials.
>
> (NPC, 2012: 27)

As mentioned in Chapter 5, the National Planning Commission has started a series of community-based dialogues to begin to assess progress and invite participation in delivering on the NDP. What role can civil society play to ensure that notions of justice and inclusivity are being sufficiently addressed in the design and implementation of South Africa's sustainability transition?

While social dialogue has been central in the early stages of South Africa's transition narrative – through the formulation of the Green Economy Accord, for instance – the country's transition pathway can be characterised as largely state- and business- or market-led. There have been promising developments from civil society recently around wide-ranging issues such as energy democracy, food sovereignty and health, which could signal the restoration of the dynamic social justice-oriented environmental movement of the 1990s. Undoubtedly, the progressive environmental policy framework and tradition of participatory environmental policymaking is in need of revival. However, as Cock and Fig (2001: 15) note, "key civil society activists were drawn into the post-apartheid state, and without the democratic movement having a coherent strategic plan to maintain grassroots structures, civil society was decimated". Civil society was further weakened by the repressive measures such as the "harassment of activists and social movements by state security agencies" (HBS, 2016: 17) and an ever-present state intelligence.

The shrinking space for civil society action – especially marked in the Zuma era – has to be reclaimed to coalesce the voices calling for a just and inclusive transition. These include, for instance, calls for greater links between social and sustainable development policy plans, strategies and actions (Musyoki, 2012; Ganda and Ngwakwe, 2014) such as land reform, rural development, social protection, social finance and skills development. The inclusion of women and youth, informal economy actors and grass-roots enterprises in sustainability transitions is briefly explored to illustrate the challenges (but also the necessity) for a just transition.

Unemployment, poverty and inequality in South Africa has both an age *and* gender dimension, with youth and women disproportionately affected. Musyoki (2012: iv) calls for sustainability transitions to "address women's empowerment and gender equity issues by ensuring that women and men have equal access to resources such as land, technology information, extension services and decision making". Youth employment, on the other hand, was highlighted as the country's *most pressing challenge* by incumbent President Ramaphosa (The Presidency, 2018), while a focus on gender emerged as one of the country's key action areas. Of note is the fact that the President mentioned youth as the key beneficiaries of the employment emanating from government programmes central to the transition, the Solar Water Heaters installation programmes and the War on Leaks programme, urging the further engagement of youth in tackling the country's key challenges. Amongst South African youth, unemployment stood at almost 58 per cent in 2017 (Stats SA, 2017). In 2015, Stats SA unemployment figures also showed higher unemployment amongst women (28.7 per cent) than men (24.4) (Stats SA, 2015). The feminisation of poverty outlined in the report, *The State of Women in the South Africa Economy* (The Presidency, 2015), not only affirmed the vulnerability of women in the labour market, but also showed stark inequalities in women's access to skills, assets and educational opportunities. In spite of this knowledge, there has been very little focused effort that seeks to address social inclusion – of women, youth and other marginalised groups, in the country's transition pathway. This is a key area where civil society voices need to articulate the need for "going green with equity".

Informal economy activities are

> mostly invisible, in part because of a lack of conceptual consensus and interpretation but also as a result of insufficient recognition or awareness of the informal economy's role within the green economy space or how to engage with it successfully.
>
> (Smit and Musango, 2015: 9)

A focus on integrating the informal economy activities that contribute to sustainable development, can contribute substantially towards developing a socially inclusive transition. Smit and Musango (2015) list a range of activities which are largely in the ambit of the informal economy, such as bioprospecting and biotrade, recycling and waste picking and small-scale subsistence farming. Globally, informal waste picking and recycling far outweigh formal employment. This holds true in South Africa where it has been estimated that the informal sector could be "two to three times the size of formal sector, with an estimated 60,000–90,000 people earning a livelihood from the collection and sorting of recyclables, mostly from paper and packaging waste" (Godfrey *et al.* 2016: 3). There are many inroads into linking sustainable development policies and actions, which will incorporate informal sector actors and activities in the country's transition pathway. These include wide-ranging approaches such as sustainable livelihoods, community-based natural resource management, indigenous and local knowledge, ecosystem-based adaptation and grass-roots green entrepreneurship.

The South African government has acknowledged the role of small, micro and medium-sized enterprises (SMMEs) in growing the economy and in creating jobs. This is evident through a number of policy frameworks, financing mechanisms and incentives that seek to promote SMME activity, but also in the establishment of a dedicated ministry, the Department for Small Business Development. According to Creech *et al.* (2014: 8), since SMMEs "account for the largest share of enterprises and employment across the world, it is necessary that 'Green Economy' and 'Green Growth' strategies consider fully the production, technology and management practices of these enterprises". The "radical environmental innovations that are often neglected by established firms" (Marks and Hidden, 2017: 10), can be adopted by grass-roots green enterprises in the production and manufacturing of environmental goods, services and technologies in response to growing societal demands for resource efficiency and climate resilience. In fact, these enterprises could be at the forefront of climate responses and innovations, both adaptation and mitigation, building resilient and adaptive community structures and processes. Grass-roots enterprises can also play a role in strengthening not only the productive but also the social networks, and in developing more inclusive pathways to sustainability by offering opportunities for greater social impact of transition pathways.

Civil society is indeed the missing voice in South Africa's green growth transition narrative, yet plays a central role in promoting inclusive transition pathways. Social and environmental movements – including organised labour, need to find rallying points around which to build and strengthen political and social consensus around just transition narratives. They have to develop and present the green transformation and revolution narratives by highlighting the "[s]ocial dimensions, which include equity, human rights and justice – critical social factors in poverty reduction, pro-poor growth and environmental sustainability – [which] are relegated to the margins of the mainstream green growth agenda" (Khan and Mohamed, 2016: 187) in South Africa's transition narrative.

Beyond growth, back to development

An economic growth orientation remains strong in South Africa's transition narrative, reflecting the ecological modernisation and neo-liberal turn in the country's sustainable development trajectory (Oelofse *et al.*, 2006; Sharife and Bond, 2011; Cock, 2015). Concepts such as green growth, circular economy or low-carbon emission development strategies are largely representative of "market-centered pathway[s] to sustainable development" which have not been able to shift economic policies away from a "growth-centred approach to development" and towards versions of the sustainable development discourse which "reference equity, pro-poor agency, power dynamics, and resilience" (Perreira, 2014: 176).

South Africa's planning blueprint, the National Development Plan, uses the language of a just transition but inflects it towards a green neoliberal approach, in which market mechanisms are used to mitigate greenhouse gas emissions, promote technofixes (such as carbon capture and storage), incentivize energy efficiency in business, and support the expansion of fossil fuel extractivism by mining coal and shale gas.

(Satgar, 2014: 148)

Several commentators however, posit that a green development state which moves beyond the "haphazard adoption of 'green economy' approaches" and which is focused on reinvigorating a "new development paradigm with sustainability at its core" (Swilling and Annecke, 2012: 313) could present inroads into reorienting the carbon-intensive development pathway of South Africa. As noted in Chapter 1, the varieties of sustainable development which prioritised and effectively linked social and environmental outcomes, were well articulated by the environmental justice movement in post-apartheid South Africa. These included a focus on addressing the concerns of the urban and rural poor for good quality housing, access to land, water and sanitation, food security and open spaces in tandem with environmental sustainability. Pro-poor and socially inclusive transition discourses, which respond to the developmental challenges of poverty, inequality and unemployment, have to build on this tradition to craft an inclusive sustainability transition in South Africa. Transition pathways will thus have to move beyond adjustments of the existing systems which have perpetuated the deep poverty, high unemployment and growing inequality in the country (Turok *et al.*, 2011) to address the structural constraints facing the development of just transition pathways – bringing to the fore green transformation and green revolution narratives of sustainability in South Africa.

While the NDP and many other government policies and strategies affirm that, "[s]ince the late 19th century, South Africa has exploited its mineral wealth with little or no regard for the environment" (NPC, 2012: 47), the country continues to pursue a resource- and carbon-intensive growth path. While resource scarcity and climate impact are amongst the primary business risks identified in the country, this path dependency is illustrated by regime- and landscape-level systems, processes and institutions which could slow down or even derail sustainability transitions. Several chapters in this book, for instance, detail the impact of this path dependency on the vested interests which exist around the country's coal-based energy system, which "is fast approaching natural and non-natural limits" (Fakir, 2017: 9), but which remains core to the long-term development vision of the country. Critical commentators have detailed the devastating impact which the minerals energy complex (MEC) has had on the economy, environment and society in South Africa (Sharife and Bond, 2011; Cock, 2015), while the sustainable development governance framework of the country still largely reflects the continued neo-liberal approach of ecological modernisation, detailed in Chapter 1. According to Satgar, South Africa's "so-called green developmental state … is merely reproducing the minerals-energy complex as part of a new post-apartheid resource nationalism and green neoliberal capitalism" (Satgar, 2014: 148).

The reflections in this book present visions of a green development state. It draws together the strands that show how the just transition movement in South Africa has been able to harness, with various levels of success, the policy impetus for sustainability transitions. Research for impact, partnerships for sustainability and inclusive finance approaches form part of the growing suite of approaches which seek to claim the discursive space created by transitions to "move the economy away from its dependence on the MEC and to transform resource intensive growth to a more efficient pathway" (Fakir and Gulati, 2015: 106). A broad suite of concepts, methods and approaches – from well-being economies, doughnut economics, just transitions, vulnerability and resilience and transitions theory, has been employed to present opportunities for shifting the trajectory of the country's development pathway. What is needed now, and which is in fact essential for the evolution of this just transitions movement, is to link these with the widespread grass-roots actions in rural and urban South Africa.

Conclusion

Almost five decades ago global efforts to link the environment and development were first initiated in Stockholm. The formulation of the Sustainable Development Goals has deepened this development narrative considerably. South Africa has kept pace with these shifts, enacting an enabling and supportive policy vision and framework for transitioning towards sustainable development. However, it appears that a neo-liberal emphasis on economic growth continues to feature strongly in sustainable transition narratives in the country, in spite of an abundance of rights-based approaches which promote both social justice and environmental sustainability, like just transitions. These are central in presenting sustainability transition pathways, which are inclusive *by intent*, and which seek to ensure that transitions are both green *and* fair.

Building greater political and social consensus towards just transitions requires, first, enhancing environmental knowledge, understanding and action with the intent of achieving a cultural shift – or at times a revival, of the intricate and multifaceted relationships between society and nature. Social dialogue processes, a second area, is core to just transitions and not only supports consensus-building, but is a platform for surfacing divergent views, which is a necessary step in participatory democracy. And third, multi-stakeholder and multi-level actions, illustrative of the development pathways that address social justice and environmental sustainability, need to be presented as empowering alternatives to the litany of technological innovations which replicate the institutional systems and power structures of the "old economy".

Sustainability transitions offer new ways of shifting the trajectory of South Africa's resource- and carbon-intensive economy towards socially and environmentally just pathways, and could "accelerate progress in building an equitable society". Transition planning, management and implementation processes will have to be more deliberate about South Africa's transformative development agenda, prioritising the social *and* environmental dimensions of sustainability transitions.

References

Academy of Science of South Africa (ASSAF), 2014. *The State of Green Technologies in South Africa.* Assaf, Pretoria.

Alfreds, D., 2018. Ramaphosa should shift to Green Energy – Greenpeace. *News 24,* 20 February 2018. Available at www.news24.com/Green/News/ramaphosa-should-shift-to-green-energy-greenpeace-20180220 (accessed 26 February 2018).

Cock, J., 2015. *Alternative Conceptions of a "Just Transition" from Fossil Fuel Capitalism.* Sustainable Development 03/2015. Rosa Luxemburg Stiftung, Johannesburg.

Cock, J. and Fig, D., 2001. The Impact of Globalization on Environmental Politics in South Africa, 1990–2002. *African Sociological Review,* 5(2): 15–35.

Cole, M., 2015. *Is South Africa Operating in a Safe and Just Space? Using the doughnut model to explore environmental sustainability and social justice.* Oxfam Research Report. Oxfam, Johannesburg.

Conway, D., 2015. iShack Off-Grid Solar Electricity Utility: An Incremental Model for Faster, Greener Informal Settlement Upgrading. *Green Fund Policy Brief 6.* Development Bank of Southern Africa, Midrand.

Creech, H., Paas, L., Gabriel, G.H., Voora, V., Hybsier, C. and Marquard, H., 2014. Small-Scale Social-Environmental Enterprises in the Green Economy: Supporting Grassroots Innovation. *Development in Practice,* 24: 3, 366–378, DOI: 10.1080/09614 524.2014.899561.

Death, C., 2014. The Green Economy in South Africa: Global Discourses and Local Politics. *Politikon: South African Journal of Political Studies,* 41: 1, 1–22.

Douwes, E., Buthelezi, N., Mavundla, K. and Roberts, D. 2015. Ethekwini Municipality Community Reforestation Programme: A Model of Ecosystem-Based Adaptation. *Green Fund Policy Brief 4.* Development Bank of Southern Africa, Midrand.

DST (Department of Science and Technology), 2012. *Department of Science and Technology Ministerial Review Committee on the Science, Technology and Innovation Landscape in South Africa. Final Report.* DST, Pretoria.

Energy Sector Management Assistance Programme (ESMAP), 2012. *Planning for a Low Carbon Future. Low Carbon Growth Country Studies Program: Lessons Learned from Seven Country Studies.* Knowledge Series 011/12. ESMAP, Washington.

Fakir, S., 2017. *Transition Realism: The Implications of Rent-Seeking to Achieve South Africa's Low-Carbon Technology Solutions.* WWF South Africa, Cape Town.

Fakir, S. and Gulati, M. 2015. The Role of State-owned Companies in National Development Towards a Low-Carbon Future in South Africa. In Holm Olsen, K. and Fenhann, J. (eds.), *Transformational Change for Low Carbon and Sustainable Development.* UNEP DTU Partnership, Denmark.

Fioramonti, L., 2017. *Wellbeing Economy: Success in a World without Growth.* Pan Macmillan, Johannesburg.

Ganda, F. and Ngwakwe, C.C., 2014. The Role of Social Policy in Transition Towards a Green Economy: The Case of South Africa. *Environmental Economics,* 5(3): 32–41.

Godfrey, L., Vozza, A. and Mohamed, N., 2016. Transitioning South Africa to a Green Economy: Opportunities for Green Jobs in the Waste Sector. *Green Fund Policy Brief* 8. DBSA, Midrand.

Green Fund, 2014. *Mapping the Green Economy Landscape of South Africa: Insights from the Green Fund.* DBSA, Midrand.

Hart, T., Jacobs, P. and Mangqalaza, H., 2012. *Key Concepts in Innovation Studies: Towards working Definitions.* RIAT Concept Paper Series – Concept Paper 2. Human Sciences Research Council, Pretoria.

HBS (Heinrich Böll Stiftung), 2016. A View from the Ground: State-Civil Society Relations in South Africa. Interview: Chumile Sali. In *Under Pressure: Shrinking Space for Civil Society in Africa.* Perspectives, Issue 3. HBS, Cape Town.

Hlahla, S., Goebel, A. and Hill, T.R., 2016. Green Economy: A Strategy to Alleviate Urban Poverty and Safeguard the Environment? KwaZulu-Natal, South Africa. *Urban Forum,* 27: 113–127.

ILO (International Labour Organization), 2015. *Guidelines for a Just Transition. Towards Environmentally Sustainable Economies and Societies for all.* ILO, Geneva.

Khan, F. and Mohamed, S., 2016. From the Political Economy of the MEC to the Political Ecology of the "Green Economy". In Swilling, M., Musango, J.K. and Wakeford, J. (eds.), *Greening the South African Economy: Scoping the Issues, Challenges and Opportunities.* UCT Press, Cape Town.

Marks, J and Hidden, K., 2017. *SMMEs and the Green Economy: Muddy Waters and Murky Futures. An Investigation into the Sustainable Practices of Small Medium and Micro Manufacturing Enterprises in South Africa's Gauteng Province.* Gordon Institute of Business Science, Pretoria.

Musyoki, A., 2012. *The Emerging Policy for Green Economy and Social Development in Limpopo, South Africa.* UNRISD Occasional Paper 8. UNRISD, Geneva.

National Planning Commission (NPC), 2012. *National Development Plan 2030: Our Future – Make It Work.* NPC, Pretoria.

Nicholls, S., Vermaak, M. and Moolla, Z., 2016. *The Power of Collective Action in Green Economy Planning. It's the Economy, Stupid.* The National Business Initiative, Johannesburg.

Oelofse, C., Scott, D., Oelofse, D. and Houghton, J., 2006. Shifts within Ecological Modernization in South Africa: Deliberation, Innovation and Institutional Opportunities. *Local Environment,* 11(1): 61–78.

PAGE (Partnership for Action on Green Economy), 2017 *PAGE Annual Report 2015.* PAGE, Geneva.

Perreira, L., 2014. The Role of Substantive Equality in Finding Sustainable Development Pathways in South Africa. *McGill International Journal of Sustainable Development Law and Policy,* 10(2): 147–178.

Rotmans, J., Kemp, R. and Van Asselt, M., 2001. More Evolution Than Revolution: Transition Management in Public Policy. *Foresight,* 3(1): 15–31.

Satgar, V., 2014. South Africa's Emergent Green Developmental State. In Williams, M. (ed.), *The End of the Developmental State?* UKZN Press, Pietermaritzburg.

Sharife, K. and Bond, P., 2011. Above and Beyond South Africa's Minerals Energy Complex. In Pillay, D., Daniel, J., Naidoo, P. and Southall, R. (eds.), *New SA Review 2. New Paths: Old Compromises.* Wits University Press, Johannesburg. www.ee.co.za/wp-content/uploads/legacy/Sharife-Bond-MEC-in-New-SA-Review-2.pdf (accessed 21 February 2018).

Smit, S. and Musango, J.K., 2015. Exploring the Connections Between Green Economy and Informal Economy in South Africa. *South African Journal of Science*, 111 11/12.

Stats SA (Statistics South Africa) 2015. *Labour Market Dynamics in South Africa, 2015*. Stats SA: Pretoria. Available at www.statssa.gov.za/publications/Report-02-11-02/Report-02-11-022015.pdf (accessed 17 January 2018).

Stats SA, 2017. *Quarterly Labour Force Survey. Quarter 1: 2017*. Stats SA: Pretoria. Available at www.statssa.gov.za/publications/P0211/P02111stQuarter2017.pdf (accessed 17 January 2018).

Swilling, M. and Annecke, E., 2012. *Just Transitions: Explorations of Sustainability in an Unfair World*. UCT Press, Claremont.

Swilling, M., Musango, J. and Wakeford, J., 2015. Developmental States and Sustainability Transitions: Prospects of a Just Transition in South Africa. *Journal of Environmental Policy & Planning*, DOI: 10.1080/1523908X.2015.1107716.

The Presidency, 2015. *The Status of Women in the South African Economy*. Ministry in the Presidency Responsible for Women: Pretoria.

The Presidency, 2018. President Cyril Ramaphosa: 2018 State of the Nation Address. 16 February 2018. The Presidency, Pretoria. Available at www.gov.za/speeches/president-cyril-ramaphosa-2018-state-nation-address-16-feb-2018-0000. (accessed 26 February 2018).

Turok, B., 2011. *The Controversy about Economic Growth*. Jacana Media, Auckland Park.

United Nations Economic Commission for Africa (UNECA), 2015. *Inclusive Green Growth in South Africa: Selected Case Studies*. UNECA, Addis Ababa.

United Nations Environment (UNEP), 2013. *Green Economy Modelling Report of South Africa – Focus on Natural Resource Management, Agriculture, Transport and Energy Sectors*. UNEP, Nairobi.

Index

Page numbers in **bold** denote tables and boxes, those in *italics* denote figures.